The Law Commission
Consultation Paper No. 132

Aggravated, Exemplary and Restitutionary Damages

A Consultation Paper

HMSO

ISBN 0 11 730216 3

THE LAW COMMISSION

AGGRAVATED, EXEMPLARY AND RESTITUTIONARY DAMAGES

TABLE OF CONTENTS

PART I

INTRODUCTION

SCOPE OF THE PAPER

1.1   Under Item 11 of our Fifth Programme of Law Reform,[1] we are currently engaged upon a review of the principles governing the present law of damages and the effectiveness of this remedy, and we are publishing a series of consultation papers on various aspects of this subject. This is the second paper in the series. Unlike the first paper,[2] which dealt with structured settlements, interim and provisional damages, and the method of determining future loss, this paper is neither confined to, nor indeed focused on, awards of damages for personal injuries.

1.2   It is widely assumed that the principle which primarily informs civil actions for damages is compensatory,[3] - that damages are first and foremost awarded in order to compensate the plaintiff. Accordingly they purport to correspond to the losses suffered as a result of the defendant's wrong. However, in some circumstances damages may be awarded on a non-compensatory basis, by reference either to a punitive or to a restitutionary principle.[4] In both cases the aim is to deter the commission of such wrongs, the former by making an award of damages to deter and condemn the defendant's behaviour, the latter by an award which deprives the defendant of any resulting benefit which may have accrued.[5] It is with these non-compensatory damages that this paper is concerned.

---

[1]   (1991) Law Com. No. 200.

[2]   Structured Settlements and Interim and Provisional Damages (1992), Law Com. Consultation Paper No. 125.

[3]   See, for example, *Livingstone* v. *Rawyards Coal Co.* (1880) 5 App. Cas. 25, 39, *British Transport Commission* v. *Gourley* [1956] A.C. 185, 208 and *Stoke-on-Trent City Council* v. *W. & J. Wass Ltd.* [1988] 1 W.L.R. 1406, 1410G-H (torts); *Robinson* v. *Harman* (1848) 1 Exch. 850, 855, 154 E.R. 363, 365 and *Tito* v. *Waddell (No. 2)* [1977] Ch. 106, 328-334 (breach of contract); P.B.H. Birks, *Civil Wrongs: A New World* (Butterworth Lectures 1990-91), particularly at 56-57, 58, 77-80; A.S.Burrows, *Remedies for Torts and Breach of Contract* (1987), pp.15-33; *McGregor on Damages* (15th ed., 1988), paras. 9, 10; G.H. Treitel, *The Law of Contract* (8th ed., 1991), pp.825-830; *Winfield & Jolowicz on Tort* (13th ed., 1989), pp.600, 608-9.

[4]   See para. 1.15 below for an explanation of these terms. In English law, damages awarded on the basis of a punitive principle are generally referred to as exemplary damages.

[5]   See paras 1.11 ff. for discussion of the terminological difficulties.

1.3   While compensatory damages enjoy unquestioned acceptance in the law of obligations, non-compensatory damages have tended to be regarded as problematic and as requiring justification. There seem to be two related reasons for this, both of which derive from the assumption that the compensatory principle occupies a position of paramountcy, perhaps even exclusivity, in relation to civil actions for damages. First, there is an understanding, which receives wide adherence, about the function of remedies for breach of obligations, namely that they exist solely to provide compensation for loss.[6] This view has been expressed most often in connection with exemplary, rather than restitutionary, damages. The aims of exemplary damages are to deter and condemn the defendant's behaviour. It is said that exemplary awards confuse the civil and the criminal functions of the law.[7] Second, sums awarded in excess of plaintiffs' losses look like a pure and undeserved windfall and there is some discomfort with the fact that plaintiffs thereby profit from the wrong done to them, being placed in a better position (in pecuniary terms) than they were before the wrong.[8] Exemplary and restitutionary awards therefore attract controversy simply by virtue of the fact that they *are* non-compensatory.

1.4   However, in two categories of case there is an obvious difficulty in applying the principle of compensatory damages. Where the damage caused is financial, or readily expressed in money terms, for instance loss of earnings or damage to property, the view that the compensatory principle occupies a position of paramountcy or exclusivity causes no difficulty. But there are cases in which it is impossible to quantify the damage suffered as a precise sum of money. The law of obligations protects many interests such as bereavement, pain and suffering,[9] personal liberty and reputation in respect of which it is either difficult or impossible to determine a monetary equivalent. There have also been calls for the law to protect other such interests, for

---

[6]   This would deny, for instance, any admonitory function to tort law.

[7]   *Rookes* v. *Barnard* [1964] A.C. 1129, 1221 (*per* Lord Devlin); *Broome* v. *Cassell* [1972] A.C. 1027, 1086C-D (*per* Lord Reid) and 1127H-1128A (*per* Lord Diplock). A corollary of this is that defendants are deprived of the safeguards which have been developed for their protection by the criminal law. Restitutionary awards may also be punitive in effect. See paras. 7.2 and 7.18 below.

[8]   *Broome* v. *Cassell* [1972] A.C. 1027, 1086B-C (*per* Lord Reid); 1126D (*per* Lord Diplock).

[9]   These, together with loss of amenity and mental disturbance amounting to a recognised psychiatric illness, will be discussed in our next consultation paper on damages.

example privacy and freedom from harassment.[10] Another difficulty for the compensatory view of damages consists of those cases where interests, such as property, are protected without proof of damage or loss. Where there has been no damage, it is fanciful to see the damages as strictly compensatory, and if there has been damage but it is not quantified, the relationship between the award and the loss must necessarily be questionable.[11] Although this second category is well established and recognised, some argue that the cases in the first category are inherently unsuitable for compensatory damages and that even if the law were informally to adopt, for pragmatic reasons, a 'tariff' to ensure that awards are both reasonable and consistent, it is likely that some litigants would express discontent, with plaintiffs seeing awards as inadequate or derisory and defendants characterising them as penal. Because this review is not concerned with the range of interests protected by the law, we simply note this argument for the sake of completeness. However, we also believe that to exclude such interests would lead to a significant and in our view undesirable narrowing of the scope of the civil law. The main question for consideration in this paper, therefore, is whether awards of exemplary and restitutionary damages are ever justified, and if so in what circumstances.

1.5   As a result of the leading House of Lords decision in *Rookes* v. *Barnard*,[12] exemplary damages have only been available in England in recent years in three very limited categories of case - oppressive, arbitrary and unconstitutional action by government servants, conduct calculated by the defendant to make a profit in excess of the compensation payable to the plaintiff, and cases where an exemplary award is authorised by statute. This decision has not been followed in the Commonwealth: Australia, Canada and New Zealand all adhere to a broad punitive principle and have rejected the limitations placed upon it by *Rookes* v. *Barnard*. In these countries and in the United States exemplary damages are justified for flagrant or conscious wrongdoing; or where a person acts maliciously or vindictively, arrogantly or high-handedly with a contumelious disregard for the plaintiff's rights and civil liberties. The present

---

10   *Khorasandjian* v. *Bush* [1993] 3 W.L.R. 476; *Kaye* v. *Robertson* [1990] T.L.R. 232; Report of the Committee on Privacy and Related Matters (1990), Cmnd. 1102, ch. 12 and para. 17.13; Review of Press Self-Regulation (1993), Cmnd. 2135, paras. 7.33 - 7.42; Infringement of Privacy (July 1993), Lord Chancellor's Department & the Scottish Office, Consultation Paper, paras. 3.13, 6.11 and 6.12.

11   See paras. 2.24-2.25 below.

12   [1964] A.C. 1129, discussed at paras. 2.3, 3.2 ff., and 3.33 ff. below.

condition of the English law on exemplary damages has led to calls that it be reconsidered and statements that the law "... cries aloud ... for Parliamentary intervention".[13]

1.6 In the first place, concern has been expressed that in the assessment of exemplary damages too much is left to the exercise of discretion according to indeterminate principles. Whilst the assessment of compensatory damages may be difficult where future losses and non-pecuniary losses are involved, in personal injury actions the judiciary has been able, since the almost complete removal of juries from such cases,[14] to develop a tariff system by virtue of which a measure of consistency and uniformity has been achieved. There has been no similar development in the context of exemplary damages, which still remain in many instances within the province of the jury[15] and this has given rise to concern about their indeterminacy. In theory, principles for the assessment of exemplary damages should be generated by the purpose(s) which the remedy is intended to serve.[16] However, it is commonly recognised that where damages are assessed according to what the defendant ought to pay because of the way in which the wrong was committed,[17] there is little to be gained by referring to awards which have been made in other cases since these can only be understood if the full facts are known, and they depend very much on subjective evaluations.[18] That consistency cannot be achieved between awards of exemplary damages is sometimes given as a reason in favour of

---

[13] E.g. *Riches* v. *News Group Newspapers Ltd.* [1986] 1 Q.B. 256, 269C (*per* Stephenson L.J.). This approach has sometimes included calls for abolition: e.g Report of the Committee on Defamation (1975), Cmnd. 5909, para. 360 (as regards defamation); L.J. Anderson, "An Exemplary Case for Reform", (1992) 11 C.J.Q. 233; A.S. Burrows, *Remedies for Torts and Breach of Contract* (1987), p. 247; *McGregor on Damages* (15th ed., 1988), para. 406; A. Ogus, *The Law of Damages* (1973), pp. 32-34. Lord Reid in *Broome* v. *Cassell* [1972] A.C. 1027, 1083-1093, clearly favoured the abolition of exemplary damages but believed that only Parliament had the power to achieve this.

[14] By s. 69 of the Supreme Court Act 1981 and its predecessor, s. 6 of the Administration of Justice (Miscellaneous Provisions) Act 1933. In *Ward* v. *James* [1966] 1 Q.B. 273, the full Court of Appeal held that, when exercising the discretion under the 1933 Act, a judge ought not, in a personal injury case, to order trial by jury save in exceptional circumstances. Since then there has been only one reported instance of an order for trial of a personal injury case with a jury.

[15] There is a prima facie presumption in favour of trial by jury in the case of libel, slander, malicious prosecution and false imprisonment contained in s. 69(1) of the Supreme Court Act 1981. These are some of the principal torts giving rise to awards of exemplary damages.

[16] See paras. 1.12, 1.15 and 5.1-5.27 below for further discussion of the purposes for which an exemplary award is made.

[17] See para. 3.86 below.

[18] *Warby* v. *Cascarino*, *The Times*, 27 October 1989, *per* Lord Donaldson M.R. (C.A.).

jury trial where judges exercise their discretion under section 69(3) of the Supreme Court Act 1981.[19] Perhaps somewhat contradictorily, lack of consistency has led to accusations from some quarters that jury awards of exemplary damages are arbitrary and unprincipled. Criticism has also been made of the levels of awards, particularly in defamation cases,[20] although in many such cases the awards criticised have been compensatory. One issue which this paper therefore addresses is whether, if exemplary damages can be justified, there are changes which can be made to the rules governing and incidental to their assessment, with a view to structuring this discretion. A related issue is whether the jury is the appropriate tribunal for determining liability for, and for assessing, such damages.

1.7 An additional reason for a review of exemplary damages is the confusion which surrounds the circumstances of their availability, the purpose for which awards of aggravated damages are made and the relationship between aggravated and exemplary damages.[21] This confusion is evinced in the misuse of terminology,[22] in the difficulty which judges have in directing juries[23] and in the reasons which are sometimes given for rejecting awards.[24] It is to be hoped that an examination of the principles which are involved will assist in the understanding and clarification of this area of the law.

---

[19] *H* v. *Ministry of Defence* [1991] 2 Q.B. 103, 112E-F (C.A.); *Singh* v. *London Underground, The Independent*, 25 April 1990 (Q.B.D.). Cf. *Racz* v. *Home Office*, [1992] T.L.R. 624 (C.A.) (at pp. 18F, 22D-E, 23B-C of transcript). By virtue of s. 69(3) there is a prima facie presumption *against* trial with a jury in all cases which fall outside s. 69(1), unless the court in its discretion orders otherwise.

[20] This criticism is usually reinforced by (the unfavourable) comparison with the levels of awards made in personal injury cases: *Groom* v. *Crocker* [1939] 1 K.B. 194, 231 (*per* MacKinnon L.J.); *McCarey* v. *Associated Newspapers Ltd. (No. 2)* [1965] 2 Q.B. 86, 108D-E, 109B-110B; *Broome* v. *Cassell* [1972] A.C. 1027, 1130H (*per* Lord Diplock); *Rantzen* v. *Mirror Group Newspapers* (1993) 143 N.L.J. 507.

[21] See the pleas of Stephenson L.J. in *Riches* v. *News Group Newspapers Ltd.* [1986] 1 Q.B. 256, 269C. Cf. A. Ogus, *The Law of Damages* (1973), pp. 29 and 238; and D. Kemp, *Damages for Personal Injury and Death* (5th ed., 1993), para. 3.22.

[22] *Riches* v. *News Group Newspapers Ltd.* [1986] 1 Q.B. 256, 269B; *Lloyd* v. *Francis*, 17 January 1990 (Unreported, C.A.). See paras. 1.11 ff. below.

[23] See, for example, the direction given by the trial judge in *Holden* v. *Chief Constable of Lancashire* [1987] 1 Q.B. 380, and the comments of the Court of Appeal in *Riches* v. *News Group Newspapers Ltd.* [1986] 1 Q.B. 256, 268A-C (*per* Stephenson L.J.) and 289C (*per* Parker L.J.).

[24] For instance, *A.B.* v. *South West Water Services Ltd.* [1993] Q.B. 507, 527-528, where Stuart-Smith L.J.'s reasons for rejecting the plaintiffs' claims for aggravated damages seem to be in conflict with what was said by the House of Lords in *Broome* v. *Cassell* [1972] A.C. 1027. See paras. 3.8-3.9 below.

1.8   It is also our belief that the attempt in *Rookes* v. *Barnard* to limit the availability of exemplary damages has resulted in a body of law which can be regarded as unprincipled and illogical.[25] The recent decision of the Court of Appeal in *A.B.* v. *South West Water Services Ltd.*[26] that exemplary damages may only be awarded in respect of a cause of action for which such an award had been made prior to *Rookes* v. *Barnard* is illustrative of the way in which the law on exemplary damages has become stultified. That English law diverges from the position adopted in other common law systems further reinforces the present need to reassess the availability of exemplary damages.[27] It is our provisional view that awards of exemplary damages can be justified and in this paper we attempt to formulate principles upon which they can be based and on which we seek consultees' views.

1.9   Restitutionary damages - being non-compensatory - are subject to the same fundamental objection which is made in relation to exemplary damages,[28] but they also raise slightly different issues. Restitutionary damages have not yet acquired a profile comparable to that of exemplary damages nor have they been criticised and restricted by the House of Lords in the way that exemplary damages have been in *Rookes* v. *Barnard*. The position is rather that the law in this field is under-developed. The scattered caselaw evinces an acceptance of the restitutionary principle, but unfamiliarity with restitutionary analysis still means that judges on occasion question their ability to invoke it.[29] Indeed, the term 'restitutionary damages' is by no means yet universal or even common and there is some debate as to whether certain money remedies are properly characterised as restitutionary. This unfamiliarity has also led to some confusion between exemplary and restitutionary damages, and to decisions based on assertions and assumptions the implications of which may not have been fully worked out. There is a need therefore to give a simple account of the law relating to restitutionary damages, with the aim of promoting clarification and understanding. Because we believe that restitutionary damages have an important role to play in the law of civil wrongs, we make provisional recommendations regarding the circumstances in which they should be available.

---

[25]   Cf. Lord Reid in *Broome* v. *Cassell* [1972] A.C. 1027, 1087A-B. See paras. 3.31 and 3.55-3.56 below.

[26]   [1993] Q.B. 507.

[27]   Cf. Lord Hailsham in *Broome* v. *Cassell* [1972] A.C. 1027, 1067H-1068A.

[28]   See para. 1.3 above.

[29]   See, for instance, *Stoke-on-Trent City Council* v. *W. & J. Wass Ltd.* [1988] 1 W.L.R. 1406, 1415G-H.

1.10   We do not, however, deal with all forms of non-compensatory damages. Thus, contemptuous damages (a derisory sum awarded to indicate that the plaintiff ought not to have pursued the claim) and nominal damages (awarded in the case of torts actionable *per se*, where the plaintiff's rights have been infringed but no 'actual' loss has been suffered) will not be considered. In this paper we are principally concerned with those non-compensatory damages which represent a sum in excess of the plaintiff's loss, and which have for that reason generated more controversy. There is no significant body of caselaw relating to contemptuous or nominal damages. However, although an examination of nominal damages is excluded from the scope of this paper, it should be noted that it is in some of those cases where a plaintiff can recover only nominal damages that exemplary or restitutionary damages may be especially useful.[30]

TERMINOLOGY

1.11   We make an attempt here to explain some of the terms which will be used throughout this paper. In doing so, however, we wish to emphasise that, due to the confusion which bedevils this area of the law and to the nature of the issues involved, this is necessarily a tentative exercise, and what is said below should not therefore be treated as a touchstone for all purposes.

1.12   Part of the difficulty we have experienced in formulating a precise terminology stems from the fact that awards which aim to compensate a plaintiff may also have the *effect* of deterring or punishing the defendant.[31] However, the difficulty also stems from the inconsistent way in which descriptive labels have been used in relation to non-compensatory damages, and particularly to exemplary damages. Prior to *Rookes* v. *Barnard*[32] various appellations were used interchangeably and without distinction in order to describe exemplary damages. The contrast was between compensatory damages on the one hand, and "punitive",[33]

---

30   See below, paras. 2.20-2.28 and n. 76. Cf. also Report on Exemplary Damages (1991), Ontario Law Reform Commission, p. 10. n.35.

31   See further, paras. 3.89 - 3.90 below.

32   [1964] A.C. 1129.

33   *Lavender* v. *Betts* [1942] 2 All E.R. 72, 73H-74A.

7

"retributory",[34] "vindictive",[35] "exemplary",[36] "aggravated",[37] "liberal"[38] or "large"[39] damages on the other. In many of the cases in which these damages had previously been awarded, the plaintiff could also be said, by reason of the way in which the defendant had committed the wrong, to have suffered a certain form of intangible loss, namely losses associated with injury to personality,[40] such as insult, humiliation, degradation, indignation, offence, outrage and hurt to feelings. Thus it was possible to conceptualise these damages as compensating the plaintiff for intangible losses, rather than as punishment for the defendant.[41]

1.13   In *Rookes* v. *Barnard*, Lord Devlin sought to remove this ambiguity in the purpose(s) for which damages 'at large' are awarded by distinguishing exemplary damages (which were punitive) from aggravated damages (which were compensatory).[42] Unfortunately, this attempt to dispel a source of confusion has not been entirely successful in that aggravated damages may still be awarded by reference to the gravity of the defendant's conduct as well as the plaintiff's loss, and judges may therefore at times confuse exemplary and aggravated damages. The fact that the treatment of these intangible interests remains problematic must mean that any terminology adopted cannot be regarded as absolute. Indeed, one issue which we raise for

---

[34]   *Bell* v. *Midland Railway Co.* (1861) 10 C.B. (N.S.) 287, 308, 142 E.R. 642, 471.

[35]   *Emblen* v. *Myers* (1860) 6 H. & N. 54, 158 E.R. 23; *Cruise* v. *Terrell* [1922] 1 K.B. 664, 670; *Whitham* v. *Kershaw* (1886) 16 Q.B.D. 613, 618.

[36]   *Huckle* v. *Money* (1763) 2 Wils. K.B. 205, 95 E.R. 768; *Emblen* v. *Myers* (1860) 6 H. & N. 54, 158 E.R. 23; *Merest* v. *Harvey* (1814) 5 Taunt. 442, 128 E.R. 761.

[37]   *Lavender* v. *Betts* [1942] 2 All E.R. 72, 74B.

[38]   *Tullidge* v. *Wade* (1769) 3 Wils. K.B. 18, 95 E.R. 909.

[39]   *Merest* v. *Harvey* (1814) 5 Taunt. 442, 128 E.R. 761.

[40]   H. Stoll, "Penal Purposes in the Law of Tort", (1970) 18 Am.J.Comp.L. 3, 5. These losses are described variously in the legal literature: M.G. Bridge, "Contractual Damages for Intangible Loss: A Comparative Analysis", (1984) 62 Can. B.R. 323 ('intangible losses') and P.R. Handford, "Moral Damage in Germany", (1978) 27 I.C.L.Q. 849 ('injury to the dignitary interest').

[41]   See *Mafo* v. *Adams* [1970] 1 Q.B. 548, 559A-B. This possibility has become more evident in recent years as the law has become increasingly prepared to recognise non-proprietary, non-economic and non-physical harms as 'damage'.

[42]   [1964] A.C. 1129, 1221-1233.

consideration is whether it is proper to attempt this sort of demarcation at all.[43] However, for expository purposes we make every effort to adhere to the terminology presented below. Further, although the decision in *Rookes* v. *Barnard*[44] is the source of the modern meaning to be attributed to the terms 'exemplary' and 'aggravated' damages, it purported to establish a retrospective classification of awards labelled variously in the past but generally considered until *Rookes* to be punitive in aim.[45] In this paper we generally refer to exemplary, rather than punitive, damages because although these terms may still be used interchangeably this now reflects the language of the English case law in this area.[46] However, it should not be forgotten that the language (and meaning) of the English cases underwent a transition as a result of *Rookes* v. *Barnard* and we also refer to 'punitive damages' as including both aggravated and exemplary damages, which before *Rookes* v. *Barnard* were not differentiated - in particular, where dealing with the position before that case.[47]

1.14   When we turn to restitutionary damages the problem is not inconsistency of usage but the fact that such damages are underdeveloped and the term 'restitutionary damages' is relatively unfamiliar to courts. Instead, restitutionary remedies have simply been described as such or have tended to be known by other names. Furthermore, some doubt has been expressed as to whether certain remedies for wrongs, particularly equitable wrongs, are properly regarded as restitutionary or are capable of being described as 'damages'.[48]   Even among jurists specialising in the law of restitution there is some difference of opinion.[49] For these reasons it is particularly important to make clear the sense in which the term is used in this paper.

---

[43]   *Broome* v. *Cassell* [1972] A.C. 1027, 1115C-1116C (*per* Lord Wilberforce). Cf. H. Stoll, "Consequences of Liability: Remedies", Int. Enc. Comp. L. XI/2 Torts (1986), ch. 8, s.8.

[44]   [1964] A.C. 1129.

[45]   But some doubts were beginning to be expressed at the time that *Rookes* v. *Barnard* [1964] A.C. 1129 was decided. See para. 2.2 below.

[46]   Exemplary awards are often referred to in the literature as punitive damages.

[47]   See, especially, Part II.

[48]   For example, the equitable remedy of an account of profits and equitable compensation.

[49]   Compare, for instance, P.B.H. Birks, *Civil Wrongs: A New World* (Butterworth Lectures 1990-91), p. 57, with A.S. Burrows, *Remedies for Torts and Breach of Contract* (1987), ch. 6.

1.15   Given the reservations expressed above, we have nevertheless tried to adhere to the following terminology:

(i) *Compensatory damages* - are primarily awarded in order to compensate the plaintiff for all pecuniary and non-pecuniary losses suffered as a result of the defendant's wrong. They are therefore measured by the extent of the plaintiff's loss. There is a prior question, however, as to what qualifies as a 'loss' in law. If the law is prepared to conceptualise interference with intangible interests of personality as 'losses', then damages awarded in respect of them may be described as compensatory. Since this is one of the issues which has to be addressed in any examination of exemplary and aggravated damages, we have tried to refer to compensatory damages which are awarded for pecuniary losses, pain and suffering and loss of amenity, or psychiatric injury and lesser forms of mental or emotional distress, *not including* aggravated damages, as *pure* compensatory damages.

(ii) *Aggravated damages* - a term of art[50] for those damages which purport to compensate the plaintiff for intangible injury to personality (insult, humiliation, degradation, indignation, outrage, distress, hurt feelings, etc.) where this has been caused by the way in which the defendant committed the wrong. Aggravated damages are traditionally regarded as compensatory, but the fact that the defendant's exceptional behaviour is a precondition to their being awarded raises the question whether they do not in fact contain a punitive element. This is one of the issues considered below.

(iii) *Exemplary (or punitive) damages* - are awarded by reference to the defendant's conduct and are intended to deter similar conduct in the future (whether by the defendant or others) and to signify condemnation or disapproval. They can therefore serve deterrent, symbolic and retributory functions. In deterring and condemning undesirable behaviour exemplary damages can also serve the distinct purpose of vindicating an individual's rights and the strength of the law.[51] It has been suggested that exemplary damages may also serve a placatory function.[52]

---

[50]   *Broome* v. *Cassell* [1972] A.C. 1027, 1072C.

[51]   See, for instance, Lord Devlin in *Rookes* v. *Barnard* [1964] A.C. 1129, 1226 and Lords Hailsham, Morris and Diplock in *Broome* v. *Cassell* [1972] A.C. 1027, at 1073F, 1099H and 1130D respectively.

[52]   See, e.g. D.D. Ellis, "Fairness and Efficiency in the Law of Punitive Damages", (1982) 56 S. Cal. Law Rev. 1, 3, 9-10; and L.J. Anderson, "An Exemplary Case for Reform", (1992) 11 C.J.Q. 233, 235; *Lamb* v. *Cotogno* (1987) 164 C.L.R. 1. Cf. *White* v. *Metropolitan Police Commissioner, The Times*, 24 April 1982, final col. ("Conduct of the kind in the present case could do gross damage to race

The kind of conduct in respect of which exemplary damages may be awarded varies according to jurisdiction and time but in English law they may now only be awarded where the cause of action is one in respect of which an award of exemplary damages had been made prior to 1964[53] and the fact situation comes within one of Lord Devlin's categories.[54] To this extent, as English law does not adhere to a broad punitive principle,[55] the term 'exemplary damages' is, in English law, a term of art.[56]

(iv) *Restitutionary damages* - are money awards following a civil wrong[57] which are measured by the defendant's gain and made with the intention of removing any profits or other benefits which the defendant has obtained as a result of the wrong to the plaintiff. There is debate as to the juridical basis of such awards; that is, whether all or some of the benefit-based remedies are generated by independent restitutionary claims or whether at bottom the cause of action is the civil wrong.

ARRANGEMENT OF THE PAPER

1.16   The bulk of the paper is concerned with and considers the principles governing the availability and assessment of exemplary damages with reference also being made to the position adopted in other jurisdictions. This is done in Parts II-VI. Because there has been some debate as to the proper classification of aggravated damages,[58] these are examined alongside exemplary damages. We preface our analysis with a discussion in Part II of the background and of the problems which intangible losses, particularly those concerning injury to interests of personality, have posed for the law, since we believe that an understanding of this issue is essential both to any explanation of the development of exemplary and aggravated damages, and to the formulation of any proposals for reform. The existing law is discussed in Part III

---

relations.").

[53]   *A.B.* v. *South West Water Services Ltd.* [1993] Q.B. 507 (C.A.).

[54]   *Rookes* v. *Barnard* [1964] A.C. 1129. See paras. 3.36-3.54 below.

[55]   Cf. para. 1.5 above.

[56]   Cf. *Broome* v. *Cassell* [1972] 1027, 1072C (*per* Lord Hailsham).

[57]   That is, a tort, breach of contract or equitable wrong.

[58]   That is, as to whether they are strictly compensatory or also contain a punitive element.

and Part IV considers the position in a number of other jurisdictions. In Part V we set out the arguments for and against awards of damages based upon a punitive principle and consider whether such awards can ever be justified and, if so, in what circumstances. Part VI sets out the options for reform and the consultation issues and discusses some of the specific issues which are incidental to the availability and assessment of aggravated and exemplary damages, and asks whether there are ways in which the discretion to award them can be structured so as to dispose of the practical objections which are often made about them.

1.17 Part VII considers restitutionary damages, albeit more briefly. We begin by examining how they are related to exemplary damages and the sense in which they are to be regarded as non-compensatory. We then summarise the present law on the subject, an exercise which is not an easy one. We consider whether restitutionary damages can be justified and what their proper scope should be. Our provisional conclusion is that they have an important role to play in remedying civil wrongs and we seek consultees' views as to whether further development should be left to the courts or whether legislation is needed. Part VIII of the paper summarises our provisional recommendations for reform and the issues upon which we seek the views of consultees.

1.18 In March 1992 we organised a conference with the torts group of the Society of Public Teachers of Law and the Faculty of Law at the University of Manchester at which papers on exemplary damages were presented by Professor David Owen of the University of South Carolina, Professor Anthony Ogus of the University of Manchester and Mr Keith Stanton, Head of the Department of Law at the University of Bristol. This paper in part draws on the discussion at the conference but is intended to stimulate responses and comment from all interested parties.

1.19 The Commission is most grateful to Mr Keith Stanton, who prepared a draft of this Consultation Paper in collaboration with us and who has made a substantial contribution to the development of this project; and to Professor David Owen, who prepared a background paper for us on the position in the United States. The views expressed, however, are those of the Commission.

PART II

PUNITIVE DAMAGES - THE BACKGROUND

INTRODUCTION

2.1   Despite the controversy that has surrounded punitive damages[1] in more recent times,[2] it has long been possible in English law for damages to be awarded in excess of the loss actually suffered, for the purpose of deterring and condemning the conduct involved.[3] However, the type of conduct regarded by the law as deserving of such disapproval, and hence the circumstances in which the punitive principle may operate in the civil law, has varied with time. So too has the judicial classification of these awards of increased damages. The reasons for this can be understood by examining the development of punitive awards and the context in which these awards have operated rather than by focusing on an abstract understanding of the punitive principle. This examination reveals a connection between punitive damages, particular wrongs and certain forms of non-pecuniary harm.

2.2   The earliest reported cases of punitive damages appear to have been decided in the eighteenth century[4] and until 1964, when *Rookes* v. *Barnard*[5] was decided, the discretion to award such damages was wide. It was thought that awards could be made wherever the defendant's conduct or motive in committing the wrong had been wanton or wilful - that is "high-handed, insolent, vindictive or malicious or had in some other way exhibited a contumelious disregard

---

1   In this part the term 'punitive damages' includes what since *Rookes* v. *Barnard* [1964] A.C. 1129 have been reclassified as 'aggravated' and 'exemplary' damages, but which before that decision were undifferentiated awards.

2   See paras. 1.3-1.8, above, and Part V below.

3   For a brief outline, see H. Street, *Principles of the Law of Damages* (1962), pp. 28-29.

4   *Wilkes* v. *Wood* (1763) Lofft. 1, 98 E.R. 489 (trespass through unlawful search and seizure); *Huckle* v. *Money* (1763) 2 Wils. K.B. 205, 95 E.R. 768 (false imprisonment). Both cases arose out of the unlawful seizure under general warrants of persons and papers connected with the publication of *The North Briton*. See para. 3.38 below. However, although punitive damages are usually regarded as having their origins in these cases, Pratt L.C.J. refers in *Wilkes* v. *Wood* (1763) Lofft. 1, 18 and 98 E.R. 489, 498 to having " ... formerly delivered it as my opinion on another occasion ... that a jury have it in their power to give damages for more than the injury received." It seems, therefore, that the practice of awarding punitive damages may have a longer history than is generally supposed. Cf. the comments of Windeyer J. in *Uren* v. *John Fairfax & Sons Pty Ltd.* (1966) 117 C.L.R. 118, 152.

5   [1964] A.C. 1129.

13

of the plaintiff's rights."[6] However, legal commentators pointed at the same time to two areas of uncertainty. First, the precise nature of the relationship between punitive awards and particular wrongs was not explicitly articulated and it was unclear whether the punitive principle could be applied to *all*, or only to some, of the wrongs which were accompanied by such conduct.[7] Secondly, doubts were expressed concerning the purpose with which many of the awards labelled in the past as 'punitive'[8] had been made. It was suggested that some of these awards at least could be explained as increased compensation for the plaintiff's non-pecuniary harm - that is, as having been awarded by reference to an enhanced compensatory, rather than a punitive, principle.[9] In addition, there was growing concern that the levels of awards being made by juries in defamation cases were not only too high, but also virtually uncontrollable.[10]

2.3   Against this background and in the context of a claim for damages for intimidation, the House of Lords in *Rookes* v. *Barnard* subjected the punitive principle to reexamination and placed the significant limitations mentioned in Part I upon the circumstances in which it may be invoked.[11] Lord Devlin's speech in *Rookes* now forms the basis of, and hence must be the starting point for any treatment of, the modern English law on exemplary damages. On the assumption that exemplary damages are anomalous because they confuse the civil and criminal functions of the law,[12] he identified three categories in which they could exceptionally be awarded. At common law he limited their scope to two classes of case, where they could be

---

6   *Uren* v. *John Fairfax & Sons Pty Ltd.* (1966) 117 C.L.R. 129 (*per* Taylor J.).

7   See, for instance, the argument of counsel in *Rookes* itself: [1964] A.C. 1129, 1159, 1160, 1162, 1164 Cf. H. Street, *Principles of the Law of Damages* (1962), p. 31.

8   Or as 'exemplary', 'vindictive', 'retributory', 'aggravated' and so on. See para. 1.12, above.

9   See for example, *Mayne and MacGregor on Damages* (12th ed., 1961), para. 212; C.T. McCormick, *The Law of Damages* (1935), p. 278; H. Street, *Principles of the Law of Damages* (1962), pp. 22-25, 28-30; A. Samuels, "Problems of Assessing Damages for Defamation", (1963) 79 L.Q.R. 63, 76. See para. 1.12, n.39 above.

10   The jury could be given little guidance as to how they should assess damages and the power of an appellate court to interfere with the verdict of a jury was limited to instances where the award could be described as 'excessive', i.e. no reasonable jury could have made it. See Salmon L.J.'s explanation of Lord Devlin's attempt to restrict the availability of exemplary awards, in the Court of Appeal's decision in *Broome* v. *Cassell* [1971] 2 Q.B. 354, 388C-F. See paras. 3.86 and 3.103 below.

11   [1964] A.C. 1129.

12   *Ibid.*, 1221.

14

said to serve a useful social purpose[13] and where their availability was justified by precedent. These were oppressive arbitrary and unconstitutional action by government servants, and conduct calculated by the defendant to make a profit in excess of compensation payable to the plaintiff. He also identified a third class of case where an exemplary award is permitted by statute.[14] In doing so, Lord Devlin also addressed the second source of uncertainty referred to above concerning the function of increased damages awards. His speech was an attempt not only to restrict the operation of the punitive principle but, further, to extract the compensatory element from previously undifferentiated awards made in excess of the plaintiff's proprietary, economic and physical injury.[15] The result was clearly an attempt to separate 'aggravated damages', which aim to compensate the plaintiff for injured feelings of pride and dignity or insult and humiliation suffered as a result of the defendant's outrageous conduct; and 'exemplary damages', which aim solely to deter and condemn the defendant's behaviour and are accordingly punitive.

2.4   It was thought that the effect of *Rookes* v. *Barnard* would be to relegate exemplary damages and the punitive principle "to a role of insignificance in English law."[16] But, as we shall see, whilst reaffirming the status of the decision in *Rookes*, the House of Lords in *Broome* v. *Cassell*[17] reinterpreted Lord Devlin's categories in a less restrictive way.[18] In addition, the distinction between aggravated and exemplary damages was enlarged upon and there was some discussion of the kinds of wrongs which could give rise to an exemplary award. Recognising that what was said in *Rookes* had been intended as illustrative,[19] their Lordships urged that Lord Devlin's speech should not be read literally, as a statute, but should instead be interpreted broadly and with flexibility.[20]

---

13   *Ibid.*, 1223, and 1226; *Broome* v. *Cassell* [1972] A.C. 1027, 1124B, 1128E, and 1129H (*per* Lord Diplock).

14   See paras. 3.36-3.54 below.

15   Cf. Taylor J. in *Uren* v. *John Fairfax & Sons Pty Ltd.*(1966) 117 C.L.R. 118, 130.

16   H. Stoll, "Penal Purposes in the Law of Tort", (1970) 18 Am. J. Comp. Law 3, 13. Cf. *Mafo* v. *Adams* [1970] 1 Q.B. 548, 559B.

17   *Broome* v. *Cassell* [1972] A.C. 1027.

18   See paras. 3.39 and 3.45 below.

19   *Broome* v. *Cassell* [1972] A.C. 1027, 1068B and 1074F-G (*per* Lord Hailsham).

20   *Ibid.*, 1068A-B, 1074G, 1077G, 1085A-D.

2.5   *Broome* v. *Cassell* thus paved the way for the continued development of aggravated and exemplary damages. Since that decision, these damages have enjoyed a robust existence at lower court level, especially in cases concerning the harassment and eviction of tenants by 'Rachman-type' landlords[21] and in cases of unlawful and oppressive police action. Aggravated and exemplary damages have also been extended subsequently to cases of race and sex discrimination.[22] However, exemplary damages continue to attract controversy and criticism, particularly at appellate level and among academics.[23] Moreover, for a number of reasons the decisions in *Rookes* and *Broome* may have contributed to, rather than resolved, the uncertainty which pervades this area of the law.

2.6   Firstly, after *Broome* v. *Cassell* it remained unclear whether the requirement that the plaintiff's case satisfy one of Lord Devlin's categories was the only precondition to an exemplary award, or whether the nature of the wrong committed might also preclude it. The link between the punitive principle and exemplary awards had been somewhat obscured by the discussion in *Rookes* of the categories of case in which it was permissible for an exemplary award to be made. Thus, although Lord Devlin had said that flagrant, wilful or malicious wrongdoing was insufficient in itself to give rise to an exemplary award,[24] it was unclear whether this nevertheless remained a necessary condition. This uncertainty has, additionally, permitted a debate to take place as to whether certain wrongs, because of the state of mind required to establish them and because of the nature of the losses which they typically involve, are capable of giving rise to exemplary damages. The debate has recently been resolved by the Court of Appeal in *A.B.* v. *South West Water Services Ltd.*,[25] where it was held that exemplary damages may only be awarded in respect of those torts for which an award had been made prior to *Rookes* v. *Barnard*. Rather than rediscover the connection between certain types of wrong or loss and punitive awards[26] (by examining the kind of conduct which is required

---

[21]   Cf. the comments of Lord Hailsham in *Broome* v. *Cassell* [1972] A.C. 1027, 1079E-F.

[22]   See paras. 3.41 and 3.66 below. Exemplary awards for discrimination can no longer be made following *A.B.* v. *South West Water Services Ltd.* [1993] Q.B. 507; see *Deane* v. *Ealing L.B.C.* [1993] I.C.R. 329.

[23]   See paras. 1.3-1.8, above, and 5.4-5.12 below.

[24]   [1964] A.C. 1129, 1229.

[25]   [1993] Q.B. 507.

[26]   See paras. 2.8-2.10 and 2.20-2.28 below.

over and above that implicit in Lord Devlin's categories in order to sustain an exemplary award), the Court of Appeal therefore chose to adopt a strict precedent-based approach to the issue rather than one based on principle. The case appears to preclude any further extension by analogy of exemplary awards.

2.7   Secondly, confusion remains with regard to the respective roles of aggravated and exemplary damages.[27] It has been questioned whether the distinction between them can be sustained, either in theory or in practice.[28] In particular, because the precise role of the defendant's conduct (both in determining the availability and in the calculation of aggravated damages) is not entirely clear, the function of aggravated awards remains ambiguous.[29] This makes it possible for a perfectly plausible argument to be put forward to the effect that, despite what was said in *Rookes* v. *Barnard*,[30] aggravated damages are at least partly punitive in character, and indeed this view gains some credence from the speeches in *Broome* v. *Cassell*.[31]   The availability of aggravated damages, if this is correct, therefore allows punitive awards to be made in circumstances other than those which, according to the House of Lords, justify them and the present distinction between aggravated and exemplary damages would seem for this reason alone to be unacceptable.

2.8   This uncertainty concerning the nature of aggravated damages is remarkably similar to that which existed immediately prior to *Rookes* v. *Barnard* in relation to previously undifferentiated awards. Indeed, functional ambivalence has characterised the history and development of increased damages awards. The ambiguity which seems to be inherent in these increased

---

[27]   See, for example, H. Stoll, "Consequences of Liability: Remedies", Int. Enc. Comp. Law XI/2 Torts (1986), ch. 8, s. 109; M.G. Bridge, "Contractual Damages for Intangible Loss: A Comparative Analysis", (1984) 62 Can. B.R. 323, 365; L.J. Anderson, "An Exemplary Case for Reform", (1992) 11 C.J.Q. 233, 240, 248-249; A. Ogus, *The Law of Damages* (1973), p. 238; D. Kemp, *Damages for Personal Injury and Death* (5th ed., 1993), para. 3.22.

[28]   *Uren* v. *John Fairfax & Sons Pty. Ltd.* (1966) 117 C.L.R. 118, 149, 152; H. Stoll, "Penal Purposes in the Law of Tort", (1970) 18 Am. J. Comp. Law 3, 14; J. Stone, "Double Count and Double Talk: The End of Exemplary Damages?", (1972) 40 A.L.J. 311; F.D. Rose, "Contract - Damages - Non-Pecuniary Losses - Injured Feelings and Disappointment - Remoteness", (1977) 55 Can. B.R. 333, 335, n.11.

[29]   See paras 3.24 ff. below.

[30]   [1964] A.C. 1129.

[31]   [1972] A.C. 1027, 1071G, 1073D, 1076F-H, 1079F-H, 1080F, 1083A (*per* Lord Hailsham); 1089D-F (*per* Lord Reid) 1126D (*per* Lord Diplock). See A. Ogus's comments to this effect: *The Law of Damages* (1973), p.238.

(punitive, or exemplary and aggravated) awards is in our view linked to the role which such damages have played in English law in the vindication of rights, the protection of interests, and the redress of non-pecuniary harm.

2.9 The protection of certain interests, particularly interests of personality,[32] presents special difficulties for the law. Interference with interests of personality "require[s] energetic measures of redress because they are concerned with moral values which are, or should be, the values most precious to the individual."[33] Further, interference with these interests typically gives rise to a certain form of non-pecuniary harm: diminution of reputation, loss of self-esteem and dignity, feelings of outrage, humiliation, insult, degradation and the like.

2.10 A glance at other legal systems reveals a variety of ways in which such interests are protected.[34] In English law, they seem to have been protected (at least in part) for many years by undifferentiated punitive awards,[35] more recently by exemplary and aggravated damages and yet more recently by compensatory damages for injury to feelings.[36] The general trend of the law in using monetary awards to protect these interests has therefore been a movement from punishment to compensation.[37] Thus, in English law the punitive principle and the redress of intangible losses caused by the infringement of personality interests have an interdependent history. Although a number of arguments have been used to explain or

---

[32] Defined by P. Ollier and J. Le Gall, Various Damages : Int. Enc. Comp. L. XI/2 Torts (1986), ch. 10, s. 70, as "the collection of values enjoyed by an individual within the society of which he is a member: injury to honour or reputation, deprivation of liberty...injury to feelings, convictions, beliefs."

[33] P. Ollier & J. Le Gall, Various Damages : Int. Enc. Comp. L. XI/2 Torts (1986), ch. 10, s. 105. Monetary awards in respect of their infringement may therefore tend to act as an indication of the value which society places upon them. Cf. the condemnatory role of punitive damages, which looks not merely to the quality of the defendant's conduct but also to the value attached to the interest infringed.

[34] See, further, Part IV below.

[35] Significantly, at a time when all awards of damages in tort cases were in the control of the jury, and when intangible losses were not yet recognised as legal 'damage'.

[36] The most recent example of this is the proposal contained in the consultation paper published jointly by the Lord Chancellor's Department and the Scottish Office, that a right to privacy be recognised as a new tort. See Infringement of Privacy (July 1993), Lord Chancellor's Department & the Scottish Office, Consultation Paper, paras. 3.13, 3.18 and 5.22.

[37] See Lord Devlin's analysis of the older cases in *Rookes* v. *Barnard* [1964] A.C. 1129, at 1223 and 1229.

criticise the availability of punitive damages,[38] these have usually focused on their punitive, quasi-criminal nature, and we believe that an examination of the difficulties which intangible losses pose for the law is particularly helpful in explaining the development of punitive awards which we have outlined above and in accounting in part for their problematic status. We therefore consider these difficulties before proceeding to set out in more detail the current state of English law on aggravated and exemplary damages and to examine the full range of the arguments for and against such awards.

---

[38] These are considered in Part V below.

THE PROBLEM OF INTANGIBLE LOSSES AND THE REDRESS OF INTERFERENCE
WITH INTERESTS OF PERSONALITY

(1) The problem of intangible losses

2.11   The reparation of non-pecuniary harm[39] poses special problems for the law. In the case of intangible losses[40] this is manifested in a reluctance to award damages for such harm except under certain conditions and also in conceptual uncertainty regarding the nature of the money awards which are made in respect of them. These problems, examination of which suggests a close relationship between intangible losses and punitive awards, can be reduced to three: incommensurability, subjectivity or difficulties of proof, and the convergence of the different purposes which damages associated with intangible losses can be said to serve.

(a) Incommensurability

2.12   Compensation[41] involves the reparation of harm by the delivery of an equivalent or equivalent value.[42] Compensation which takes the monetary form of compensatory damages therefore encounters peculiar difficulties when the harm is non-pecuniary. There is no exact equivalent and no standard measure of assessment by reference to which the harm can be converted into monetary form.[43] Although some forms of non-pecuniary detriment, such as the non-performance of services, can be valued, no market exists in the intangible losses which are inflicted by the violation of personality interests; hence the harm cannot be quantified or valued precisely. This incommensurability gives rise to real danger of indeterminacy and of inconsistent awards. Further, it means that, unless special effort is made to itemize awards, one cannot identify with certainty which part of an award actually corresponds to loss suffered

---

[39]   Meaning pain and suffering, loss of amenity, mental disturbance amounting to a recognised psychiatric illness and intangible losses. As indicated, these will be discussed in our next consultation paper on damages, but the issues raised here to some extent inevitably overlap.

[40]   Meaning lesser forms of emotional distress typically involved when personality rights are infringed, as to which see para. 2.9 above.

[41]   See Structured Settlements and Interim and Provisional Damages, (1992) Law Com. Consultation Paper No. 125, Part II, para 2.1.

[42]   H. Stoll, Consequences of Liability: Remedies, Int. Enc. Comp. L. XI/2 Torts (1986), ch. 8, s.9.

[43]   Except by reference to levels of awards made in comparable cases. See para. 2.13 below.

and which part (if any) corresponds to an amount in excess of it, especially when the assessment of these awards is within the control of a tribunal which need not articulate the process by which it arrived at the sum awarded.[44] Where the harm is non-pecuniary, an award of damages is therefore more susceptible to the accusation that it is not in fact (entirely) compensatory, but instead contains a punitive element.

(b) Subjectivity or difficulties of proof

2.13   Incommensurability is a feature not only of intangible losses, but also of non-pecuniary harm which takes the form of pain and suffering, loss of amenity and psychological injury. However, compensation is less of a problem in those cases than is the case with regard to intangible losses. This is because difficulties of proof are exacerbated where the non-pecuniary harm involved is intangible. Damages for pain and suffering and loss of amenity are predicated on *bodily* injury, which is visible,[45] usually has an element of permanency and is capable of objective determination. Thus although such injury may be difficult to assess, it is not in general difficult to prove that it has occurred. Special restrictions beyond normal duty and breach requirements are not imposed in the case of bodily injury, which is compensated without more. Moreover, since the removal of the jury in personal injury cases,[46] the judiciary has developed a tariff for pain and suffering and loss of amenity, whereby certain conventional figures for specific injuries have emerged, giving rise to a measure of consistency between comparable cases. This is possible because the injury involved is considered less subjective.

2.14   Psychological injury might be thought to raise similar difficulties to intangible loss, since it is neither observable nor capable of easy measurement and is also vulnerable to fabrication. Indeed, mental disturbance amounting to psychiatric injury at first enjoyed no independent

---

[44] Uncertainty as to the precise purpose (compensation or punishment) with which awards have in the past been made is due in part, therefore, to the fact that the jury was formerly the appropriate tribunal for assessment in all civil actions. Cf. D.E.R. Venour, "Punitive Damages in Contract", (1988) 1 Can. J. Law & Juris. 87, 95-97.

[45] Nervous shock is a special case and is dealt with in para 2.14 below. Disease raises special problems of its own which will not be considered here. See J. Stapleton, *Disease and the Compensation Debate* (1986).

[46] Through the judicial interpretation of s. 69 of the Supreme Court Act 1981 and its predecessor s. 6 of the Administration of Justice (Miscellaneous Provisions) Act 1933.

protection in English law.[47] However, since psychiatric injury has begun to be recognised by the medical profession, this form of non-pecuniary loss has come to be perceived as objective and identifiable in scientific or medical terms - that is, it is now recognised as being susceptible to diagnosis. The law has now followed the medical, psychiatric and psychological professions by recognising psychiatric injury as constituting 'damage' for the purpose of an action in negligence, even where this is not consequential on some physical harm. As a result, a tariff similar to that employed in relation to bodily injury has also developed for such injury. However, because (inter alia) the difficulties of proof remain greater in this context, the law imposes additional restrictions on the recovery of damages for pure psychiatric injury. The significance of this observation becomes apparent when we examine aggravated damages below.[48]

2.15 These problems are particularly evident where intangible losses are concerned.[49] The subjectivity inherent in the assessment of such losses was explicitly recognised in *Broome* v. *Cassell* as of contextual importance in explaining the incidence and development of punitive damages.[50] When interference with personality rights gives rise to intangible losses such as injury to reputation, dignity or feelings the problems of triviality and authenticity are increased. Such losses are inherently subjective and difficult to prove, unless controlled by an objective test.

2.16 Further, where the loss is intangible other factors tend to become significant in determining liability and assessment: "all the circumstances" may be taken into account,[51] and in particular the gravity of the defendant's conduct. However, the *precise* role of the defendant's conduct has long remained unclear. Hence, because the defendant's conduct is considered relevant, where these intangible losses have been suffered it is possible to regard the damages which are awarded as being punitive or as containing a punitive element.[52]

---

[47] This will be examined in our next paper on damages.

[48] See paras. 3.2 ff. below.

[49] Cf. *Broome* v. *Cassell* [1972] A.C. 1027, 1071B-C.

[50] [1972] A.C. 1027, 1070D-1072H. The starting point of Lord Devlin's decision in *Rookes* was also an analysis of damages 'at large', i.e. where the award need not be confined to the pecuniary loss proved.

[51] *Rookes* v. *Barnard* [1964] A.C. 1129, 1221.

[52] Cf. *Walsh* v. *Ministry of Defence* [1985] N.I. 62, 66F-H (*per* Lord Lowry L.C.J.).

(c) Convergence of purposes: compensation, satisfaction and punishment

2.17   The problems we have just discussed explain in part people's ambivalence about the function of increased damages awards.[53] Because they are incapable of precise assessment and because factors other than the plaintiff's loss are taken into account where the harm is intangible, awards can be analysed as *either* compensation *or* punishment. Alternatively, because the law is here concerned with the plaintiff's feelings, awards can also be interpreted as a satisfaction - that is made with the purpose of assuaging the plaintiff's outraged sense of justice.[54] When the harm to the plaintiff's personality interests is non-pecuniary, the ideas of compensation, satisfaction and punishment thus tend to coincide.[55] This permits variation in the characterisation of these awards between jurisdictions[56] and at different times, a possibility which is seen in the shift in the characterisation of these awards in English law, from punitive (pre-*Rookes*) to compensatory (post-*Rookes*).[57] We shall see that these features are particularly apparent in the case of aggravated damages.

2.18   The incommensurability and subjectivity of intangible losses do not, however, entirely account for the convergence of the purposes which money remedies in respect of them may be said to serve. Although not all intangible losses are redressed by the law, those which arise as a result of the infringement of personality rights generally are. The kind of conduct which is involved in the serious violation of interests of person and personality is precisely the kind of conduct at which the community in general tends to be most outraged. The effect is that the line between compensation and punishment, one aim of which is to express disapproval, is blurred.

---

53   See para. 2.8 above.

54   Cf. *Wilkes* v. *Wood* (1763) Lofft. 1, 18-19, 98 E.R. 489, 498; and Lord Hailsham's interpretation of aggravated damages as a "solatium" in *Broome* v. *Cassell* [1972] A.C. 1027, 1073D, 1076F-1077B, 1079F-G, 1083A-B.

55   Cf. H. Stoll, Consequences of Liability : Remedies, Int. Enc. Comp. L. XI/2 Torts (1986), ch. 8., s.8; P. Ollier & J. Le Gall, Various Damages, Int. Enc. Comp. L. XI/2 Torts (1986), ch. 10, s.105; C. Magruder, "Mental and Emotional Disturbance in the Law of Torts", (1936) 49 Harv. L.R. 100, 101, n. 4; M.G. Bridge, "Contractual Damages for Intangible Loss: A Comparative Analysis", (1984) 62 Can. B.R. 323, 331, 334.

56   See Part IV below.

57   See para 2.3 and also n. 2 above. See paras. 3.24 ff. below.

2.19   Further, because of the nature of the interests involved, the 'compensation' of intangible losses can appear closer to a sanction, the law perhaps seeming to be as much concerned with the *fact* of violation as with the effect it has on the plaintiff.[58] In other words, in the case of personality rights freedom from harm is not the primary or only concern, and the infringement of the right is in itself objectionable. For this reason an award of damages may look more like vindication or punishment than compensation. Hence it is not merely the nature of the loss but the nature of the interest infringed which leads to uncertainty as to the function which damages may be serving in these cases.

(2) The link between the problems posed by intangible losses, the redress of interests of personality and the historical development of punitive damages

2.20   Prior to *Rookes* v. *Barnard*,[59] any flagrant or wilful wrongdoing was said to be capable of giving rise to an award of exemplary, that is punitive, damages in English law.[60] After that case the type of conduct capable of giving rise to such an award is defined by the requirements of Lord Devlin's categories.[61] An examination of the context in which punitive damages, or increased awards, have in fact been used discloses a more refined description of the conduct required which, although not explicitly articulated, seems to have been implicitly assumed.

2.21   That a connection exists between the punitive principle and certain wrongs has always been suspected and there are a number of observations by judges and jurists to this effect. Initially these took the form of simple assertions that punitive damages might be awarded in respect of certain nominate torts, for example in defamation cases or cases of false imprisonment,[62] thereby implying that the nature of the wrong itself was relevant to the availability of a such an award. Sometimes a more sophisticated connection was made between particular wrongs

---

[58] E.g. *John Lewis & Co. Ltd.* v. *Tims* [1952] A.C. 676, 680; *Murray* v. *Ministry of Defence* [1988] 1 W.L.R. 692, 703B. Thus also, many of the torts protecting such interests are actionable *per se*, i.e. without proof of special damage.

[59] [1964] A.C. 1129.

[60] See para. 2.2, above.

[61] These are examined in detail in paras. 3.36 - 3.54 below.

[62] E.g. *Phillips* v. *South Western Ry. Co.* (1879) 4 Q.B.D. 406, 409 (punitive damages for slander, but not personal injury). See Lord Hailsham in *Broome* v. *Cassell* [1972] A.C. 1027, 1068E, quoting *Mayne and MacGregor on Damages* (12th ed., 1961), para. 207.

and the nature of the harm to which they typically gave rise.[63] After the decision in *Rookes* v. *Barnard*, however, the relevance of the wrong itself or of the harm involved was obscured somewhat by the rigid categorisation of the circumstances in which the punitive principle could be invoked.

2.22 A literal reading of Lord Devlin's speech might suggest that it exhaustively defined the prerequisites for an exemplary award. What had previously acted as a kind of unspoken but tacitly understood limitation upon the scope of the punitive principle was now, paradoxically given the desire to restrict awards, open to question. Thus, in the years following *Rookes* v. *Barnard* it was argued on a number of occasions that exemplary damages might be made in cases where they had not previously been considered appropriate, but where the conduct of the defendant nevertheless fell within one of Lord Devlin's categories. A notable example is provided by deceit[64] but such arguments were also put in other cases.[65] In *A.B.* v. *South West Water Services Ltd.*[66] the Court of Appeal reinstated a limitation upon exemplary damages by reference to the wrong, but it was of a different and more formal kind than the limitation which had previously existed: exemplary awards were to be permissible only where the cause of action was one in respect of which an exemplary award had been made prior to *Rookes* v. *Barnard*.

2.23 A closer look at the case law suggests that there may be a more substantive and more principled relationship with the nature of the wrong committed. It is possible to identify a number of factors which demonstrate that the punitive principle has played an important role in the protection of personality interests and in the redress of intangible losses.

2.24 First, there are torts actionable *per se* - that is torts actionable without proof of special damage - the existence of which can be traced back to the origins of the common law. In these cases,

---

63 See Lord Morris in *Broome* v. *Cassell* [1972] A.C. 1027, 1099F, quoting Sir Frederick Pollock, *The Law of Torts* (4th ed., 1895), p. 174.

64 See, for example, *Mafo* v. *Adams* [1970] 1 Q.B. 548, 558G-H; *Catnic Components Ltd.* v. *Hill* [1983] F.S.R. 512; *Morton-Norwich Products Inc.* v. *Intercen Ltd.* (No. 2) [1981] F.S.R. 337. Some judges considered that precedent compelled them to dismiss the argument; others accepted or rejected the argument on the facts by reference to the quality of the conduct which must be shown in order to justify an exemplary award.

65 E.g. see the cases on infringement of intellectual property rights, cited at para. 3.73.

66 [1993] Q.B. 507.

the interest protected by the tort is considered important enough for its infringement to be actionable without proof of loss. Thus although the compensatory principle (which presupposes loss) has attained prominence today, with the growth of the cause of action in negligence,[67] the historical significance of torts actionable *per se* suggests that tort law was, and still is, as much concerned with the protection of particular interests as with protection from conduct which causes loss.

2.25   Defamation,[68] false imprisonment, trespass to the person (assault and battery), and trespass to land and goods are all torts which are actionable *per se*. Even if unable to prove actual loss, the plaintiff is not necessarily restricted to nominal damages but will receive substantial damages for any loss which the court presumes to flow from the tort.[69] These torts are also the ones in respect of which the punitive principle has been employed most often by the courts. Malicious prosecution, a cause of action where punitive damages have been equally conspicuous, requires proof of actual damage "[b]ut in practice this rule has been almost entirely nullified by the benevolent fiction that certain kinds of damage will of necessity follow as a consequence of prosecution",[70] namely injury to reputation, humiliation, mental suffering or injury to feelings.[71] This is not to say that it is *only* torts which are actionable *per se* which give rise to punitive awards, but these torts do tend to involve non-pecuniary harm and are the kinds of wrong which incorporate values to which the law attaches special importance, demonstrating this by substantial awards.

2.26   Secondly, defamation, false imprisonment and trespass to the person are all wrongs which directly protect personality interests and by nature import a particular form of intangible loss: diminution of reputation, insult, outrage, distress, loss of dignity, self-esteem or self-respect,

---

67   See paras 5.30 below.

68   All libel is actionable *per se*, but only four categories of slander are actionable without proof of damage: see *Clerk & Lindsell on Torts* (16th ed., 1989), para. 21-21.

69   A. Ogus, *The Law of Damages* (1973), p. 23.

70   P. Ollier and J. Le Gall, Various Damages, Int. Enc. Comp. L. XI/2 Torts (1986), ch. 10, s. 73. Cf. *McGregor on Damages* (15th ed., 1988), para. 1627: "...it is because these kinds of damage flow from these kinds of legal proceedings that they are made actionable in the first place, and these kinds of damage are then in all cases presumed to flow from these kinds of legal proceedings."

71   *McGregor on Damages* (15th ed., 1988), paras. 1627, 1629, 1631.

degradation, humiliation.[72] In the case of defamation the interest protected, reputation, is more intangible than the interests protected by false imprisonment and trespass to the person, and gives rise to problems of its own.[73] In particular, the nature of the basic tort in defamation has elements of the outrage associated with the punitive principle which are taken into account in the assessment of compensatory damages, irrespective of aggravation or exemplification. However, defamation remains the prime illustration of the recognition of personality interests by the law and for this reason we consider that defamation cases should not be separated out of any review of this area of the law.[74] Although trespass to land or goods do not so obviously protect these interests they can do so where the manner of the infringement is such as to give rise to insult, offence, affront, and the other forms of intangible loss.[75] Prior to *Rookes* v. *Barnard* the legal concept of 'damage' did not embrace such losses, but they could be reflected in punitive awards. It is possible therefore to see part of the role of punitive damages in the past as the redress of non-pecuniary harm.[76] In *Rookes* v. *Barnard*, this compensatory element within previously undifferentiated awards was extracted and renamed aggravated damages, although the culpability of the defendant's conduct remains a condition of their availability. The development of punitive damages has thus been closely allied to the development in the legal conceptualisation of these intangible losses and to the problematic issues which such losses raise.

---

[72] These feelings may be understandably exacerbated by or attributable also to the status of the defendant. For example, when the wrongs of false imprisonment or malicious prosecution are committed by the police, whose actions carry a certain legitimacy, they affect the plaintiff's reputation in the eyes of others *and* appear to be more outrageous. Cf. Lord Devlin's first category, paras. 3.37-3.43 below; and see also para. 3.60 below.

[73] Conduct subsequent to the wrong can be seen as an extension of the libel itself, for example. See para. 3.5 below. False imprisonment does affect reputation but to a much lesser degree.

[74] Especially since *Broome* v. *Cassell* [1972] A.C. 1027, itself a libel case, added much to the existing law on exemplary damages.

[75] See *Merest* v. *Harvey* (1814) 5 Taunt. 442, 128 E.R. 761; and *Sears* v. *Lyons* (1818) 2 Stark. 317, 171 E.R. 658. In more recent times these torts have been extensively used in order to protect tenants from harassment by their landlords, which usually involves trespass. See paras. 3.46 and 3.61 below.

[76] Cf. H. Stoll, Consequences of Liability : Remedies, Int. Enc. Comp. L. XI/2 Torts (1986), ch. 8, s. 35 and s. 109. The operation of punitive damages can also be linked to the development of judicial control over jury verdicts, juries being permitted a wider discretion in tort cases due to the nature of the interests and losses involved. Cf. Lord Devlin's warning in *Rookes* v. *Barnard* [1964] A.C. 1129, 1229, that the reasons given by judges in the past for not interfering with jury awards ought not to be taken as a positive statement of the type of case in which punitive damages can be awarded.

2.27   However, despite the importance which we have attached in this analysis to the relevance of intangible losses in explaining the development of punitive damages, it should be emphasised that they are not *merely* a means of compensating loss which the law finds difficult to fit within its existing conceptual tools. Exemplary awards remain prevalent in relation to the torts identified in paragraph 2.26 above. This may reflect a continuing confusion about the capacity of the law to compensate the victims of these torts and about the notion of what constitutes 'loss', or it may reflect the implausibility of the distinction which has been created between aggravated and exemplary damages.[77] But it also suggests that the punitive principle has an independently significant role in the protection of certain interests, particularly interests of personality. The interests concerned are precisely the kinds of interests which demand vigorous protection and yet which may not be adequately protected by compensation. It is here that the law may be especially concerned to prevent or deter infringement. It may also be more, or as, interested in the *fact* of infringement and the focus on loss may be somewhat misplaced. Where personality interests are involved, money awards are inevitably seen as an indication of the value which the law attaches to them and for this reason the symbolic function of punitive awards makes them particularly suited to this task.[78]

2.28   Accordingly, the third strand in the argument that there is a more substantive relation between the punitive principle and the nature of the wrong is that punitive damages have been and remain an important means of vindicating or reflecting the intrinsic value of an individual's rights.[79] In a country which has no written constitution, and where the freedoms which citizens can expect to be protected in their relations with the state therefore fall to be determined in large part by ordinary tort law, awards of what were before *Rookes* v. *Barnard* undifferentiated punitive damages have proved to be a valuable judicial technique for the protection of civil liberties.[80] This has remained possible after *Rookes* v. *Barnard* because

---

[77]   See paras. 3.32 below.

[78]   Cf. *Dumbell* v. *Roberts* [1944] 1 All E.R. 326, 329H-330A. Alternatively, the symbolic aspect of the award means that it can be interpreted as punitive.

[79]   Nominal damages are a symbolic indemnification of rights, but may nowadays look like more of an insult (and therefore closer to being contemptuous damages) than a vindication. See *Wileman* v. *Minilec Engineering Ltd.* [1988] I.R.L.R. 144: a nominal sum of £50 was awarded, but the E.A.T. clearly took a dim view of the plaintiff's claim.

[80]   Cf. the origins of punitive damages in cases such as *Wilkes* v. *Wood* (1763) Lofft. 1, 98 E.R. 489, and *Huckle* v. *Money* (1763) 2 Wils. K.B. 205, 95 E.R. 768; with their modern counterpart in cases of misconduct by the police and prison officials. In other jurisdictions which have a written constitution, it has been argued that an award of substantial damages should be made for the infringement of *per se*

one of the two categories of case in which exemplary damages were still regarded by Lord Devlin as fulfilling a useful purpose was the unconstitutional action of government officials.

(3) Implications for law reform

2.29   As indicated, any consideration of the reform of such damages must address a wider range of issues than those we have raised in this section of our paper. The other arguments for and against non-compensatory damages are considered in Parts V and VI of the paper. However, the matters raised in this section do have several implications for law reform. One implication which does not fall for consideration in the present context, although consultees may have views on it, is whether the difficulties of according a monetary value to intangible losses and interests of personality suggest that the law should not protect such interests. Those which do fall for consideration in the present context are:-

(a)   Given the recognition of the special problems which intangible losses entail, what level of legal protection should interests of personality enjoy and how is this best formulated? Do they fit more easily into a compensatory or into a punitive model of redress, or are they necessarily hybrid in character? (see paragraphs 6.48 and 6.54 below.)

(b)   What additional problems would arise if the requirement of culpable conduct, which is now a prerequisite for an aggravated award,[81] was abandoned as one of the preconditions to the recoverability of intangible losses? (see paragraphs 6.50 - 6.53 below.)

(c)   If the links between exemplary damages and the protection of personality interests which we have identified are accepted as meaningful, does this suggest the extension of the punitive principle to other cases where interference with personality is the very harm contemplated by the conduct which is wrongful? (see paragraph 6.8 ff. below).

---

constitutional rights. See paras 4.9 and 4.21 below.

[81]   See para. 3.3 -3.4 below.

PART III

AGGRAVATED AND EXEMPLARY DAMAGES - THE PRESENT LAW

INTRODUCTION

3.1   The development of the law relating to punitive damages has been outlined in the introduction to Part II of our paper.[1] As we have observed,[2] such damages have a long history in English law, but the foundation of the modern law on the subject is the speech of Lord Devlin in *Rookes* v. *Barnard*[3] (subsequently reaffirmed with some amplification by the House of Lords in *Broome* v. *Cassell*),[4] in which significant limitations were placed upon the circumstances in which the punitive principle might operate and a new terminology was adopted. As the law now stands exemplary damages (which are punitive) are to be distinguished from aggravated damages (which are compensatory). Exemplary damages are restricted to three categories of case and are permissible only where the cause of action is one in respect of which such an award had been made prior to *Rookes* v. *Barnard*.[5] Aggravated damages, on the other hand, may be awarded wherever the motive or conduct of the defendant in committing the wrong [6] was such as to injure the plaintiff's proper feelings of pride or dignity or to diminish the plaintiff's sense of self-esteem and self-respect. The relevance of the defendant's conduct to

---

[1]   Paras. 2.2-2.5 above.

[2]   See para. 2.2 above.

[3]   [1964] A.C. 1129, 1203-1233. See para. 2.3 above. *Rookes* was an intimidation case in which the plaintiff was initially awarded £7,500 damages after a direction by the trial judge that any deliberate illegality might be punished with exemplary damages. Because the sum was awarded by a jury it is not clear how much was added as exemplary damages, but Lord Reid at 1178 thought it "fairly obvious that they must have added a considerable sum." The House of Lords ordered a new trial as to damages on the ground of misdirection.

[4]   [1972] A.C. 1027. But the Privy Council in *Australian Consolidated Press Ltd.* v. *Uren* [1969] 1 A.C. 590 accepted that the High Court of Australia was not wrong in deciding that *Rookes* should not be followed in Australia, where there was "a well settled judicial approach" to exemplary damages in libel cases.

[5]   *A.B.* v. *South West Water Services Ltd.* [1993] Q.B. 507 (C.A.). In this case, 180 people brought a group action seeking compensatory, aggravated and exemplary damages from the defendants, for ill effects suffered by drinking water which had been accidentally contaminated. The exemplary and aggravated damages were sought on the grounds that the defendants acted in an arrogant and high handed manner in ignoring complaints; wilfully misled the plaintiffs in a circular letter which stated that the water was fit to drink; and wilfully withheld any accurate or consistent information following the incident, thus causing the plaintiffs to consume the water for longer than they otherwise would have.

[6]   Or conduct committed after the wrong in some cases. See para. 3.5 below.

the availability of an aggravated award has led some to doubt its compensatory character.[7] It has also been questioned whether the distinction between exemplary and aggravated damages can be maintained.[8] In our survey of the present law we therefore examine the principles governing the availability and assessment of aggravated damages, as well as examining those which govern exemplary awards.

AGGRAVATED DAMAGES

(1) Availability

(a) Exceptional conduct such as to give rise to intangible loss

3.2   Aggravated damages emerged as a distinct category of damages in *Rookes* v. *Barnard*.[9] Prior to Lord Devlin's speech in that case, the terms 'punitive', 'exemplary' and 'aggravated' had been used interchangeably in relation to awards of increased damages,[10] which were generally regarded as punitive in aim. Lord Devlin, however, detected a compensatory element within these supposedly punitive awards. Where damages were 'at large' - that is, not limited to the pecuniary loss which can be proved and hence where the damage suffered cannot be exactly converted into a sum of money[11] - it was permissible for the jury to look at "all the circumstances" in arriving at the appropriate figure for compensation.[12] In particular, they were entitled to take into account the motives or conduct of the defendant where these aggravated the injury to the plaintiff.[13] Many of the earlier increased awards in which there had been malevolence, spite or the like could therefore be explained as including an element

---

7   See paras. 3.24-3.32 below.

8   See para. 2.7 above, and paras. 3.24 - 3.32 below.

9   [1964] A.C. 1129.

10   See the authorities cited at para. 1.12 above.

11   But see para. 3.12 below.

12   *Rookes* v. *Barnard* [1964] A.C. 1129, 1221. Cf. para. 2.16 above.

13   *Ibid.*.

of compensatory aggravated damages.[14] The failure to separate this compensatory element of the award from its punitive element, or to recognise that many awards could be explained without reference to punitive principles at all, was regarded by Lord Devlin as a "source of confusion" which he hoped his new analysis would eliminate.[15]

3.3   In *Rookes* v. *Barnard* Lord Devlin said that aggravated awards were appropriate where the manner in which the wrong was committed was such as to injure the plaintiff's proper feelings of pride and dignity,[16] or gave rise to humiliation,[17] distress,[18] insult or pain.[19] Examples of the sort of conduct which would lead to these forms of intangible loss were conduct which was "offensive"[20] or which was accompanied by malevolence, spite,[21] malice, insolence or arrogance;[22] in other words, the type of conduct which had previously been regarded as capable of sustaining a punitive award.[23] It would therefore seem that there are two elements relevant to the availability of an aggravated award: first, exceptional or contumelious conduct or motive on the part of the defendant in committing the wrong; and second, intangible loss suffered as a result by the plaintiff, that is, injury to personality.

3.4   As regards the first requirement, examples of outrageous wrongdoing are the wrongful eviction of a tenant accompanied by circumstances of harassment and abuse,[24] police

---

[14]   Thus although *Rookes* is the origin of the meaning to be attributed to the term 'aggravated damages', it purports to establish a retrospective classification of awards formerly labelled as 'punitive' in aim.

[15]   *Rookes* v. *Barnard* [1964] A.C. 1129, 1230.

[16]   [1964] A.C. 1129, 1221.

[17]   *Ibid.*, 1226, 1233.

[18]   *Ibid.*, 1233.

[19]   *Ibid.*, 1231.

[20]   *Ibid.*, 1232.

[21]   *Ibid.*, 1221.

[22]   *Ibid.*, 1229, 1232.

[23]   See para. 2.2 above. Hereafter 'exceptional' or 'contumelious conduct'.

[24]   E.g. *McMillan* v. *Singh* (1984) 17 H.L.R. 120; *Asghar* v. *Ahmed* (1984) 17 H.L.R. 25; *Jones* v. *Miah*, [1992] E.G.C.S. 51. See *Arden and Partington on Quiet Enjoyment* (3rd ed., 1990), pp. 31-42.

misconduct[25] and malicious libels.[26] Some exceptional conduct directed at the plaintiff must be identified. Hard words or pig-headedness will not suffice.[27] Nor will flagrant wrongdoing against A which also constitutes a separate and different wrong against B give rise to an award of aggravated damages to B if there is no offensive conduct directed at B.[28] The requirement that some exceptional conduct must accompany the wrongdoing would also seem to entail that wrongs which are committed merely negligently cannot give rise to awards of aggravated damages, even though the plaintiff may have been insulted or offended. However, in *Barbara* v. *Home Office*, Leggatt J. was of the opinion that a negligently committed trespass to the person, although not capable of being punished by exemplary damages, *could* justify an aggravated award for injury to feelings and dignity.[29] It has subsequently been held that aggravated damages ought not to be available in actions based on the tort of negligence,[30] and this view has recently been endorsed by the Court of Appeal in *A.B.* v. *South West Water Services Ltd.*.[31]

---

[25]   E.g. *White* v. *Metropolitan Police Commissioner*, *The Times*, 24 April 1982. See R. Clayton & H. Tomlinson, *Civil Actions Against the Police* (2nd ed., 1992), pp. 385, 387-389.

[26]   E.g. *Ley* v. *Hamilton* (1935) 153 L.T. 384, as interpreted by Lord Devlin in *Rookes* v. *Barnard* [1964] A.C. 1129, 1230-1231. *Broome* v. *Cassell* [1972] A.C. 1027, 1079 F-H.

[27]   *Rookes* v. *Barnard* [1964] A.C. 1129, 1232.

[28]   *Ibid.*, 1232-1233. The plaintiff in *Rookes* relied on the defendants' flagrant breach of contract with a third party, which also constituted the tort of intimidation actionable by the plaintiff. But "this was not conduct that affected" the plaintiff. This also illustrates the fact that aggravated damages are parasitic. Exceptional conduct causing mere mental distress is insufficient; it must also amount independently to an actionable wrong.

[29]   (1984) 134 N.L.J. 888.

[30]   *Kralj* v. *McGrath* [1986] 1 All E.R. 54 (*per* Woolf J.).

[31]   [1993] Q.B. 507. But Lord Bridge in *Hicks* v. *Chief Constable of S. Yorkshire Police* [1992] 2 All E.R. 65, 69D-E, left open the question whether damages should be increased in a personal injury case on account of the terrifying circumstances in which they were inflicted. Where fear was the only 'loss' suffered, it clearly could not give rise to a cause of action in negligence. Cf. H. Luntz, *Assessment of Damages for Personal Injury and Death* (3rd ed., 1990), para. [1.7.11], n. 20.

3.5   It seems that conduct subsequent to the wrong may give rise to aggravated damages.[32] This is well established in defamation cases where the subsequent conduct of the defendant clearly permits an increase in the level of damages. Relevant aggravating conduct includes:

> ... a failure to make any or any sufficient apology and withdrawal; a repetition of the libel; conduct calculated to deter the plaintiff from proceeding; persistence, by way of a prolonged or hostile cross-examination of the plaintiff or in turgid speeches to the jury, in a plea of justification which is bound to fail; the general conduct either of the preliminaries or of the trial itself in a manner calculated to attract further wide publicity; and persecution of the plaintiff by other means.[33]

The extent of the rule and whether it is confined to defamation or cases involving conduct similar to defamation is unclear.[34] In cases of defamation later conduct of the sort referred to is closely bound up with the wrong itself and the harm to which the wrong typically gives rise; indeed, it can be seen as an extension or prolongation of the libel. The conduct of the defendant at trial has also been considered relevant to aggravated damages in cases of malicious prosecution,[35] false imprisonment[36] and discrimination[37] where the persistence by the defendant in damaging allegations about the plaintiff or in attempts to tarnish character can be viewed as analogous to attempts to sully reputation, that is, as a form of defamation.[38] In discrimination cases, it appears that further victimisation of the plaintiff following the discriminatory treatment can justify an award of aggravated damages.[39] Here again the later conduct which merits the award is closely connected to the wrong itself. Where

---

[32]   Conduct prior to the wrong may also be put forward as an aggravating feature, but here its relevance may be that it goes towards evidence of malice: *Prince Ruspoli* v. *Associated Newspapers Plc.*, 11 December 1992 (Unreported, C.A.).

[33]   *Sutcliffe* v. *Pressdram Ltd.* [1991] 1 Q.B. 153, 184E-F (*per* Nourse L.J.).

[34]   See para. 2.26 above.

[35]   *Marks* v. *Chief Constable of Greater Manchester*, [1992] T.L.R. 23 (C.A.).

[36]   *Warby* v. *Cascarino*, *The Times*, 27 October 1989.

[37]   *Duffy* v. *Eastern Health & Social Services Board* [1992] I.R.L.R. 251; *Alexander* v. *Home Office* [1988] 1 W.L.R. 968, 978B-D.

[38]   The wrongs referred to have been said to involve a defamatory element: *Walter* v. *Alltools Ltd.* (1944) 61 T.L.R. 39, 40 "A false imprisonment does not merely affect a man's liberty; it also affects his reputation" (*per* Lawrence L.J.). K. O'Donovan & E. Szyszczak, *Equality and Sex Discrimination Law* (1988), p. 222, point to a close analogy between defamation and discrimination.

[39]   *Duffy* v. *Eastern Health & Social Services Board* [1992] I.R.L.R. 251, 257, para. 15.

the later conduct is not so intimately connected it may not be possible for an award of aggravated damages to be made. It may even be that in cases other than defamation aggravated damages in respect of conduct subsequent to the wrong may only be awarded where the conduct constituting the wrong itself justifies them.[40]

3.6   The kinds of injury to which the defendant's exceptional conduct must give rise have been described above.[41] Lord Devlin said that malice or malevolence might be *such as to* injure the plaintiff's feelings. In other words, malice, malevolence, or insolence accompanying the wrong *import* a particular form of injury. They import insult, outrage, mental hurt and the like. The injury which is relevant to an aggravated award therefore consists of those subjective sensations which affect the plaintiff's consciousness: injuries to personality.

3.7   The requirement of injury to feelings and the like means that a plaintiff who is unaware of the defendant's exceptional motive or conduct cannot claim aggravated damages, although the conduct might otherwise excite outrage or offence.[42] But where knowledge of the exceptional behaviour does give rise to wounded feelings, injury to pride or dignity, mental distress, humiliation, pain or insult it is clear that an aggravated award is possible. In *Broome* v. *Cassell*,[43] the House of Lords referred to mental distress,[44] injury to feelings, insult, indignity,[45] humiliation,[46] and a heightened sense of injury or grievance.[47] Lord Hailsham L.C. also identified feelings of outrage and indignation as permissible elements of an aggravated award, although he spoke of effect being given to them in those cases where they

---

40   In *A.B.* v. *South West Water Services Ltd.* [1993] Q.B. 507, the defendant's conduct following the wrong was described as "highly reprehensible" but the wrong itself had been committed merely negligently and had not been accompanied by any exceptional conduct. However, the plaintiffs' claims for aggravated damages were struck out on the different ground that feelings of anger and indignation were not 'damage' which the law recognised. See para. 3.8 and n.52 below.

41   See paras. 3.3 above.

42   *Alexander* v. *Home Office* [1988] 1 W.L.R. 968, 976C-D. Cf. H. Luntz, *Assessment of Damages for Personal Injury and Death* (3rd. ed., 1990), p. 71, para. [1.7.14].

43   [1972] A.C. 1027.

44   *Ibid.*, 1085E.

45   *Ibid.*, 1089C-D.

46   *Ibid.*, 1121H.

47   *Ibid.*, 1124G.

were experienced by the jury, rather than by the plaintiff.[48] Nevertheless it seems that the kinds of sensation mentioned in *Broome* v. *Cassell* necessarily also embrace feelings of outrage or indignation experienced by the plaintiffs themselves, and indeed subsequent caselaw has confirmed this.[49]

3.8   However, in *A.B.* v. *South West Water Services Ltd.* the Court of Appeal struck out claims for aggravated damages based on feelings of indignation at the defendant's highhanded conduct following a negligently committed public nuisance.[50] It was held that any greater pain or suffering and real anxiety or distress which were suffered as a result of the defendant's subsequent conduct were to be compensated by way of general damages for pain and suffering.[51] But in the Court of Appeal's view feelings of anger and indignation were not a proper subject for compensation[52] and could not attract an award of aggravated damages, since they were neither damage directly caused by the defendant's tortious conduct[53] nor damage which the law had ever previously recognised.[54] On the face of it, this would appear to conflict with previous law on aggravated damages.

3.9   It is nevertheless probable that feelings of anger and indignation can still form the basis of an aggravated award where the plaintiff's basic claim is not based on a complaint of negligence, or where the nature of the wrong itself imports injury to feelings. Sir Thomas Bingham M.R. accepted that indignation aroused by a defendant's conduct could in effect increase a plaintiff's damages in defamation cases, because in such cases "injury to the plaintiff's feelings and self-

---

[48]   *Ibid.*, 1073D, 1076G-H, 1077D, 1079F-H. He explicitly recognised a punitive element to aggravated awards, which he called a "solatium".

[49]   E.g. *McMillan* v. *Singh* (1984) 17 H.L.R. 120, 125 (sense of outrage); *Ansell* v. *Thomas, The Times*, 23 May 1973 (outrage and grave contumely); *Columbia Picture Industries Inc.* v. *Robinson* [1987] Ch. 38, 88H (contumely and affront).

[50]   [1993] Q.B. 507.

[51]   *Ibid.*, 527H, 528E-F, 532F-G.

[52]   *Ibid.*, 527H-528E.

[53]   See para. 3.5 above. Thus it seems that only the conduct constituting the wrong itself, or subsequent conduct so closely associated with it that it can be said to be an extension of the wrong itself, are relevant to aggravated awards.

[54]   [1993] Q.B. 507, 533B (*per* Bingham M.R.).

esteem is an important part of the damage for which compensation is awarded."[55] It would follow that awards of aggravated damages should still be permissible in respect of anger and indignation in other similar actions of which this can also be said.[56] Again, Stuart-Smith L.J. relied on Woolf J.'s judgment in the negligence case of *Kralj* v. *McGrath*[57] in support of his view that feelings of anger and indignation cannot be compensated. Although the statements in *A.B* v. *South West Water Services Ltd.* on the availability of aggravated damages and the legal concept of damage appear to be made in general terms, this part of the decision is linked to the fact that the plaintiffs' claims were for personal injury following a *negligently* committed nuisance and therefore, it may be argued, it does not embrace those causes of action where aggravated damages have previously been regarded as legitimate.

3.10   In *Messenger Newspapers Group Ltd.* v. *National Graphical Association*, it was held that a limited company could be awarded aggravated damages, although such awards would be lower than those which a human being, who has feelings, could receive.[58] Caulfield J. was able to come to this conclusion by concentrating on the first precondition to an award of aggravated damages and by not emphasising the second.[59] The better view is that a corporation cannot receive an aggravated award since it cannot experience the intangible losses which are an inherent part of human personality.[60]

3.11   So far as their availability is concerned, aggravated damages are therefore both wider and narrower than exemplary damages. They are wider in that they need not satisfy the *A.B.* v. *South West Water Services Ltd.*[61] cause of action test[62] and *any* exceptional or contumelious conduct may give rise to such an award, whereas exemplary damages may only be awarded in three special sets of circumstances: aggravated awards extend beyond Lord Devlin's

---

55   [1993] Q.B. 507, 533A.

56   E.g. false imprisonment, malicious prosecution, assault and battery, discrimination.

57   [1986] 1 All E.R. 54.

58   [1984] I.R.L.R. 397, 407, paras. 77-78.

59   The *nature* of the injury was considered irrelevant by him.

60   *Columbia Pictures Industries Inc.* v. *Robinson* [1987] Ch. 38, 88H,(*per* Scott J).

61   [1993] Q.B. 507.

62   But see paras. 3.13-3.17 below.

categories. But they are at the same time more circumscribed than exemplary damages in two respects.[63] First, exceptional conduct is a necessary precondition to aggravated damages and not merely a sufficient one. Exemplary damages, on the other hand, may be awarded even in the absence of any aggravating circumstances.[64] Second, aggravated damages are tied to the injury to feelings and the like which the plaintiff has experienced, whilst exemplary damages may be awarded where the defendant's conduct falls within one of Lord Devlin's categories even though no intangible loss has been suffered.[65]

(b) Which wrongs

3.12   Aggravated damages are available in respect of those wrongs where damages are 'at large'. Lord Devlin used this expression to mean those cases where the award is not limited to the pecuniary loss that can be specifically proved.[66] It is because it is impossible to equate the plaintiff's loss (which is non-pecuniary) to a sum of money that it is permissible to have regard to the conduct of the defendant, as a means of determining the sum that should be awarded and as a guide to that process. However, in personal injury actions based on negligence, damages are also at large in that the plaintiff may be compensated for non-pecuniary harm which takes the form of pain and suffering and loss of amenity. Yet aggravated damages are thought to be unavailable in such cases.[67] It is therefore perhaps preferable to adopt Lord Hailsham's view, and to restrict the term 'at large' to those wrongs for which it has been held that the plaintiff may recover damages for intangible losses.[68]

---

[63]   And also because aggravated sums tend to be smaller than exemplary awards.

[64]   *Huckle* v. *Money* (1763) 2 Wils. K.B. 205, 95 E.R. 768; *Broome* v. *Cassell* [1972] A.C. 1027, 1128H, 1134D-E; *Holden* v. *Chief Constable of Lancashire* [1987] Q.B. 380. See para. 3.38 below.

[65]   *Broome* v.*Cassell* [1972] A.C. 1027, 1111D (*per* Viscount Dilhorne).As a matter of *practice* however, exemplary damages tend to be awarded where this is the case. See paras. 2.20-2.28 above, and 3.33-3.112 below.

[66]   *Rookes* v. *Barnard* [1964] A.C. 1129, 1221.

[67]   See para. 3.4 above and para. 3.14 below.

[68]   *Broome* v. *Cassell* [1972] A.C. 1027, 1073G-H.

3.13 As a consequence of the Court of Appeal's recent decision in *A.B.* v. *South West Water Services Ltd.*,[69] exemplary damages may only be awarded in respect of those wrongs for which such an award had been made prior to *Rookes* v. *Barnard*.[70] This cause of action test does not appear to extend to aggravated damages.[71] However, it seems that not *all* wrongs are capable of sustaining an aggravated award, partly as an implicit consequence of its definitional elements and partly as a result of the judicial perception that an award which takes into account the culpability of the defendant's conduct is not strictly compensatory and therefore inappropriate for certain wrongs.

3.14 It has been held, for instance, that aggravated damages ought not to be awarded where the plaintiff's cause of action is based on negligence.[72] This seems to be sound in principle. The exceptional conduct which is a precondition of an aggravated award would seem to be incompatible with conduct which is merely negligent. There is also the additional consideration that in personal injury cases based on negligence pure compensatory principles appear to be paramount and considerations of culpability misplaced.[73] Where the defendant's conduct *does* satisfy the test appropriate for an award of aggravated damages, it will usually also amount to some other nominate tort, such as battery, which directly protects the victim's personality, for which it is well recognised that an aggravated award can be made.

3.15 In the same way, it has also been held that an award of aggravated damages cannot be made where the wrong of which the plaintiff complains is a breach of contract.[74] This is so despite the fact that, in contrast to personal injury cases, a breach of contract which is accompanied

---

[69] [1993] Q.B. 507.

[70] [1964] A.C. 1129. See paras. 3.55-3.78 below.

[71] Although Lord Diplock's statement in *Broome* v. *Cassell* [1972] A.C. 1027, 1131A, upon which the Court of Appeal relied, refers also to aggravated damages not being intended to extend to torts for which they had not previously been awarded.

[72] *Kralj* v. *McGrath* [1986] 1 All E.R. 54, 61E-G, approved by the Court of Appeal in *A.B.* v. *South West Water Services Ltd.* [1993] Q.B. 507, 527H-528E. See para. 3.4 above.

[73] *Kralj* v.*McGrath* [1986] 1 All E.R. 54, 61F-G. Although see *Hicks* v. *Chief Constable of South Yorkshire* [1992] 2 All E.R. 65, 69D-E, where Lord Bridge left open the question whether damages in a personal injury case might be increased on account of the terrifying circumstances in which physical injuries were inflicted.

[74] *Addis* v. *Gramophone Co. Ltd.* [1909] A.C. 488 (a pre-*Rookes* case in which the damages referred to can be interpreted as aggravated); *Kralj* v. *McGrath* [1986] 1 All E.R. 54, 61E-G (*per* Woolf J.); *Levi* v. *Gordon*, 12 November 1992, (Unreported, C.A.).

by some exceptional conduct will not necessarily amount at the same time to a nominate tort for which aggravated damages can be awarded.[75] Subject to the limited possibility of a restitutionary award discussed in Part VII of this paper,[76] the reason for this seems to be that in assessing the appropriate award for a breach of contract, as in the case of the tort of negligence, pure compensatory principles prevail.[77] Moreover, contract is primarily concerned with pecuniary losses,[78] rather than with the non-pecuniary losses which form the basis of an aggravated award. Nevertheless, where the plaintiff is able to frame an alternative claim in tort, aggravated damages can be awarded where there has been (but not *for*) a contumelious breach of contract, a possibility which is particularly evident in those housing cases where a breach of repairing covenants or of the covenant for quiet enjoyment amounts also to the tort of trespass or nuisance.

3.16 The fact that damages for mental distress can be awarded for breach of contract in certain limited circumstances may mitigate the rule which precludes aggravated (and exemplary) awards in contract cases. In general, damages are not recoverable for disappointment, distress, upset and frustration caused by a breach even where it was within the contemplation of the parties that the breach would have such effects.[79] However, it now appears that damages for distress are recoverable where the contract is intended to prevent distress, give peace of mind or provide enjoyment[80] or where the plaintiff's distress is directly caused by physical loss arising from the breach of contract.[81]

---

[75] This is another way of saying that where the cause of action is contract the quality of the defendant's conduct is not necessarily merely negligent and therefore may be consistent with the exceptional conduct required for an aggravated award.

[76] See also the references there to *Surrey C.C.* v. *Bredero Homes Ltd.*, *The Times*, 16 April 1993 (C.A.).

[77] *Addis* v. *Gramophone Co. Ltd.* [1909] A.C. 488; *Kralj* v. *McGrath* [1986] 1 All E.R. 54, 61F-G.

[78] *McGregor on Damages* (15th ed., 1988), para. 91.

[79] *Bliss* v. *S.E. Thames R.H.A.* [1987] I.C.R. 700 (contract of employment); *Hayes* v. *James & Charles Dodd* [1990] 2 All E.R. 815 (solicitor's contract to provide professional services); *Branchett* v. *Beaney* [1992] 3 All E.R. 910 (covenant for quiet enjoyment of property). See also A.S. Burrows, *Remedies for Torts and Breach of Contract* (1987), pp. 204-206.

[80] *Jarvis* v. *Swan Tours Ltd.* [1973] Q.B. 233, 238, (*per* Lord Denning M.R.).

[81] *Perry* v. *Sidney Phillips & Son* [1982] 1 W.L.R. 1297 (anxiety and distress of living in a house in poor condition which had been bought in reliance on negligence in breach of contract in a surveyor's report); *Calabar Properties Ltd* v. *Stitcher* [1984] 1 W.L.R. 287 (unpleasantness of living in deteriorating premises until they became uninhabitable because of landlord's delay in repairing).

3.17   Wrongs for which there is clear authority that aggravated damages may be awarded include assault and battery,[82] false imprisonment,[83] malicious prosecution,[84] defamation,[85] intimidation,[86] discrimination,[87] trespass to land,[88] deceit,[89] nuisance[90] and unlawful interference with business.[91] Aggravated damages have also been awarded in respect of a breach of a cross-undertaking given by a plaintiff when obtaining an *Anton Piller* order.[92]

---

[82]   E.g. *Ansell* v. *Thomas, The Times*, 23 May 1973; *Flavius* v. *Metropolitan Police Commissioner* (1982) 132 N.L.J. 532; *Ballard* v. *Metropolitan Police Commissioner* (1983) 133 N.L.J. 1133; *W.* v. *Meah* [1986] 1 All E.R. 935. See R. Clayton & H. Tomlinson, *Civil Actions Against the Police* (2nd ed., 1992), pp. 396-7.

[83]   *Smith* v. *Metropolitan Police Commissioner* [1982] C.L.Y. 899; *Warby* v. *Cascarino, The Times*, 27 October 1989; *Barnes* v. *Metropolitan Police Commissioner* [July 1992] Legal Action 14; *White* v. *Metropolitan Police Commissioner, The Times*, 24 April 1982. See R. Clayton & H. Tomlinson, *Civil Actions Against the Police* (2nd ed., 1992), pp. 400, 401.

[84]   *White* v. *Metropolitan Police Commissioner, The Times*, 24 April 1982; *Marks* v. *Chief Constable of Greater Manchester*, [1992] T.L.R. 23, *The Independent*, 21 January 1992. See R. Clayton & H. Tomlinson, *Civil Actions Against the Police* (2nd ed., 1992) p. 404.

[85]   *Ley* v. *Hamilton* (1935) 153 L.T. 384, as interpreted by Lord Devlin in *Rookes* v. *Barnard* [1964] A.C. 1129, 1230-1231; *McCarey* v. *Associated Newspapers Ltd. (No. 2)* [1965] 2 Q.B. 86, 107D; *Broome* v. *Cassell* [1972] A.C. 1027.

[86]   *Messenger Newspapers Group Ltd.* v. *National Graphical Association* [1984] I.R.L.R. 397; *Godwin* v. *Uzoigwe*, [1992] T.L.R. 300. This is implicit in *Rookes* v. *Barnard* [1964] A.C. 1129, 1232-1233.

[87]   *Alexander* v. *Home Office* [1988] 1 W.L.R. 968; *Morris* v. *Higgs & Hill Building Ltd.*, (Jan/Feb 1992) 41 Equal Opportunities Review, 30, 33; *Duffy* v. *Eastern Health & Social Services Board* [1992] I.R.L.R. 251; *Hynes* v. *Warner Howard Ltd.* [March 1993] Legal Action 18.

[88]   *Merest* v. *Harvey* (1814) 5 Taunt. 442, 128 E.R. 761, *Sears* v. *Lyons* (1818) 2 Stark. 317, 171 E.R. 658, *Williams* v. *Currie* (1845) 1 C.B. 841, 135 E.R. 774, and *Emblen* v. *Myers* (1860) 6 H. & N. 54, 158 E.R. 23, as interpreted by Lord Devlin in *Rookes* v. *Barnard* [1964] A.C. 1129, 1223, 1229; *Drane* v. *Evangelou* [1978] 1 W.L.R. 455, 461H, 462E. Cases of trespass where landlords have harassed and intimidated tenants represent a significant body of the case law on aggravated damages.

[89]   *Mafo* v. *Adams* [1970] 1 Q.B. 548, 558D-E; *Archer* v. *Brown* [1985] Q.B. 401, 426D-E.

[90]   *Thompson* v. *Hill* (1870) L.R. 5 C.P. 564, which after *Rookes* must be interpreted as a case of aggravated damages since the defendant does not appear to have been motivated by profit.

[91]   *Messenger Newspapers Group Ltd.* v. *National Graphical Association* [1984] I.R.L.R. 397.

[92]   *Columbia Picture Industries Inc.* v. *Robinson* [1987] Ch. 38.

(c) Miscellaneous rules governing availability

3.18 By virtue of R.S.C., O. 18, r. 8(3), a claim in the High Court for exemplary damages must be specifically pleaded together with the facts on which the party pleading relies.[93] R. 8(3) does not extend to aggravated damages, but it is advisable that they be specifically pleaded. In *Prince Ruspoli* v. *Associated Newspapers Plc.*,[94] the Court of Appeal accepted the defendants' argument that, at least on the facts of the case before it,[95] the combined effect of R.S.C., O. 18, rr. 8(1)(b),[96] 12(1)(b),[97] and 12(1)(c)[98] was that the plaintiff's claim for aggravated damages should have been pleaded.[99] Whether or not a claim is pleaded can therefore affect the availability of an aggravated award.

3.19 If Lord Kilbrandon's view in *Broome* v. *Cassell* is correct,[100] the death of the plaintiff may also preclude a claim for aggravated damages. This is because he interpreted the phrase "exemplary damages" in section 1(2)(a) of the Law Reform (Miscellaneous Provisions) Act 1934, which provides that these damages shall not survive for the benefit of the estate of a deceased person, as referring in fact to aggravated damages. He was, however, alone in expressing this view.[101]

---

[93] By virtue of C.C.R. 1981, O. 6, r. 1B, a claim for aggravated or exemplary damages in the County Court must be specifically pleaded (inserted by County Court (Amendment No. 4) Rules 1989, S.I. 1989, No. 2426).

[94] 11 December 1992 (Unreported).

[95] The plaintiff sought to rely on *previous* conduct as aggravation and as evidence of the defendants' state of mind at the time they published the defamatory statement.

[96] Which requires facts which may take the opposite party by surprise to be pleaded.

[97] Which requires "any condition of mind" including malice to be pleaded.

[98] Which requires facts relied on in mitigation of, or otherwise in relation to, the amount of damages to be pleaded.

[99] See also *The Supreme Court Practice 1993*, vol. 1, p. 310, note 18/12/9. Cf. *Deane* v. *Ealing L.B.C.* [1993] I.C.R. 329, 331F, where in the context of a claim for aggravated and exemplary damages in respect of discrimination, the E.A.T. suggested that it would "be sound practice for an indication to be given as early as possible that such damages were to be claimed."

[100] [1972] A.C. 1027, 1133F.

[101] In *Halford* v. *Brookes* [1992] 1 P.I.Q.R. 175, the plaintiff, suing as administratrix of the estate of her daughter, claimed (inter alia) aggravated damages in respect of a battery which resulted in the daughter's death. In disapplying the statutory time limit for the claim, the Court of Appeal did not take the point that s. 1(2)(a) of the Law Reform (Miscellaneous Provisions) Act 1934 precluded the claim

(2) Assessment

3.20   If aggravated damages really are compensatory, as Lord Devlin maintained,[102] then they should be governed by compensatory principles of assessment. Consequently, matters such as the means of the defendant or factors such as provocation by the plaintiff ought not to enter into the jury's or the court's assessment of the sum to which the plaintiff is entitled, and indeed there are judicial statements to this effect.[103] The tribunal of assessment should look only to the extent of the plaintiff's loss and attempt to quantify it.

3.21   However, the starting point for Lord Devlin's analysis of aggravated and exemplary awards in *Rookes* was his recognition that where the plaintiff's loss is non-pecuniary, and particularly where it is intangible, it cannot be precisely quantified or converted into monetary form.[104] Hence other factors, such as the defendant's conduct, can be used as a guide to assessment. Lord Reid described the process in *Broome* v. *Cassell* in the following terms:

> Where the injury is material and has been ascertained it is generally possible to assess damages with some precision. But that is not so where he [i.e. the plaintiff] has been caused mental distress or when his reputation has been attacked - where, to use the traditional phrase, he has been held up to hatred, ridicule or contempt. Not only is it impossible to ascertain how far other people's minds have been affected, it is almost impossible to equate the damage to a sum of money. Any one person trying to fix a sum as compensation will probably find in his mind a wide bracket within which any sum could be regarded by him as not unreasonable - and different people will come to different conclusions. So in the end there will probably be a wide gap between the sum which on an objective view could be regarded as the least and the sum which could be regarded as the most to which the plaintiff is entitled as compensation.
>
> It has long been recognised that in determining what sum within that bracket should be awarded, a jury, or other tribunal, is entitled to have regard to the conduct of the defendant. He may have behaved in a highhanded, malicious, insulting or oppressive manner in committing the tort or he or his counsel may at the trial have aggravated the injury by what they there said. That would justify going to the top of the bracket

---

for aggravated damages: [1991] 1 W.L.R. 428. Damages were awarded in the sum of £10,641 but whether they included an aggravated sum does not appear from the report of Rougier J.'s judgment in the trial of the action.

[102] *Rookes* v. *Barnard* [1964] A.C. 1129, 1221, 1228 - 1231.

[103] *Rookes* v. *Barnard* [1964] A.C. 1129, 1222 (mitigating factors), 1228 (means of the parties) and 1230 (both); *Godwin* v. *Uzoigwe*, [1992] T.L.R. 300 (at p. 15D of the transcript) (means of the defendant irrelevant).

[104] [1964] A.C. 1129, 1221.

and awarding as damages the largest sum that could fairly be regarded as compensation.[105]

3.22   It would seem that in practice, because of the nature of the loss involved and the subjectivity of the factors which can legitimately be taken into account, the process of assessing aggravated damages cannot be equated to that which is followed in relation to pecuniary losses, or even non-pecuniary losses which take the form of pain and suffering or loss of amenity. Moreover, aggravated damages may be particularly appropriate in precisely those actions which remain within the control of a jury.[106] In contrast to the position in personal injury cases, these considerations combine so as to impede the development of a criterion of comparability by reference to which some standardisation of awards could be achieved.[107] In actions where a judicial assessment of damages is made and where a significant body of caselaw on aggravated damages exists, such as housing and discrimination cases, it is possible to identify some consistency in and guidance as to levels of awards,[108] but this may be attributable in part to statutory maximum limits on awards,[109] which necessarily control and determine levels, confining them within a limited range. Ultimately, the process seems to be an inherently discretionary one.

3.23   The incommensurability and subjectivity of the intangible losses with which an aggravated award is concerned ensure that perfect compensation cannot be achieved: there can only be fair and reasonable compensation. But the significance of matters other than the plaintiff's loss

---

[105] [1972] A.C. 1027, 1085D-G.

[106] Libel, slander, malicious prosecution and false imprisonment: s. 69 of the Supreme Court Act 1981.

[107] In *W.* v. *Meah* [1986] 1 All E.R. 935, 942B, a case of intentional trespass to the person, Woolf J. thought that the award he made, which included an aggravated sum, had to "bear a proper relationship to the awards which the court makes in more conventional personal injury cases." But although this consideration is sometimes referred to by the courts, it has never been consistently applied.

[108] On housing, see M. Partington & J. Hill, *Housing Law: Cases, Materials and Commentary* (1991), p. 277; and *Arden & Partington on Quiet Enjoyment* (3rd ed., 1990), pp. 31-44. On discrimination, see (Jan/Feb 1992) 41 Equal Opportunities Review 30; C. Bourn, "Harassed by discrimination law?", (1992) 142 N.L.J. 1059, 1060; A. Watson, "Remedies for Sexual Harassment at Work", (Dec. 1992) 12 Litigation 91, 95; and the recent guidance on damages for injury to feelings in *Sharifi* v. *Strathclyde Regional Council* [1992] I.R.L.R 259.

[109] As regards housing, the limit was £5,000 for county court actions (but now see para. 3.46). As regards discrimination, the limit was £11,000 for claims made in an industrial tribunal, but this limit no longer operates in claims made by public sector employees: see para. 5.37 below. There would seem to be no limit to claims for discrimination which are brought in the county court: D. Pannick, *Sex Discrimination Law* (1985), p. 89.

suggests that the principles applied in the assessment of aggravated damages do not encompass merely compensatory aims. It has been said, for instance, that aggravated awards should be moderate,[110] a concern traditionally associated with exemplary damages.[111] In addition, matters in mitigation[112] do seem to affect the assessment of aggravated damages, particularly in defamation cases, despite Lord Devlin's contrary view.[113] Lord Hailsham L.C.in *Broome* v. *Cassell* thought that the plaintiff's own bad conduct or an apology by the defendant were matters to be taken into account when assessing an aggravated award in defamation cases.[114] He was of the opinion, further, that the rule relating to multiple defendants in the context of exemplary damages,[115] was equally applicable in the case of aggravated damages. The assessment of aggravated damages therefore may not be wholly reconcilable with strict compensatory principles, even if one does not take into account the problems raised by the nature of the losses involved. It should be noted, however, that Lord Hailsham's views were a product of the way in which he perceived aggravated damages to contain within them a punitive aspect, a proposition which we consider in the next section.

(3) Function

3.24   Uncertainty regarding the function of aggravated damages and their close association with exemplary damages, having emerged out of awards formerly considered punitive in aim, has led to their inclusion in this paper. Lord Devlin clearly regarded them as being compensatory in aim, and it has commonly been argued since then that this is the case.[116] However, a

---

[110] *W.* v. *Meah* [1986] 1 All E.R. 935, 942D-E (*per* Woolf J.).

[111] *Rookes* v. *Barnard* [1964] A.C. 1129, 1227-1228.

[112] E.g. *O'Connor* v. *Hewitson* [1979] Crim.L.R. 46; *Lewis* v. *Chief Constable of Greater Manchester, The Independent*, 23 October 1991 (see transcript).

[113] *Rookes* v. *Barnard* [1964] A.C. 1129, 1222, 1230.

[114] [1972] A.C. 1027, 1071F, G.

[115] Namely, that where there are multiple defendants the exemplary damages should reflect only the lowest figure for which any of them can be held liable. See paras. 3.97-3.98 below.

[116] E.g. *Salmon & Heuston on Torts* (20th ed., 1992) at pp. 517-518); *Winfield and Jolowicz on Tort* (13th ed., 1989), p. 602; A. Ogus, *The Law of Damages* (1973) pp. 29, 231-2 and 238. Indeed, this is the basis upon which courts have since proceeded, at least in form.

number of features of aggravated awards have led to suggestions that they may be partly punitive in character.[117]

3.25   First, the legal significance of the defendant's conduct is unclear. It may be interpreted in a way which is compatible with either compensatory or punitive aims.[118] For instance, it may be argued that the defendant's conduct is only relevant in a purely causal sense. The assessment of an appropriate compensatory sum is affected and indeed measured by the extent of the injury suffered by the plaintiff. Where the conduct of the defendant which accompanies the wrong has increased the plaintiff's injury, it is clearly relevant to determining the extent of loss. For example, a defamatory statement which has been widely (or selectively) distributed by the defendant will cause greater hurt to the plaintiff and injury to reputation than one which receives a narrow or untargeted circulation. Again, the manner in which a discriminatory dismissal is carried out may cause greater hurt, for example by advertising the position without the knowledge of the dismissed employee. If, in an award of aggravated damages, the defendant's conduct is only relevant in this causal sense, it is clear that aggravated damages can be regarded as purely compensatory in function.

3.26   This does not, however, explain why the defendant's conduct must be exceptional, unless the idea is that conduct of this kind *necessarily* gives rise to or increases injury to the plaintiff's feelings and the like. In other words, where the defendant's conduct is exceptional, intangible loss can be presumed or inferred. The subjectivity of these losses has meant that they have traditionally been remedied only with caution. The availability of aggravated awards can be seen as an illustration of how protection will at least be extended to them in extreme cases, since here the defendant's conduct is designed to injure, or contemplates injury to, the plaintiff. The defendant's culpable conduct thus transforms what might otherwise be regarded as a purely subjective injury attributable to the plaintiff's own value system or peculiar sensitivity, or which is too trivial to merit protection, into an objective and serious one. The defendant's conduct therefore, may also be an objective test of injury.[119]

---

[117] *Uren* v. *John Fairfax & Sons Pty. Ltd.* (1966) 117 C.L.R. 118, 151-152 (*per* Windeyer J.); J Stone, "Double Count and Double Talk : The End of Exemplary Damages?", (1972) 46 A.L.J. 311.

[118] Cf. H. Stoll, "Penal Purposes in the Law of Tort", (1970) 18 Am. J.C.L. 3, 3-6.

[119] Cf. paras. 2.15 above, and 6.48 below.

3.27   However, compensatory awards should take account of injury to feelings, pride and dignity in any case where damages are at large,[120] and aggravated damages increase the award where that same injury is exacerbated (aggravated) by the manner in which the defendant committed the tort.[121] To obtain an award of aggravated damages it is not sufficient that the plaintiff should prove that the nature of the defendant's conduct caused increased injury to pride and dignity, as would be the case were aggravated damages merely a variation of ordinary compensatory damages. In addition the defendant's conduct is relevant in determining whether an award of aggravated damages should be made at all.[122] In other words, it seems that an award of aggravated damages may be based on the defendant's conduct, that is, that it may be awarded upon a punitive basis.

3.28   Further, upon examining the case law, one interpretation is that in practice the defendant's conduct is not used to cast light upon the plaintiff's injury, but is instead used to punish, deter or condemn the defendant's conduct. A sum of aggravated damages increases the size of an award significantly,[123] and more attention appears to be paid to the defendant's conduct and its gravity than to trying to assess the extent of the plaintiff's injury.[124] For example in *Morris* v. *Higgs and Hill Building Ltd.,*[125] where an award of £4,000 for injury to feelings and £2,000 aggravated damages was made the tribunal said:

> The factors which have led us to make this increased award are firstly, that the respondents advertised the job behind her back, something which she found out about. This is an extremely insulting and high-handed and oppressive thing to do. Secondly, there is the manner of her dismissal, sending her a letter whilst she was away on holiday to await her return, which was bound to cause the maximum amount of shock and distress. Thirdly, since the application was made the respondents have persisted

---

[120] *Rookes* v. *Barnard* [1964] A.C. 1129, 1221, (*per* Lord Devlin).

[121] *Winfield and Jolowicz on Tort* (13th ed., 1989), p. 601.

[122] *Rookes* v. *Barnard* [1964] A.C. 1129, 1221 *per* Lord Devlin.

[123] For example, in a survey of 249 discrimination cases from 1988 to 1990 the average award of damages for injury to feelings was £857. In over half the cases where the tribunal identified the aggravated element of the award, the aggravated element was over £1,000: (Jan/Feb 1992) Equal Opportunities Review 30.

[124] E.g. *Hynes* v. *Warner Howard Ltd.* [March 1993] Legal Action 18; *Deane* v. *Ealing L.B.C.* [1993] I.C.R. 329, 335B-F, H. Cf. *Messenger Newspapers Group Ltd.* v. *National Graphical Association* [1984] I.R.L.R. 397, 407, para. 78.

[125] (Jan/Feb 1992) 41 Equal Opportunities Review, 30, 33.

in various untrue allegations, both about her work and about her conduct, and fourthly, the company as a whole ... have failed to acknowledge the wider problems which have been exposed by this case in their lack of fair procedures and by the absence of any equal opportunities policy and have taken no steps to try and install such a policy.

Of the four reasons given here, only one refers to the plaintiff's injury. Whilst in form judges maintain that aggravated damages are compensatory, the way these awards are used in practice suggests that they are also used in order to pursue punitive aims. This point is further illustrated by the Supreme Court Procedure Committee's *Report on Practice and Procedure in Defamation* (1991) which states:

> We think that in those cases where a defendant's behaviour particularly merits disapproval the jury can adequately deal with this by an award of aggravated damages without stepping outside the notion of compensation.[126]

3.29   Second, the availability of pure compensatory damages for mental distress, injury to feelings and the like in many of the actions for which awards of aggravated damages are traditionally made undermines the claim that aggravated damages are entirely compensatory. Since the former may now be awarded without proof of exceptional conduct, it can no longer be maintained that aggravated damages are simply a particular head of loss corresponding to one form of non-pecuniary injury (namely injury to feelings and the like) or that the role of the defendant's conduct is merely a means of restricting the recovery of intangible losses. The concurrent availability of compensatory damages for injury to feelings and aggravated damages may of course suggest only that the conceptualisation of awards in respect of these losses has not yet been completed and is still in a state of transition. But it also suggests that aggravated damages do not solely perform a strictly compensatory function and that they contain a distinct non-compensatory element. Aggravated damages do not merely duplicate compensatory damages for mental distress,[127] but serve to *increase* the damages that could otherwise be awarded; and they increase awards *because of* the defendant's conduct. This looks like punishment. Further, by separating out aggravated damages and labelling them as such, the

---

[126] At p. 42, para. IV 10.

[127] Cf. *Deane* v. *Ealing L.B.C.* [1993] I.C.R. 329, 335C, where the respondents conceded that the issue of aggravated damages was separate from that of damages for injury to feelings.

conduct upon which they are based is thereby marked out for disapproval, which is of course a punitive aim.[128]

3.30   A third feature of the law relating to aggravated damages which tends to confirm this interpretation of their character is the rejection of these awards in cases where the cause of action is negligence or breach of contract.[129] As we noted above, their rejection in such cases seems to be a consequence in part of a judicial perception that aggravated damages have a punitive aspect to them, thereby making them inappropriate in a context where compensatory principles are thought to prevail.[130] In addition, we think that the considerations taken into account in the assessment of aggravated damages cannot be completely reconciled with compensatory principles as they are traditionally understood.[131]

3.31   Finally, apart from the way in which judges may use aggravated damages in practice, there are some explicit judicial statements to the effect that aggravated damages are indeed a hybrid form of award, incorporating both compensatory and punitive functions. For instance, Lord Hailsham L.C. in *Broome* v. *Cassell* clearly believed that aggravated damages contained a punitive aspect. He expressed the view that in certain cases:

> ... aggravated damages ... can, and should in every case lying outside [Lord Devlin's] categories, take care of the exemplary element, and the jury should neither be encouraged nor allowed to look beyond as generous a solatium as is required for the injuria simply in order to give effect to feelings of indignation. It is not that the exemplary element is excluded in such cases. It is precisely because in the nature of things it is, and should be, included in every such case that the jury should neither be encouraged nor allowed to look for it outside the solatium and then to add to the sum awarded another sum by way of penalty additional to the solatium.[132]

---

128   Cf. F. Trindade and P. Cane, *The Law of Torts in Australia* (2nd ed., 1993), p. 6, n. 23.

129   See paras. 3.14 and 3.15 above.

130   Negligence is incompatible with the requirement of exceptional conduct, and this is one reason why aggravated damages are unavailable. But some breaches of contract will satisfy the requirement and the reason for refusing aggravated awards in this context must therefore be found elsewhere.

131   See para. 3.23 above.

132   [1972] A.C. 1027, 1076G-H. See also, 1071G, 1072E-H, 1073D, 1079G, 1080F, 1082A, 1083A. Lord Wilberforce did not believe that it was possible to separate the compensatory and punitive elements of an award in the case of wrongs accompanied by contumely or affront: 1115C-1116B.

3.32 In *Rookes* v. *Barnard*, even Lord Devlin observed that his distinction between aggravated and exemplary damages would make little difference to the substance of the law.[133] In the face of this claim, it has rightly been questioned what the real nature of the exercise was in that case.[134] Lord Devlin's interpretation of many increased awards as aggravated damages, by characterising this form of liability as compensatory, thereby rendered it less objectionable and able to conform with the proposition that punishment ought to take place only within the context of the criminal law. But it appears there was also a genuine attempt to identify a real (albeit intangible) loss. One possible interpretation is that these awards are necessarily hybrid, containing both compensatory and punitive elements. The nature of the 'losses'[135] and of the interests involved permits some flexibility in the characterisation of money awards redressing and protecting them. It suggests that the question of how to frame the legal treatment of these losses or interests is a matter of policy rather than one of logic. This is not to say that the issue is simply a choice between concepts (compensation or punishment). The way in which the redress of these interests is perceived can have important substantive implications, and we therefore address these problems Part VI below.[136] Further, if aggravated awards *are* at present being used partly to pursue punitive aims this perhaps suggests a choice between two options for law reform: their abolition;[137] or the removal of the restrictions[138] which have been placed upon exemplary awards.[139]

---

[133] [1964] A.C. 1129, 1230.

[134] *Uren* v. *John Fairfax & Sones Pty Ltd.* (1966) 117 C.L.R. 118, 152; *Broome* v. *Cassell* [1972] A.C. 1027, 1121A-B (*per* Lord Wilberforce). Cf Lord Diplock at 1130G-H.

[135] Whether it is a loss or not becomes a question of legal policy, not observation.

[136] Cf. also para. 2.29 above.

[137] Because punitive considerations are objectionable and because the availability of purely compensatory mental distress damages now makes aggravated awards unnecessary.

[138] I.e. the requirements that the plaintiff's case fall within one of Lord Devlin's categories and that the wrong satisfy the cause of action test. See paras. 3.37-3.78 below.

[139] Because the use of aggravated damages in this way reflects a need for punitive awards.

EXEMPLARY DAMAGES

(1) Availability

3.33   Damages which are intended to punish, deter or convey disapproval were referred to in *Rookes* v. *Barnard* as "exemplary".[140] This terminology was approved in *Broome* v. *Cassell*[141] and has become commonplace so that in English law damages which are purely punitive in aim are now generally known as exemplary damages, a term which perhaps better expresses the modern emphasis on admonition, rather than retribution.[142]

3.34   As indicated above, the availability of exemplary damages was significantly curtailed in *Rookes* v. *Barnard*.[143] Lord Devlin examined the authorities on increased damages in order to discover the scope of the punitive principle.[144] But by reinterpreting many of them as aggravated awards, he was able to conclude that exemplary awards were permissible (and justified) in just three categories of case.[145] It is recognised that, given the previous understanding as to these awards,[146] this effected a radical restriction of the circumstances in which a claim for exemplary damages may be made.[147] The reason for so doing was Lord Devlin's assumption that the availability of an exemplary award in civil actions is anomalous because the punitive considerations which it incorporates properly belong exclusively to the criminal law.[148] In addition, he believed that no serious gaps would be left by limiting exemplary damages in this way, since aggravated damages could do most, if

---

[140]   [1964] A.C. 1129, 1196-1197, 1220-1233.

[141]   [1972] A.C. 1129, 1073E-G, 1124H-1125A. Lord Reid insisted on calling them punitive damages throughout his judgment, perhaps because they appear more objectionable when so described.

[142]   *Ibid.*, 1073F

[143]   [1964] A.C. 1129.

[144]   *Ibid.*, 1221-1225.

[145]   *Ibid.*, 1226-1230. See paras. 3.37-3.54 below.

[146]   See para. 2.2 above.

[147]   *Rookes* v. *Barnard* [1964] A.C. 1129, 1226; *Uren* v. *John Fairfax & Sons Pty. Ltd.* (1966) 117 C.L.R. 118, 132, 145, 146-147, 158-159; *Broome* v. *Cassell* [1972] A.C. 1027, 1077A, 1082E, 1107G, 1120B, 1124B, C-D, 1127B, 1129D-G.

[148]   *Rookes* v. *Barnard* [1964] A.C. 1129, 1221.

not all, of the work done by exemplary awards and that, where they did not, the wrong would generally be punishable as a crime.[149] In other words, he believed that while achieving doctrinal purity, the restriction would have little substantive effect. But because he accepted that, first, the weight of authority favouring exemplary awards made it impossible to remove them from the law completely; and, second, that they could in certain circumstances serve the useful purpose of "vindicating the strength of the law",[150] restriction was preferred to outright abolition.

3.35   Since *Rookes* v. *Barnard* the plaintiff's claim for an exemplary award can only succeed if it falls into one of Lord Devlin's categories. As indicated above, the Court of Appeal has recently held that a further obstacle exists,[151] namely that the cause of action upon which the plaintiff's claim is based must be one in respect of which an exemplary award had been made prior to *Rookes* v. *Barnard* (which we will call the 'cause of action test').[152] There there are therefore at present two preconditions for an exemplary award being made. Furthermore, even if these two requirements are satisfied, the jury or court retains an overriding discretion to refuse the plaintiff's claim: exemplary damages *may*, not must, be awarded.[153] Although this discretion has been somewhat difficult to structure because the decision whether to award exemplary damages so often lies within the control of the jury,[154] appellate courts have begun to develop principles defining its scope and thus further determining the availability of exemplary awards.[155] We shall discuss these principles after

---

[149] *Ibid.*, 1230.

[150] *Ibid.*, 1225-1226.

[151] *A.B.* v. *South West Water Services Ltd.* [1993] Q.B. 507, 523B, 528E-F, 530G.

[152] *Ibid.*, 530H. Reliance was placed on discussion in some of the speeches in *Broome* v. *Cassell* [1972] A.C. 1027 as to the kinds of wrong which could *not* give rise to exemplary damages. See paras. 3.55-3.78, below. The availability of exemplary damages is thus partly contingent upon the interpretation of pre-*Rookes* awards as either aggravated or exemplary. For instance, in *A.B.* v. *South West Water Services Ltd.*, 523C-D the plaintiff's reliance on *Emblen* v. *Myers* (1860) 6 H. & N. 54, 158 E.R. 23, as showing that negligence satisfied the cause of action test was rejected by Stuart-Smith L.J. because "it was regarded as a case of trespass by Lord Devlin *for which aggravated and not exemplary damages were awarded*" (emphasis added).

[153] *Holden* v. *Chief Constable of Lancashire* [1987] 1 Q.B. 380, 385F, 387H-388B, 388D-E, 389B-C; *Broome* v.*Cassell* [1972] A.C. 1027, 1060B-C.

[154] See para. 1.6 above, and para. 3.87 below.

[155] See paras. 3.86-3.88 below.

examining the current state of English law as identified by Lord Devlin's categories and the effect of the cause of action test.

Lord Devlin's Categories

3.36 The three categories of case in which exemplary damages may be awarded were described by Lord Devlin in *Rookes* v. *Barnard* as:[156]

(i) oppressive, arbitrary or unconstitutional action by the servants of the government;

(ii) wrongful conduct which has been calculated by the defendant to make a profit for himself which may well exceed the compensation payable to the plaintiff; and

(iii) any category which such an award is expressly authorised by statute.

According to Lord Devlin, it is only in these cases that an award of exemplary damages can be justified as serving a useful purpose in vindicating the strength of the law and thus affording a practical justification for admitting into the civil law a principle which he considered ought logically to belong to the criminal law.[157] In *Broome* v. *Cassell* Lord Diplock explained that the fact situations described by the requirements of the categories each evinced "some special reason still relevant in modern social conditions for retaining the power to award exemplary damages".[158] Although the categories are now firmly established as representing English law they have been the subject of much criticism, mainly on the ground that they are rigid and not soundly based on principle.[159] They have exerted an obvious effect upon the context in

---

[156] [1964] A.C. 1129, 1226-1227.

[157] *Rookes* v. *Barnard* [1964] A.C. 1129, 1226.

[158] [1972] A.C. 1027, 1128E. Lord Reid rejected the proposition that the categories could be justified as serving a useful purpose. In his view it was only precedent which forced the House of Lords to recognise the operation of the punitive principle in these categories of case: 1087B-C.

[159] E.g. the Court of Appeal in *Broome* v. *Cassell* [1971] 2 Q.B. 354; Viscount Dilhorne and Lord Wilberforce in the House of Lords in *Broome* v. *Cassell* [1972] A.C. 1027, 1108E-G, H-1109B, 1119F, H, 1120C, F-G; L.J.Anderson, "An Exemplary Case for Reform", (1992) 11 C.J.Q. 233, 237-246, 260; *McGregor on Damages* (15th ed., 1988), para. 420. In *Broome* v. *Cassell* [1972] A.C. 1027, 1087A-B, 1088B and E, even Lord Reid, an opponent of exemplary damages, acknowledged that the limitations inherent in the categories were "illogical". *Rookes* has not been followed in other Commonwealth jurisdictions: see paras. 4.1-4.22 below.

which exemplary damages operate today, such awards being most commonly found in three areas of tort law: defamation,[160] unlawful eviction of tenants,[161] and cases of police misconduct[162] pleaded as either trespass to the person[163] or malicious prosecution.

(a) Oppressive, arbitrary or unconstitutional action by servants of the government

3.37   This category is derived from a number of eighteenth century authorities[164] which sought to protect the liberties of the subject from the power of the state and was regarded by Lord Devlin as too valuable to be lost.[165] The limitation to oppressive *governmental* action which is inherent in the category has the effect of excluding oppressive action by private individuals or corporations from the application of the punitive principle.[166] It was Lord Devlin's view that the latter form of oppression did not justify an award of exemplary damages since a powerful individual "is not to be punished simply because he is ... more powerful."[167] However, it was otherwise in the case of servants of the government, where the exercise of power should always be subordinate to their duty of service.[168] The category is therefore aimed at restraining the misuse of power by those in a peculiar position to exercise, and hence also to abuse, it.[169]

---

[160]   Category 2.

[161]   Category 2.

[162]   Category 1.

[163]   I.e. assault, battery, and false imprisonment.

[164]   *Wilkes* v. *Wood* (1763) Lofft. 1, 98 E.R. 489 (trespass to land); *Huckle* v. *Money* (1763) 2 Wils. K. B. 205, 95 E.R. 768 (trespass to the person); *Benson* v. *Frederick* (1766) 3 Burr. 1845, 97 E.R. 1130 (trespass to the person).

[165]   *Rookes* v. *Barnard* [1964] A.C. 1129, 1223 and 1226.

[166]   But an award of aggravated damages may be made.

[167]   *Rookes* v. *Barnard* [1964] A.C. 1129, 1226.

[168]   *Ibid.*.

[169]   Cf. Lord Wilberforce in *Broome* v. *Cassell* [1972] A.C. 1027, 1119E, 1120D-E; and Bingham M.R. in *A.B.* v. *South West Water Services Ltd.* [1993] Q.B. 507, 529F.

3.38   Two elements define the scope of Category 1. The first element looks to the quality of the defendant's conduct, which must be "oppressive, arbitrary or unconstitutional".[170] These terms should be read disjunctively, so that it is open to a court or jury to make an award of exemplary damages where the defendant's behaviour is unconstitutional, even if it is not at the same time oppressive or arbitrary.[171] Exemplary damages are therefore wider in this respect than aggravated damages, which require proof of some exceptional conduct.[172] However, it is also clear that not *all* forms of unconstitutional action will give rise to an award of exemplary damages. The absence of aggravating features is a circumstance which the jury or court is entitled to take into account when deciding whether or not to award exemplary damages and, if so, how much.[173] It has also been held that conduct which is merely negligent will not sustain an award within Category 1.[174] But, where the conduct of the individual officer concerned *is* deliberately unlawful or malicious, thus making the case a particularly appropriate one for exemplary damages, it is now less likely that the relevant public employer will be vicariously liable in respect of that conduct.[175] It remains to be seen whether this will significantly diminish the usefulness of Category 1, which has become an important means of controlling and marking the serious disapproval of misconduct by officials, especially by the police.

---

[170] *Rookes* v. *Barnard* [1964] A.C. 1129, 1226.

[171] *Huckle* v. *Money* (1763) 2 Wils. K.B. 205, 95 E.R. 768; *Broome* v. *Cassell* [1972] A.C. 1027, 1128H, 1134D-E; *Holden* v. *Chief Constable of Lancashire* [1987] 1 Q.B. 380, 388A-D, 388H.

[172] See paras. 3.4 and 3.12 below.

[173] *Holden* v. *Chief Constable of Lancashire* [1987] 1 Q.B. 380, 388D-E. See paras. 3.85 and 3.102 below. This may explain those cases in which claims for exemplary damages have been refused on the ground that the action, albeit unlawful, involved an honest mistake or was taken in good faith: *Eliot* v. *Allen* (1845) 1 C.B. 18, 135 E.R. 441; *Simper* v. *Metropolitan Police Commissioner* [1982] C.L.Y. 3124; and *Kay* v. *James*, 21 April 1989 (Unreported, C.A.). In Northern Ireland, the authority on this point seems almost to favour a requirement of exceptional conduct: *Kelly* v. *Faulkner* [1973] N.I. 31; *Davey* v. *Chief Constable of the R.U.C.* [1988] N.I. 139. And cf. *Uren* v. *John Fairfax and Sons Pty Ltd.* (1966) 117 C.L.R. 118, 135, 159.

[174] *Barbara* v. *Home Office* (1984) 134 N.L.J. 888. See also *A.B.* v. *South West Water Services Ltd.* [1993] Q.B. 507, 531H, at para. 3.41 below, where a negligently committed public nuisance was said to be "quite unlike the abuses of power which Lord Devlin had in mind" (*per* Bingham M.R.).

[175] See paras. 3.104-3.107 below.

3.39   The second element in the definition of Category 1 looks to the status of the defendant.[176] Lord Devlin referred to "the servants of the government",[177] a literal reading of which would confine the category to Crown servants. However, in *Broome* v. *Cassell* the House of Lords preferred a broad interpretation, indicating that the term extends to include others who exercise government functions, such as· the police and local government officials.[178] The broad approach is also reflected in cases in which courts have held that members of the armed services,[179] solicitors executing an *Anton Piller* order[180] and officers of the Intervention Board for Agricultural Produce[181] fall within the category.[182]

3.40   In adopting a broad interpretation, the House of Lords in *Broome* v. *Cassell* emphasised that what is relevant is the nature of the functions or powers being exercised.[183] Until recently English courts did not appear to have encountered difficulties in drawing the distinction between the public and private functions of "servants of the government",[184] or between governmental and non-governmental functions. Such a problem did arise in *Bradford City Council* v. *Arora* where the Court of Appeal rejected the defendant's argument that a local authority, when selecting an employee, was acting in a private capacity rather than exercising a governmental function.[185] It was held that Lord Devlin's first category could apply to such

---

[176] Or to the powers being exercised by the defendant. See para. 3.41 below.

[177] *Rookes* v. *Barnard* [1964] A.C. 1129, 1226.

[178] [1972] A.C. 1027, 1077H-1078C; 1088A-B, 1120D-E, 1130B-C, and 1134D, F-G.

[179] *Lavery* v. *Ministry of Defence* [1984] N.I. 99.

[180] *Columbia Picture Industries Inc.* v. *Robinson* [1987] Ch. 38, where Scott J. emphasised that they did so as officers of the court, thereby being placed in a position which enabled them to do that which would, without the court authority, be an inexcusable trespass.

[181] *R.* v. *Reading J.J., ex p. South West Meat Ltd.* [1992] Crim. L.R. 672.

[182] In *Moore* v. *Lambeth Registrar (No. 2)* [1970] 1 Q.B. 560, 572D, Sachs L.J. questioned whether a case of wrongful execution by an officer of the court might fall within Category 1.

[183] [1972] A.C. 1027, 1078A, 1088A-B, 1130B-C.

[184] See the discussion by L.J. Anderson, "An Exemplary Case for Reform", (1992) 11 C.J.Q. 233, 238-240 and, particularly, the decision in *Makanjuola* v. *Commissioner Metropolitan Police, The Times*, 8 August 1989, cited by the author.

[185] [1991] 2 Q.B. 507, 518E, 519C-E.

conduct.[186] As a result of this case it would appear that the category is not confined to those activities which are only conducted by public authorities. However, in *A.B.* v. *South West Water Services Ltd.*,[187] a nationalised body set up under statute for a commercial purpose (namely, the supply of water) was regarded by the Court of Appeal as falling outside Lord Devlin's first category, because in conducting its commercial operations it was not engaged in performing governmental functions[188] and was not acting as an instrument or agent of the government.[189] The Court of Appeal also rejected the plaintiffs' argument that, since the defendants were a body through which the United Kingdom performed its obligations in Community law and as such were an "emanation of the State" for the purpose of direct enforcement of EC Directives, it therefore followed that they were exercising executive power.[190]

3.41   The retention of Category 1 has allowed exemplary damages to continue to play an important role in the protection of civil liberties[191] since it enables a court or jury, through the award of a substantial sum, to deter and condemn the commission by state officials of torts which affect the liberty of the subject.[192] In practice, Category 1 has been the basis for significant development in the law concerning police misconduct and until very recently it supported a similar development in the context of race and sex discrimination by public employers. The latter development has been curtailed, however, in *A.B.* v. *South West Water Services*

---

[186] But Neill L.J. indicated that there might be cases where a junior officer of a council is carrying out some duty which cannot properly be regarded as the exercise of a public function at all: 518H.

[187] [1993] Q.B. 507.

[188] *Ibid.*, 525E-F (*per* Stuart-Smith L.J.).

[189] *Ibid.*, 532A-B (*per* Bingham M.R.). See also n. 172 above. The defendants initially conceded, as they had before Wright J., that they were a body falling within Category 1 but, at the prompting of the Court of Appeal, withdrew the concession: 531G.

[190] *Ibid.*, 525H-526A, 531G-H. In the present context Bingham M.R. also found it unhelpful to inquire whether the defendants were a body whose decisions were judicially reviewable in public law.

[191] See paras. 2.25-2.28 above.

[192] E.g. battery and assault, false imprisonment, unlawful search and seizure pleaded as trespass to land or goods, and malicious prosecution.

57

Ltd.,[193] as a result of which discrimination can no longer give rise to an award of exemplary damages.[194]

3.42   A number of criticisms have been levelled at the category, some suggesting that it is too narrow[195] and others questioning its retention.[196] The major criticism is that it is illogical in its exclusion of flagrant misconduct by businesses and other powerful non-government servants.[197] Against the argument that public bodies and their servants exercise peculiar power and therefore ought to be subject to peculiar liability, it is pointed out that in practice a large company may wield considerably more economic power than a small local authority, and may often exercise similar functions.[198] It seems strange that misconduct by a policeman, but not by a store detective, should merit an exemplary award.[199] The 'privatisation' of publicly owned industries which has occurred in recent years may be taking some of the defendants who were formerly within the scope of Category 1 outside its reach,[200] but it is difficult to see why the availability of exemplary awards should now be determined by the precise details of public ownership of particular enterprises. Alternatively, in favour of the restriction comprised in Category 1 it can be argued that non-governmental bodies are not usually in a position to exercise extraordinary powers which affect the person

---

[193]   [1993] Q.B. 507.

[194]   See *Deane* v. *Ealing L.B.C.* [1993] I.C.R. 329, 335A. This is because the tort fails the cause of action test, rather than because it necessarily falls outside Lord Devlin's categories. See para. 3.66 below. Discrimination may still give rise to an award of aggravated damages.

[195]   I.e. by those favouring the more liberal pre-*Rookes* law.

[196]   Usually by those who object *in toto* to the operation of the punitive principle in civil actions.

[197]   See particularly the judgments of the members of the Court of Appeal in *Broome* v. *Cassell* [1971] 2 Q.B. 354; and Viscount Dilhorne in the House of Lords [1972] A.C. 1027, 1108E-G. Even Lord Reid, an opponent of exemplary damages, accepted that this limitation in Category 1 was illogical; in his view, it could only be justified by reference to precedent: 1088B-C.

[198]   *Uren* v. *John Fairfax & Sons Pty Ltd.* (1966) 117 C.L.R. 118, 132-133, 137(*per* Taylor J.).

[199]   See the Canadian case of *Mckinnon* v. *F.W. Woolworth Co. Ltd.* (1968) 70 D.L.R. (2d) 280. Lord Hailsham in *Broome* v. *Cassell* [1972] A.C. 1027, 1078A-C, seemed amenable to Category 1 being extended in this respect.

[200]   And thereby perhaps diminished also its practical significance. But the police, who continue to generate a large number of the cases on exemplary damages, are by far the most important class of defendant within Category 1.

of a plaintiff, the interest with which exemplary damages have historically been concerned.

3.43   A second difficulty with this category is that the penalty will not be felt by the particular public official whose misconduct merited it but will be passed on by the rules of vicarious liability to the local authority, government department or other public body which is the employer. In such cases exemplary damages will be a charge on public expenditure. It may be asked why the general public should fund a windfall benefit for a person who has already been compensated for any loss suffered. However, where there is vicarious liability, although the penalty will not be felt by the particular public official, the award of exemplary damages may nevertheless serve an important symbolic function of marking the severity of the disapproval of the conduct.[201] American practice has differed markedly from that in this country. Instead of singling public bodies out as peculiarly liable to exemplary awards, state and federal government bodies have tended to receive statutory protection from such liability.[202] On the other hand, the recent decisions in *Weldon* v. *Home Office*[203] and *Racz* v. *Home Office*[204] may mean that exemplary damages[205] are now less likely to be passed on to public employers by the rules of vicarious liability where their employees have committed acts which were known by the employees to be outside their authority or which were committed for some malicious purpose.[206] In such cases the individual will, however, be liable.

(b) Wrongdoing which is calculated to make a profit

3.44   Lord Devlin's second category encompasses those cases where the defendant's conduct has been calculated to make a profit which may well exceed the compensation payable to the plaintiff.[207] Here, compensatory damages will be inadequate to deter the commission of the

---

[201] See para. 6.43 below.

[202] See paras. 4.15-4.17 below.

[203] [1992] 1 A.C. 58.

[204] [1992] T.L.R. 624.

[205] And even the compensatory damages on which they are parasitic.

[206] Public employers may, of course, be prepared in their discretion to pay any damages awarded.

[207] *Rookes* v. *Barnard* [1964] A.C. 1129, 1226 (*per* Lord Devlin).

tort and exemplary damages may therefore be awarded in order to ensure that the law cannot be broken with impunity:

> Exemplary damages can properly be awarded whenever it is necessary to teach a wrongdoer that tort does not pay.[208]

Category 2 is therefore concerned with one form of improper motive for wrongdoing, namely gain or advantage.

3.45   Lord Devlin's words, describing the state of mind which is required on the part of the defendant in order to satisfy category 2, have been given a liberal interpretation. Lord Devlin himself was of the view that the category extended beyond money-making in the strict sense to cases where the defendant seeks to make any gain at the plaintiff's expense;[209] but in a number of defamation cases immediately following *Rookes* v. *Barnard* plaintiffs found it difficult to satisfy its requirements.[210] The House of Lords therefore emphasised in *Broome* v. *Cassell* that a broad interpretation of Category 2 was essential.[211] It is not necessary, for instance, that the defendant should have made a precise arithmetical calculation of the benefits to be obtained from the tortious conduct; it need only be shown that the tort was knowingly committed for the purpose of obtaining some material advantage.[212] Nevertheless, their Lordships also recognised that the mere fact that the conduct occurred in a business context, for example if the defamatory matter appeared in a newspaper published for profit, was insufficient to bring a case within Category 2 so as to justify an exemplary

---

[208]   *Ibid.*,[1964] A.C. 1129, 1227 (*per* Lord Devlin). Cf. also *Broome* v. *Cassell* [1972] A.C. 1027, 1130D (*per* Lord Diplock).

[209]   *Rookes* v. *Barnard* [1964] A.C. 1129, 1227.

[210]   *McCarey* v. *Associated Newspapers Ltd. (No. 2)* [1965] 2 Q.B. 86; *Manson* v. *Associated Newspapers* [1965] 1 W.L.R. 1038. In *Uren* v. *John Fairfax & Sons Pty. Ltd.* (1966) 117 C.L.R. 118, 124, McTiernan J. gave as one of his reasons for rejecting the decision in *Rookes* the fact that Category 2 imposed "an undue burden on a plaintiff".

[211]   [1972] A.C. 1027, 1078D, H-1079A, 1094C, 1101B-C, 1121D, 1130E.

[212]   *Ibid.*. In *Catnic Components Ltd.* v. *Hill* [1983] F.S.R. 512, 539-540, Falconer J. thought that the action of the defendants in *saving* themselves the loss they would otherwise suffer if they refrained from committing the tort brought the case within Category 2. But the claim for exemplary damages was rejected on the ground that patent infringement was not a tort for which they could be awarded. See para. 3.73 below. In *Archer* v. *Brown* [1985] 1 Q.B. 401, 423F-G, Peter Pain J. said that the fact that the defendant could not in fact have profited from his wrong did not take him outside Category 2, provided he had weighed the risk of loss against the chance of getting away with it.

award.[213] In addition, it had to be shown that the defendant made a decision to proceed with the conduct knowing it to be wrong, or reckless as to whether or not it was wrong, because the advantages of going ahead outweighed the risks involved.[214] In practice, this requirement restricts the occasions on which exemplary damages can be sought in cases of defamation by the press as it can be extremely difficult to produce evidence that the defendant calculated that a particular defamation was likely to boost sales of the publication. However, the high level of compensatory damages awarded in defamation cases[215] suggests that plaintiffs may not feel it necessary to claim exemplary damages.[216]

3.46   Despite this, defamation cases still represent an important source of awards of this category of exemplary damages.[217] The high levels of awards which are often made in such cases mean they have also attracted the greatest attention. Another, numerically larger and in this sense more significant source, are the cases involving the wrongful eviction of tenants, typically in defiance of legal authority, in order to make the property available for a more profitable use.[218] The housing cases have not (in contrast to defamation) produced high levels of award, due to jurisdictional limits which until recently prevented the county court from making a total award in excess of £5,000.[219] In actions founded on contract or tort,

---

[213] *Broome* v. *Cassell* [1972] A.C. 1027, 1079B-C, 1101C-D, 1121D, 1133A. See also the direction of Widgery J. to the jury in *Manson* v. *Associated Newspapers Ltd.* [1965] 1 W.L.R. 1038.

[214] *Broome* v. *Cassell* [1972] A.C. 1027, 1079C-E, 1088G-1089A, 1094C-E, 1101D-G, 1121D, 1130D-F.

[215] *Sutcliffe* v. *Pressdram Ltd.* [1991] 1 Q.B. 153, where the C.A. substituted an award of £60,000 for a jury award of £600,000, was a case in which exemplary damages had not been claimed. The award was of aggravated compensatory damages. See also para. 2.26 above.

[216] The decision of the Court of Appeal in *Rantzen* v. *Mirror Group Newspapers* (1993) 143 N.L.J. 507, may lead to a reduction in the levels of awards in defamation cases. See para. 3.103 below.

[217] Recent examples are: *Rowland-Jones* v. *City & Westminster Financial Plc.*, 6 February 1992 and 8 July 1992 (Unreported, C.A.) (jury award of £130,000, including £20,000 exemplary damages; the C.A. ordered a retrial on the question of the £110,000 compensatory damages but upheld the exemplary award); *Armstrong-Jones* v. *News (U.K.) Ltd.*, *The Independent*, 12 April 1990 (jury award of £35,000, including £30,000 exemplary damages); and *Maxwell* v. *Pressdram Ltd. (No. 2)*, *The Times*, 22 November 1986 (jury award of £55,000, including £50,000 exemplary damages).

[218] See *Arden & Partington on Quiet Enjoyment* (3rd ed., 1990), pp. 31-44. In *Broome* v. *Cassell* [1972] A.C. 1027, 1079E-F, Lord Hailsham indicated that the unlawful eviction of a tenant by means of harassment was a prime example of a Category 2 case. This was subsequently confirmed in *Drane* v. *Evangelou* [1978] 1 W.L.R. 455, which has led to many awards of exemplary damages in housing cases.

[219] The County Courts Jurisdiction Order 1981, S.I. 1981, No. 1123.

the county court now has unlimited jurisdiction whatever the amount involved in the proceedings.[220] But there is as yet no evidence of any increase in the value of exemplary awards, which tend to be around the £1,000, £2,000 or £3,000 mark. In contrast, a claim under sections 27 and 28 of the Housing Act 1988[221] may produce a much higher award than can an aggravated or exemplary one.[222] There are signs that plaintiffs are making increasing use of sections 27 and 28, and the availability of these claims may consequently render aggravated and exemplary damages less significant in housing cases in the future.[223]

3.47 It has been held that where the defendant's conduct was calculated to make a profit for someone other than the defendant, it cannot give rise to an award of exemplary damages within Category 2.[224] This is so even where the defendant is acting as agent for the person who in fact gains by the commission of the tort. The scope of this category appears to have been further restricted by the Court of Appeal's recent decision in *A.B.* v. *South West Water Services Ltd..*[225] Stuart-Smith L.J., with whom Bingham M.R. and Simon Brown L.J.

---

[220] Art. 2, para. 1(l) of the High Court and County Courts Jurisdiction Order 1991, S.I. 1991, No. 724, with effect from 1 July 1991. Actions of which the value is less than £50,000 and which include a claim for personal injuries must be commenced in the county court (art. 5, para. (1)). Art. 7 contains a rebuttable presumption that cases of a value of less than £25,000 will be heard in a county court and those of a value of more than £50,000 will be heard in the High Court, but these limits are flexible.

[221] S. 27 introduced a new civil right to improved 'compensation' for tenants driven out by harassment or illegally evicted by their landlords. By virtue of s. 28, damages are assessed on the basis of the financial gain to the landlord in securing vacant possession of the property. The right may therefore be regarded as restitutionary, rather than compensatory, in character, as to which see Part VII.

[222] E.g. *Canlin* v. *Berkshire Holdings* [September 1990] Legal Action 10: £35,000; *Maloney* v. *Weston* [August 1991] Legal Action 4: £34,000; *Tagro* v. *Cafane* [1991] 1 W.L.R. 378: £31,000; *Chniouer* v. *Nicholades* [September 1991] Legal Action 18: £25,000; *Brook* v. *Woodcock* [September 1989] Legal Action 25: £17,000; *Dowkes* v. *Athelston* [March 1993] Legal Action 16: £12,000; *Jones* v. *Miah* [1992] E.G.C.S. 51: £8,000.

[223] But an aggravated and/or exemplary award may be made in addition to an award under ss. 27 and 28: in *Chniouer* v. *Nicholades, ibid.*, £1,000 exemplary damages were awarded in addition to £25,000 under s.28; in *Dowkes* v. *Athelston, ibid.*, £1,000 exemplary damages in addition to £12,000; in *Mason* v. *Nwcorrie* [December 1992] Legal Action 20, £1,000 exemplary damages in addition to £4,500; in *Grocia* v. *Flint* [March 1993] Legal Action 15, £1,000 exemplary damages and £1,000 aggravated damages in addition to £3,329; and in *Cadman* v. *Wood* [March 1993] Legal Action 16, £1,500 aggravated damages were awarded in addition to £3,000. That an exemplary award may be made in addition to one under ss. 27 and 28 is perhaps further proof that Category 2 should not be regarded as restitutionary, since damages on account of "the same loss" cannot be awarded both in respect of a liability arising under s. 27 and in respect of a liability arising apart from s. 27.

[224] *Ramdath* v. *O Daley* [1993] 20 E.G. 123 (C.A.).

[225] [1993] Q.B. 507.

agreed,[226] indicated that the continuation of a nuisance in an attempt to cover up the fact that a tort had been committed and thereby to limit the amount of damages payable to the plaintiff was "an entirely different concept from that involved in the second category."[227] The deliberate decision by the defendants to continue the nuisance, coupled with their recognition that this might involve them in the payment of damages, did not establish that they had knowingly committed the tort for the purpose of gaining some pecuniary or other advantage.[228]

3.48 Some commentators have regarded this category of exemplary damages as a species of restitutionary remedy under which the benefit wrongfully obtained by the defendant at the plaintiff's expense is recouped.[229] Indeed it is impossible to inflict meaningful financial punishment on a tortfeasor unless any profits obtained from the tort are removed, whether the mechanism used removes them directly or indirectly. The problem with this approach is that the present procedure makes it very difficult to see how any precise restitution of the benefits obtained by the defendant can be achieved. Awards are assessed by the jury and the jury may well lack evidence detailing the profit which has been made. As will be seen, a true restitutionary measure would also have to distinguish profits made by virtue of and attributable to the tort from profits not so attributable.[230]

3.49 Even when the profit made by the defendant by virtue of and attributable to the tort can be calculated it is possible that courts may seek to punish the defendant by making an award of exemplary damages in excess of the sum required to achieve restitution of any profits made. In *Mcmillan* v. *Singh*[231] the Court of Appeal made an award of exemplary damages of £250 in an unlawful eviction case in spite of the fact that the profit made by the defendant from the tort was only in the region of £60-70. Indeed, there would seem to be no objection to the

---

[226] *Ibid.*, 533E-F, 528E-F.

[227] *Ibid.*, 526F-H.

[228] [1993] Q.B. 507, 526E-H.

[229] E.g. *McGregor on Damages* (15th ed., 1988), para. 422. Lord Diplock adopted this approach in *McCarey* v. *Associated Newspapers Ltd. (No. 2)* [1965] 2 Q.B. 86, 107B-C, and in *Broome* v. *Cassell* [1972] A.C. 1027, 1129B-C; whilst Lord Wilberforce, at 1119H-1120A, thought that the idea behind a profit motive requirement should as a matter of logic be to take the profit out of wrongdoing.

[230] See Part VII, para. 7.13 below.

[231] (1984) 17 H.L.R. 120.

making of an award of exemplary damages in a case of tortious conduct which was 'calculated to make a profit' but which failed to produce one.[232]

3.50 A further difficulty involved in Category 2 as restitutionary is that the 'overriding principles' which structure the discretion to award exemplary damages and which govern their assessment[233] would seem to be irrelevant to, if not inconsistent with, a remedy which is directed to the recovery of profits.

3.51 A general criticism which is levelled at this category is that it is too narrow and also that it is illogical because those who commit torts out of malice should not be absolved from liability for exemplary damages merely because profit was not the motive of their act.[234]

(c) Statutory justification

3.52 Lord Devlin's third category recognises the obvious truth that awards of exemplary damages are possible whenever statute allows such an award to be made. In practice, little use has been made of statutory justifications for exemplary damages and it is possible that both of the statutes which are often cited as falling within this category are actually examples of statutes which permit aggravated as opposed to exemplary awards. As a matter of general principle, an intention on the part of Parliament to inflict punishment by means of civil process should only be established by unambiguous words.

3.53 The Landlord and Tenant Act 1730, section 1 and the Distress for Rent Act 1737, section 18, are two ancient statutory provisions still in force which allow forms of extra damages which could be said to be exemplary. However, the most commonly cited example of a statutory provision which possibly allows a court to award exemplary damages is that contained in

---

[232] Cf. *Archer* v. *Brown* [1985] 1 Q.B. 401, 423F-G.

[233] Particularly those relating to moderation and joint liability. See paras. 3.92 and 3.97-3.98 below.

[234] *Uren* v. *John Fairfax & Sons Pty. Ltd.* (1966) 117 C.L.R. 118, 138; *Broome* v. *Cassell* [1972] A.C. 1027, 1088E-F, 1108H-1109A, 1119B-F, 1120E-G. *McGregor on Damages* (15th ed., 1988), para. 420. Similar criticism has been made of the limitation in Category 1 cases to oppressive *governmental* action: see para. 3.42 above.

section 13(2) of the Reserve and Auxiliary Forces (Protection of Civil Interests) Act 1951.[235] Lord Kilbrandon in *Broome* v. *Cassell* regarded this as an example of the older usage of the term exemplary damages and thus as dealing in fact with what in modern usage would be termed aggravated damages.[236]

3.54   A more modern, and important, example of a statute which arguably justifies awards of exemplary damages is contained in the provisions of sections 97(2) and 229(3) of the Copyright, Designs and Patents Act 1988. Section 97(2) provides that:-

"The court may in an action for infringement of copyright having regard to all the circumstances, and in particular to-

(a) the flagrancy of the infringement, and

(b) any benefit accruing to the defendant by reason of the infringement,

award such additional damages as the justice of the case may require."

Section 229(3) makes similar provision for infringement of design right. The use of the word "additional" in this provision leaves open the question whether it is exemplary or aggravated damages which are being permitted.[237] In so far as section 96(2) of the Act provides a

---

[235] "In any action for damages for conversion or other proceedings which lie by virtue of any such omission, failure or contravention, the court may take account of the conduct of the defendant with a view, if the court thinks fit, to awarding exemplary damages in respect of the wrong sustained by the plaintiff."

[236] [1972] A.C. 1027, 1133G-1134A. He based his understanding on the fact that the Act applies to Scotland, which rejects the punitive principle. This seems very likely to be correct in view of the doubts which exist as to whether a true exemplary award can be made in respect of conversion.

[237] The note to s. 97(2) in *Halsbury's Statutes*, vol 11, p.11, suggests that only aggravated damages are permissible, whereas G. Dworkin in *Blackstone's Guide to the Copyright, Designs and Patents Act 1988* (1989), p. 118 state that the general view is that exemplary damages are permitted by the section, but that the issue is not settled conclusively, and W.R. Cornish, *Intellectual Property: Patents, Copyright, Trade Marks, and Allied Rights* (2nd ed., 1989), para. 11-045 states that "an exemplary award could still be made where the infringement was intended to be specially profitable." Authority on s. 17(3) of the Copyright Act 1956, which was in similar terms, was inconclusive. See *Williams* v. *Settle* [1960] 1 W.L.R. 1072; *Beloff* v. *Pressdram Ltd.* [1973] 1 All E.R. 241; and *Rank Film Distributors Ltd.* v. *Video Information Centre* [1982] A.C. 380. Lord Kilbrandon in *Broome* v. *Cassell* [1972] A.C. 1027, 1134A, was of the opinion that s. 17(3) did not authorise an award of exemplary damages. Lord Devlin in *Rookes* v. *Barnard* [1964] A.C. 1129, 1225, and Lord Hailsham in *Broome* v. *Cassell* [1972] A.C.

general remedy for copyright infringement of damages which are 'at large' as well as a remedy of account, and as the court is now enabled to award additional damages without having to consider whether effective relief is otherwise available,[238] it is difficult to see the role of subsection 97(2) if exemplary damages are not permitted by it.[239] The Whitford Committee treated the statutory predecessor of section 97(2) as conferring the power to award exemplary damages and said that the provisions for exemplary damages should if anything be strengthened.[240] The White Paper that preceded the legislation reflected this view.[241]

The cause of action test

3.55   It is now clear, following the Court of Appeal's decision in *A.B.* v. *South West Water Services Ltd.*,[242] that an additional restriction on the availability of an exemplary award is the requirement that the plaintiff's claim satisfy a cause of action test.[243] In the absence of authority to the contrary,[244] the Court of Appeal followed dicta of a majority of the House of Lords in *Broome* v. *Cassell*[245] which in its view established that awards of exemplary damages may only be made where the plaintiff's cause of action is one in respect of which prior to *Rookes* v. *Barnard* an award of this kind had already been made.

3.56   It has been pointed out that it cannot be said that precedent *dictated* acceptance of the cause of action, as well as the categorisation, test.[246] Nevertheless, unless it is overruled by the

---

1027, 1080G-1081A, thought it an open question.

[238] Contrast the Copyright Act 1956, s. 17(3).

[239] It remains difficult to see the need for s. 97(2)(b) given the existence of the remedy of account.

[240] Copyright and Designs Law (1977), Cmnd. 6732, para. 704.

[241] Intellectual Property and Innovation (1986), Cmnd. 9712, para. 12.3.

[242] [1993] Q.B. 507.

[243] *Ibid.*, 523B, 528E-F, 530G-H. See para. 3.35 above.

[244] Apparently conflicting authority, such as cases of discrimination where the punitive principle had been assumed or even acted upon, was treated as *per incuriam*.

[245] [1972] A.C. 1027. In the Court of Appeal's view, the majority consisted of Lord Hailsham, Lord Diplock, Lord Wilberforce, Lord Kilbrandon, and possibly Lord Reid.

[246] A.S. Burrows, "The Scope of Exemplary Damages", (1993) 109 L.Q.R. 358, 360-361.

House of Lords, the decision in *A.B.* v. *South West Water Services Ltd.* now precludes any future extension of exemplary awards at common law[247] to wrongs for which they have not previously been awarded[248] and, by excluding discrimination cases from the punitive principle, brings to an end a development in that area which had begun to provide another possibly significant source of exemplary awards.[249] It is therefore necessary to ask, when considering a claim for exemplary damages, whether the wrong is one which satisfies the cause of action test.

(a) Wrongs satisfying the cause of action test

(i) Defamation, trespass,[250] and malicious prosecution: personal wrongs

3.57   These torts are the principal wrongs for which exemplary damages are in fact awarded, in the sense that they represent the bulk of the case-law on this subject. This might be thought to be a reflection of the effect which Lord Devlin's categorisation in *Rookes* v. *Barnard*[251] has necessarily had upon the context in which exemplary damages are awarded,[252] but the fact that they clearly satisfy the cause of action test is evidence that they have enjoyed a much longer association with exemplary awards.

---

[247] Cf. the comments of Lord Diplock in *Broome* v. *Cassell* [1972] A.C. 1027, 1127B-E. But in *A.B.* v. *South West Water Services Ltd.* [1993] Q.B. 507, 516E, Stuart-Smith L.J. said that the law relating to exemplary damages was "not a developing field of the law."

[248] It may incidentally further encourage plaintiffs to interpret older authorities as involving awards of exemplary rather than aggravated damages; and encourage defendants to adopt the converse interpretation.

[249] See para. 3.66 below.

[250] I.e. false imprisonment, assault and battery, and trespass to land or goods.

[251] [1964] A.C. 1129.

[252] See para. 3.36 above.

3.58   Defamation clearly satisfies the test.[253] It has been described as *par excellence* the tort when exemplary damages may be claimed[254] and is often cited as a primary example of the type of wrong which can give rise to such an award. The interest which it protects is the plaintiff's right to reputation, and any consequential indignities or hurt:

> Damage or loss is not the point of a defamation action. It is brought to vindicate a right: the right to reputation.[255]

As was recognised in *Broome* v. *Cassell*,[256] the subjectivity of the loss or interest involved means that damages here cannot be calculated with anything approaching precision, a factor which, we observed above, serves to blur the distinction between compensation and punishment.[257]

3.59   Historically, the interest in reputation is one form of intangible interest which has always been protected by the common law.[258] The *level* of protection afforded it has, however, been called into question in more recent years, as overall awards of damages in defamation cases have occasionally reached sensational sums.[259] Unfavourable comparisons are increasingly made with the levels of awards made in personal injury cases,[260] and other important

---

253 E.g. *Youssoupoff* v. *Metro-Goldwyn-Mayer Pictures Ltd.* (1934) 50 T.L.R. 581; *Rook* v. *Fairrie* [1941] 1 K.B. 507, 516; *Bull* v. *Vazquez* [1947] 1 All E.R. 334. Since the cause of action test is purportedly derived from *Broome* v. *Cassell*, a defamation case in which their Lordships upheld an award of exemplary damages, this must be true.

254 *Broome* v. *Cassell* [1972] A.C. 1027, 1119C (*per* Lord Wilberforce).

255 C. Harlow, *Understanding Tort Law* (1987), pp.107-108. Cf. Lord Hailsham in *Broome* v. *Cassell* [1972] A.C. 1027, 1071D.

256 [1972] A.C. 1027, 1071B-G, 1072E-H, 1085D-G.

257 See paras. 2.17-2.19 above. Cf. Lord Diplock's observation in *Broome* v. *Cassell* [1972] A.C. 1027, 1125E-1126B, that defamation has special characteristics which "blur the edges of the boundary between" pure compensatory damages and aggravated damages.

258 C. Harlow, *Understanding Tort Law* (1987), p.107.

259 Recent examples of libel awards include: £200,000 (Jason Donovan); £450,000 (Barney Eastwood); £1.5m (Lord Aldington); £600,000 (Sonia Sutcliffe - reduced to £60,000 on appeal); £240,000 (Vladimir Telnikoff); £400,000 (Wafic Said); and £250,000 (Esther Rantzen - reduced to £110,000 on appeal). On these damages, see paras. 2.26 and 3.45 - 3.46 above.

260 *McCarey* v. *Associated Newspapers Ltd. (No.2)* [1965] 2 Q.B. 86.

principles (such as freedom of expression) begin to receive greater attention.[261] Nevertheless, the nature of the tort of defamation does provide a model for other wrongs for which exemplary damages have also been regarded as particularly appropriate. This is because defamation is a *personal* wrong, representing one form of tortious protection from attacks on person or personality.

3.60   Almost all the other wrongs which clearly satisfy the cause of action test[262] - false imprisonment,[263] assault and battery,[264] and probably malicious prosecution[265] - are wrongs which involve the infringement of personality rights and entail a particular form of injury. They are often brought to vindicate a right, rather than to make good a loss,[266] and are therefore particularly suited to the punitive principle. False imprisonment, for instance, involves not only a loss of liberty but also affects the plaintiff's reputation,[267] particularly when committed by someone with apparent lawful authority such as the police. Malicious prosecution is also concerned with injury to reputation. And in the case of battery and assault

---

[261]   The recent decision in *Rantzen* v. *Mirror Group Newspapers* (1993) 143 N.L.J. 507, influenced by Article 10 of the European Convention on Human Rights, seems symptomatic of this trend. See para. 3.103 below.

[262]   One problem with the test is that, due to *Rookes* v. *Barnard*, all cases prior to 1964 where increased damages were awarded against non-government servants (and absent a profit motive) have to be regarded as examples of aggravated damages or simply as being wrongly decided; and yet the wrongs involved were nevertheless widely acknowledged to be of a type which could in principle give rise to an exemplary award if the defendant *had* been a government servant. Hence the case law following *Rookes* abounds with awards of exemplary damages for battery, false imprisonment, malicious prosecution etc. against the police. The *dual* effect of the cause of action test and the categorisation test is that it appears that one now has to find examples of pre-*Rookes* cases where these wrongs were in fact committed by government servants, which is sometimes difficult. Taken together therefore, *Rookes* and *A.B.* v. *South West Water Services Ltd.* might be thought to force a distorted interpretation onto older cases which had not been decided on these assumptions.

[263]   *Huckle* v. *Money* (1763) 2 Wils. K.B. 205, 95 E.R. 769; possibly *Leeman* v. *Allen* (1763) 2 Wils. K.B. 160, 95 E.R. 742; *Dumbell* v. *Roberts* [1944] 1 All E.R. 326, 329H-330A.

[264]   *Benson* v. *Frederick* (1766) 3 Burr. 1845, 97 E.R. 1130.

[265]   *Leith* v. *Pope* (1779) 2 Black. W. 1327, 96 E.R. 777; *Chambers* v. *Robinson* (1726) 2 Str. 691, 93 E.R. 787. The doubt arises because, although since *Rookes* v. *Barnard* [1964] A.C. 1129 it has been said that malicious prosecution can give rise to an award of exemplary damages (e.g. *Bishop* v. *Metropolitan Police Commissioner*, *The Times*, 5 December 1989; *White* v. *Metropolitan Police Commissioner*, *The Times*, 24 April 1982), for the reasons given in n. 262 above this is no longer sufficient.

[266]   Cf. *John Lewis & Co. Ltd.* v. *Tims* [1952] A.C. 676, 680.

[267]   *Walter* v. *Alltools Ltd.* (1944) 61 T.L.R. 39, 40.

the interest protected is not merely freedom from bodily harm, but also freedom from such forms of insult as may be caused by interference with the plaintiff's person.[268]

3.61   Trespass to land and trespass to goods also satisfy the cause of action test, but they do not protect personality interests directly.[269] An examination of the cases in which these torts have been held to give rise to exemplary (and aggravated) damages, however, reveals that the majority are cases either of harassment pleaded as wrongful eviction,[270] or of forms of unlawful search and seizure which entail an attack on liberty or privacy.[271]

3.62   It appears therefore that the torts which prior to *Rookes* v. *Barnard* had been held to give rise to exemplary damages, and hence to satisfy the cause of action test, are linked by a common substantive feature: they are all personal wrongs.[272]

(ii) Private nuisance

3.63   In *A.B.* v. *South West Water Services Ltd.*,[273] the Court of Appeal found it unnecessary to decide whether exemplary damages had been awarded for nuisance prior to 1964 and thus whether nuisance is a wrong which passes the cause of action test. The point was thought to turn on the proper interpretation of *Bell* v. *Midland Railway Co.*,[274] which the Court was inclined to view as a case of nuisance for which exemplary damages had been awarded. It is therefore probable that exemplary damages can be claimed in respect of a nuisance. Although this is not a personal wrong, the only reported case following *Rookes* v. *Barnard*[275] in

---

[268]   *Salmond & Heuston on the Law of Torts* (20th ed., 1992), p.125, citing *Collins* v. *Wilcock* [1984] 1 W.L.R. 1172, 1177.

[269]   *Wilkes* v. *Wood* (1763) Lofft. 1, 98 E.R. 489; *Williams* v. *Currie* (1845) 1 C.B. 841, 135 E.R. 774.

[270]   Harassment clearly aims to annoy and distress and thereby infringes rights of personality. Cf. *Khorasandjian* v. *Bush* [1993] 3 W.L.R. 476 (C.A.), a case of injunctive relief pleaded as nuisance but in substance dealing with harassment of the plaintiff by the defendant.

[271]   *Wilkes* v. *Wood* (1763) Lofft. 1, 98 E.R. 489; *Huckle* v. *Money* (1763) 2 Wils. K.B. 205, 95 E.R. 768.

[272]   Cf. *Uren* v. *John Fairfax & Sons Pty Ltd.* (1966) 117 C.L.R. 118, 147.

[273]   [1993] Q.B. 507, 523E-H, 528E-F, 531A.

[274]   (1861) 10 C.B. (N.S.) 287, 142 E.R. 462.

[275]   [1964] A.C. 1129.

which it has been held that a nuisance can give rise to exemplary damages concerned the harassment of tenants which was difficult to plead as trespass because it took the form of disconnections and discontinuances of services and building operations, rather than entry upon the plaintiff's premises.[276]

(iii) Intimidation and other economic torts

3.64   It is implicit in Lord Devlin's speech in *Rookes* v. *Barnard* that exemplary damages may be awarded in respect of the tort of intimidation,[277] although not surprisingly there appears to be no case prior to that decision in which such an award was made. It is unclear whether other economic torts also satisfy the cause of action test. It has been held that damages are at large[278] in the case of the torts of unlawful interference with business,[279] inducing breach of contract[280] and conspiracy,[281] which perhaps suggests that an exemplary award is not necessarily excluded. The answer ultimately depends upon the proper interpretation of the pre-*Rookes* authority.

---

[276] *Guppys (Bridport) Ltd.* v. *Brookling* (1983) 14 H.L.R. 1, 27. Although it could have been pleaded as breach of the covenant for quiet enjoyment, this cannot sustain an exemplary award: see paras. 3.76-3.77.

[277] [1964] A.C. 1129, 1232-1233. Cf. *Messenger Newspapers Group Ltd.* v. *National Graphical Association* [1984] I.R.L.R. 397, 407, para. 79.

[278] See para. 3.12. The starting point for Lord Devlin's judgment in *Rookes* v. *Barnard* [1964] A.C. 1129 was an analysis of damages 'at large', which he divided according to whether they were purely compensatory, aggravated or exemplary.

[279] *Pratt* v. *British Medical Association* [1919] 1 K.B. 244, 281-282.

[280] *Street on Torts* (8th ed., 1988), p.145, citing *G.W.K. Ltd.* v. *Dunlop Rubber Co. Ltd.* (1926) 42 T.L.R. 376 and 593.

[281] *Quinn* v. *Leathem* [1901] A.C. 495, 498. Cf. *Denison* v. *Fawcett* (1958) 12 D.L.R. (2d) 537. *McGregor on Damages* (15th ed., 1988), para. 1698, n. 30 seems to accept that if the defendant's conduct satisfies Lord Devlin's second category, an exemplary award is in principle available. However, this view was stated before the introduction of the cause of action test by *A.B.* v. *South West Water Services Ltd.* [1993] Q.B. 507.

(b) Wrongs which may fail the cause of action test

3.65   The effect of the cause of action test is that the cases decided after *Rookes* v. *Barnard*[282] in which courts held that exemplary damages are or might be available, are now discredited if before 1964 there had been no such award in respect of the wrong concerned.

(i) Discrimination

3.66   There was, for instance, a growing body of authority which supported the award of exemplary damages in respect of the statutory torts created by the Sex Discrimination Act 1975 and the Race Relations Act 1976,[283] if the facts of the case fell within one of Lord Devlin's categories.[284] It might be thought that the close relationship which the tort of discrimination - a personal wrong - bears to the torts discussed above[285] justified this development. But it is now clear that torts which did not even exist at the time when *Rookes* v. *Barnard*[286] was decided necessarily fail the cause of action test and as a result exemplary damages can no longer be awarded for discrimination.[287]

---

[282]   [1964] A.C. 1129.

[283]   In Northern Ireland this line of authority had been extended to discrimination on grounds of religion contrary to the Fair Employment (Northern Ireland) Act 1976: *Duffy* v. *Eastern Health & Social Services Board* [1992] I.R.L.R. 251.

[284]   E.g. *Alexander* v. *Home Office* [1988] 1 W.L.R. 968; *Wileman* v. *Minilec Engineering Ltd.* [1988] I.C.R. 318; *Bradford City Council* v. *Arora* [1991] 2 Q.B. 507. In *A.B.* v. *South West Water Services Ltd.* [1993] Q.B. 507, 521F-522D, 528E-F, 533E-F, this line of authority was regarded by Stuart-Smith L.J., with whom Bingham M.R. and Simon Brown L.J. agreed, as *per incuriam*. Stuart-Smith L.J. also seemed to accept the defendants' argument that the relevant sections of the Sex Discrimination Act 1975 and the Race Relations Act 1976 in any event only authorised an award of compensatory damages: 522D-E.

[285]   At paras. 3.57-3.62. Cf. K. O'Donovan & E. Szyszczak, *Equality & Sex Discrimination Law* (1988), p. 222, who point to a close analogy between defamation and discrimination. Cf. the argument of counsel in *Alexander* v. *Home Office* [1988] 1 W.L.R. 968, 974H, 976C.

[286]   [1964] A.C. 1129.

[287]   See *Deane* v. *Ealing L.B.C.* [1993] I.C.R. 329, 335A. Note, however, that whilst rejecting the plaintiff's claim for exemplary damages on the basis of *A.B.* v. *South West Water Services Ltd.*, the E.A.T. increased the sum awarded to him as compensation for injury to his feelings. Aggravated damages were also awarded.

(ii) Public nuisance

3.67 The plaintiffs' claims for exemplary damages in *A.B.* v. *South West Water Services Ltd.*[288] were based (inter alia) on public nuisance. It was held that this was a cause of action for which no exemplary award had been made prior to *Rookes* v. *Barnard* and that the claims could therefore be struck out.[289]

(iii) Negligence and other personal injury cases

3.68 Prior to *A.B.* v. *South West Water Services Ltd.*[290] there was no reported case of exemplary damages having been awarded either for the tort of negligence or where the defendant's conduct was merely negligent.[291] Cases which did address the question suggested that such damages ought not to be available,[292] usually on the ground that compensatory principles prevail where the cause of action is negligence[293] and because the kind of conduct envisaged by Lord Devlin's categories involves something more than carelessness.[294]

3.69 After *A.B.* v. *South West Water Services Ltd.* it is clear that exemplary damages cannot be awarded for the tort of negligence, on the simple ground that it fails the cause of action

---

[288] [1993] Q.B. 507.

[289] *Ibid.*, 523H, 528E-F, 531B. The Court of Appeal also gave more substantial reasons why public nuisance ought not to give rise to exemplary damages: 523G-524D, 531B-E.

[290] [1993] Q.B. 507 (C.A.).

[291] *Emblen* v. *Myers* (1860) 6 H. & N. 54, 158 E.R. 23, was regarded by Lord Devlin as a case of trespass for which aggravated damages were awarded: *Rookes* v. *Barnard* [1964] A.C. 1129, 1223, 1229.

[292] E.g. *Phillips* v. *South Western Railway Co.* (1879) 4 Q.B.D. 406, 409; and cases at nn. 293 and 294 below.

[293] *Kralj* v. *McGrath* [1986] 1 All E.R. 54; *Hicks* v. *Chief Constable of South Yorkshire* [1992] 2 All E.R. 65, 68A-B ("... damages in a civil action for negligence ... are compensatory, not punitive"). Cf. para. 3.14 above.

[294] *Barbara* v. *Home Office* (1984) 134 N.L.J. 888; *A.B.* v. *South West Water Services Ltd.* [1992] 4 All E.R. 574, 584H-585B (*per* Wright J.).

test.[295] One consequence of this is that exemplary damages will only be available in respect of mass disaster claims resulting from product liability, breach of industrial safety requirements or transport accidents if some nominate tort, such as trespass to the person, can be established.

3.70   The question of the availability of exemplary awards in personal injury cases was raised by the Citizen Action Compensation Campaign at its inception in 1988.[296] It was suggested that a publicly funded judicial inquiry should be set up in all cases of large scale disaster and that such an inquiry should have the power to impose financial penalties or to recommend further punitive action if it found that a 'wanton or reckless disregard for public safety' had occurred. The suggestion was made that the money produced by such penalties might be held as a reserve compensation fund to assist victims of future disasters.

3.71   The National Consumer Council in its report 'Group Actions: Learning from Opren' said that it saw a case for 'global damages' being awarded in group actions in respect of losses suffered by unidentifiable individuals.[297] In so far as these losses could not, by definition, be quantified they would be non-compensatory. The Council believed that if any surplus existed after the distribution of this money to victims who were subsequently identified it would fall to the judge's discretion as to how it should be disposed of.

3.72   The Association of Personal Injury Lawyers in its preliminary submission to the Commission has argued that exemplary damages should not be widely available in personal injury cases, but that they could serve a useful purpose in "cases involving the most serious torts committed in the most reckless of circumstances." The Association sees the remedy as a response to the "public concern over the failure of the [criminal] law to penalise those responsible for serious and blatant acts resulting in death and injury."

---

[295]   [1993] Q.B. 523C-D, 528E-D, 530H (C.A.). But this leaves open the question whether torts which do satisfy the cause of action test, but which are committed merely negligently, can give rise to exemplary damages: cf. *Barbara* v. *Home Office* (1984) 134 N.L.J. 888.

[296]   *News from CITCOM* 1988.

[297]   (1989), pp. 3 & 24.

(iv) Infringement of intellectual property rights

3.73　There appears to be no case decided prior to 1964 in which exemplary damages were awarded for infringement of a patent and hence this wrong fails to satisfy the cause of action test.[298]

3.74　The statutory remedy of 'additional' damages for copyright infringement has already been discussed.[299]　If this provision does justify an award of exemplary damages it is based on statute and therefore the cause of action test does not arise.[300]

(v) Deceit

3.75　Although there was previously some uncertainty whether exemplary damages could be awarded for deceit,[301] following the introduction of a cause of action test[302] this must now be answered in the negative because there appears to be no case prior to *Rookes* v. *Barnard*[303] in which such an award was made.[304]

---

[298]　That exemplary damages cannot be awarded in this context is contrary to *Morton-Norwich Products Inc.* v. *Intercen Ltd. (No. 2)* [1981] F.S.R. 337 (*per* Graham J.), but in line with *General Tire & Rubber Co.* v. *Firestone Tyre and Rubber Co. Ltd.* [1975] 1 W.L.R. 819, 824C and E (*per* Lord Wilberforce) and *Catnic Components Ltd.* v. *Hill* [1983] F.S.R. 512, 541 (*per* Falconer J.). Note that a restitutionary remedy may be available: see para. 7.5 below.

[299]　See para. 3.54 above.

[300]　Nor is it necessary, of course, that the facts of the case concern either the actions of government officials or a profit motive.

[301]　In *Mafo* v. *Adams* [1970] 1 Q.B. 548, the defendants conceded that deceit could give rise to an exemplary award, but Sachs L.J. and Widgery L.J. disagreed as to whether this concession was correctly made. In *Broome* v. *Cassell* [1972] A.C. 1027, 1080C, Lord Hailsham was of the opinion that exemplary damages could not be awarded in an action for deceit, but acknowledged that this was a matter which had not yet been finally determined. Peter Pain J. in *Archer* v. *Brown* [1985] 1 Q.B. 401, 423F, assumed without deciding that exemplary damages were available.

[302]　*A.B.* v. *South West Water Services Ltd.* [1993] Q.B. 507.

[303]　[1964] A.C. 1129.

[304]　But aggravated damages and pure compensatory damages for mental distress are available: *Mafo* v. *Adams* [1970] 1 Q.B. 548, 558D-E; *Archer* v. *Brown* [1985] 1 Q.B. 401, 426D-E; *Shelley* v. *Paddock* [1979] 1 Q.B. 120, 131D-F.

(vi) Breach of contract

3.76   Even before *Rookes* v. *Barnard* was decided, it was well established that exemplary damages could not be awarded in a purely contractual action.[305] This was supported by a number of arguments. The compensatory principle is traditionally thought to be paramount in a contractual context.[306] Another consideration is that contract primarily involves pecuniary losses rather than the non-pecuniary losses with which exemplary damages seem to be concerned. In addition, it is often maintained that the need for certainty is greater in relation to commercial transactions, whereas exemplary damages are frequently criticised on the grounds of indeterminacy. The prohibition against exemplary damages is also said to reflect the fact that a contract is a private arrangement between two parties and that its breach is therefore a wrong directed against an individual rather than against the public as a whole. Further, it is said that the parties to a contract should have available the option of breaking the contract and of paying damages in lieu of performing it if they are able to find a more remunerative use for the subject matter of their promise.   Finally, the fact that the conventional measure of damages for breach of contract may include restitutionary elements may be thought to remove a significant part of the role which could be played by exemplary damages.   On the other hand, as discussed above damages for mental distress are available in relation to some breaches of contract though their availability has in recent years been curtailed [307] and the severity of the rule is undermined at least in housing cases where the plaintiff may be awarded exemplary damages if she or he is able to frame her or his claim alternatively in tort as either trespass or nuisance.[308]

3.77   Both American and Canadian law have differed from the English position by permitting awards of exemplary damages to be made in cases of wanton breaches of contract. In the United

---

[305] *Addis* v. *Gramophone Co. Ltd.* [1909] A.C. 488; *Perera* v. *Vandiyar* [1953] 1 W.L.R. 672; *Kenny* v. *Preen* [1963] 1 Q.B. 499.

[306] See cases cited para. 2.2, n.3, above. Cf. para. 3.15 above. But note that restitutionary remedies *are* available.

[307] *Hayes* v. *Dodd* [1990] 2 All E.R. 815; *Watts* v. *Morrow* [1991] 1 W.L.R. 1421. See para. 3.16.

[308] E.g. *Drane* v. *Evangelou* [1978] 1 W.L.R. 455; *Guppys (Bridport) Ltd.* v. *Brookling* (1983) 14 H.L.R. 1.

Kingdom, after *A.B.* v. *South West Water Services Ltd.*,[309] contractual claims now fail the cause of action test.

(vii) Equitable wrongs

3.78   Although, as will be seen in Part III, restitutionary awards are often canvassed and sometimes given where the defendant has committed an equitable wrong, there is no clear authority as to whether exemplary damages are available in such cases. In *Digital Equipment Corporation* v. *Darkcrest Ltd.*,[310] Falconer J. considered the possibility that, on the authority of *Smith* v. *Day*,[311] if an injunction was obtained fraudulently or maliciously, the court could give exemplary damages.[312] In *Columbia Picture Industries Inc.* v. *Robinson*, Scott J. considered that solicitors executing an *Anton Piller* order would come within Lord Devlin's first category, as officers of the court, if they executed the order in an oppressive or excessive manner.[313] These authorities are now thrown into doubt by *A.B.* v. *South West Water Services Ltd.*[314] and, in the absence of any pre-*Rookes* authority on the point, it would seem that exemplary damages cannot be awarded in respect of an equitable wrong. However in other jurisdictions there is a division of opinion on the question whether exemplary damages can be awarded in cases of equitable wrongdoing such as breach of fiduciary obligation.[315]

---

[309]   [1993] Q.B. 507.

[310]   [1984] Ch. 512.

[311]   (1882) 21 Ch.D. 421.

[312]   [1984] Ch. 512, 516.

[313]   [1987] Ch. 38, 87.

[314]   [1993] Q.B. 507.

[315]   Report on Exemplary Damages (1991), Ontario Law Reform Commission, p. 72. Note also that in England, in the context of R.S.C., O. 11, it has been held that a claim founded on a breach of duty as a constructive trustee or procuring a breach of trust is not a claim "founded on a tort": *Metall und Rohstoff A.G.* v. *Donaldson Lufkin & Jenrette Inc* [1990] 1 Q.B. 391, 474C-E (C.A.).

Overriding discretion

3.79   The award of an exemplary sum is essentially discretionary.[316] Thus, even if the plaintiff
        is able to show that the case falls within one of Lord Devlin's categories and that the wrong
        in question satisfies the cause of action test, it is still open to the court or jury to decide in its
        discretion that the case is not a proper one for exemplary damages.[317] The development of
        this discretion in the case law has led to the identification of a number of considerations
        which, subject to the court's residual discretion, further define the availability of exemplary
        awards.

        (a) The plaintiff must be the victim of the punishable behaviour

3.80   In *Rookes* v. *Barnard*, Lord Devlin indicated that there were three considerations which should
        always be borne in mind when awards of exemplary damages are being made.[318] Two of
        these are moderation and the wealth of the defendant.[319] The other consideration is that the
        plaintiff must be the victim of the punishable behaviour.[320] Lord Hailsham in *Broome* v.
        Cassell regarded this as an important contribution to the law on exemplary damages, as well
        as the identification of the categories.[321] However, its precise meaning is unclear and there
        appears to be little, if any, discussion of this requirement in the cases. McGregor points out
        that it is already generally accepted law that parties cannot assign causes of action in tort, and
        that where the victim is dead, the Law Reform (Miscellaneous Provisions) Act 1934 prevents
        the estate pursuing exemplary damages.[322] But Lord Devlin's consideration may imply
        something more, for example that the conduct must be aimed specifically at the plaintiff.[323]

---

[316] Indeed, according to Lord Hailsham in *Broome* v. *Cassell* [1972] A.C. 1027, 1060B, a punitive award,
      if it is ever permissible, *must* always remain discretionary.

[317] *A.B.* v. *South West Water Services Ltd.* [1993] Q.B. 507, 526H-527B.

[318] [1964] A.C. 1129, 1226, 1227-1228.

[319] These relate to assessment and are examined under that heading at paras. 3.92 and 3.93 below.

[320] *Rookes* v. *Barnard* [1964] A.C. 1129, 1227.

[321] [1972] A.C. 1027, 1081F.

[322] *McGregor on Damages* (15th ed., 1988), para. 425. We discuss survival of actions generally at paras.
      3.108-3.110 below.

[323] See Report on Exemplary Damages (1991), Ontario Law Reform Commission, p.10, n. 37.

3.81   The Ontario Law Reform Commission thought that it was more than a mere standing requirement, and was of the view that an exemplary award must pertain only to the conduct that actually injured the plaintiff.[324] The facts of *Rookes* v. *Barnard* itself perhaps suggest what was intended by this requirement.[325] The defendants flagrantly breached their employment contracts with an airline, conduct which also constituted the tort of intimidation against the plaintiff. Lord Devlin emphasised that the plaintiff could not increase his damages by reference to this flagrant breach since he was no more distressed by it than any of the airline's passengers.

(b) The relevance of a criminal penalty

3.82   The fact that the defendant has already been convicted and punished by means of the criminal process,[326] whilst not an automatic bar to the award of exemplary damages, nevertheless weighs heavily against them.[327] If the purpose of the award of exemplary damages is to apply a level of punishment appropriate to the wrong it is difficult to see how such an award can be justified when a criminal court has already imposed a level of punishment which it regards as appropriate to the conduct. A failure to take the criminal penalty into account risks offending elementary principles of justice by punishing a person twice for the same offence. In *A.B.* v. *South West Water Services Ltd.*, the fact that the defendants had already been convicted in respect of the nuisance was a further reason given by the Court of Appeal for refusing the plaintiffs' claims for exemplary damages.[328] In its discussion of the reasons why public nuisance was a wrong which ought not to give rise to an exemplary award, the Court regarded it as a point of particular significance that the causing of a public nuisance is a crime.[329] The decision therefore appears to magnify the relevance of a criminal conviction, or the fact that the wrong involved happens to constitute a crime, at the possible

---

[324] *Ibid.*, pp. 14-15.

[325] [1964] A.C. 1129.

[326] See Report on Exemplary Damages (1991), Ontario Law Reform Commission, pp. 43-46, for three other problematic issues which arise from the overlap with criminal law.

[327] *A.B.* v. *South West Water Services Ltd.* [1993] Q.B. 507. Cf. also *Archer* v. *Brown* [1985] 1 Q.B. 401, 423G-H.

[328] [1993] Q.B. 507, 527E, 528E-f, 533E-F.

[329] *Ibid.*, 523H-524D, 531B-D.

expense of injured plaintiffs.[330] However, there is no objection to an award of exemplary damages being made where, for instance, it relates to conduct which is different from that for which the defendant has already been punished in criminal proceedings.[331] Moreover, the fact that the defendant has already been convicted and fined should arguably be of less significance in cases which fall within Lord Devlin's first category, as opposed to cases within his second category. In *A.B.* v. *South West Water Services Ltd.* the defendants had been fined £10,000, a sum which the plaintiffs regarded as derisory and which was in any case paid by the Department of the Environment. A solicitor representing some of the plaintiffs remarked that:

> ... when you have one government department paying money to another, the size of the fine is academic .... What is important is that the jury took the view that the authority ought to be punished.[332]

The perceived inadequacy of criminal penalties may also be a reason for not attaching overwhelming significance to a criminal conviction or the possibility of one.[333]

(c) Multiple plaintiffs

3.83   Where there is a class of plaintiffs, real practical problems arise in the assessment of exemplary damages. Not all the plaintiffs may be before the court at the same time and the court is then faced with the difficult question of how it should apportion the exemplary sum. The approach which has been adopted in English law is described below.[334] But after *A.B.* v. *South West Water Services Ltd.* the number of plaintiffs has become, not just a problem of

---

[330] See Bingham M.R. in *A.B.* v. *South West Water Services Ltd.* [1993] Q.B. 507, 531B-D.

[331] *Asghar* v. *Ahmed* (1984) 17 H.L.R. 25 (C.A.), where the exemplary damages were said to be justified by the outrageous conduct which *followed* the eviction. But in *A.B.* v. *South West Water Services Ltd.* the conduct upon which the plaintiffs relied as establishing their claims for exemplary damages also appeared to be different (subsequent) to that for which the defendants had been fined. The distinction may lie in the the fact that in *Asghar* the conduct constituting the crime could itself have sustained an exemplary award, whereas this was not the case in *A.B.* v. *South West Water Services Ltd.*.

[332] (1991) 88 (2) Law Soc. Gaz. 8.

[333] This seems to be an implicit consideration in the housing cases, where the availability of fines is inadequate to deter landlords from wrongfully evicting their tenants: often they continue to harass tenants even in the face of warnings and injunctions. Note, however, the effect of s. 28 of the Housing Act 1988, discussed in para. 3.46 above.

[334] See para. 3.99-3.100 below.

assessment, but a positive reason for refusing to make an exemplary award.[335] The large number of plaintiffs affected by the nuisance was regarded by the Court of Appeal as an aspect of the case which made it a peculiarly unsuitable one for exemplary damages.[336]

(d) The plaintiff's conduct

3.84   This is a matter which relates principally to the assessment of exemplary damages,[337] but it may also operate so as to exclude them altogether, where, for example, the plaintiff induces the wrongful action by their own behaviour.[338]

(e) Absence of aggravating features

3.85   We have seen that the defendant's behaviour in committing the wrong need not be exceptional in order to give rise to an award of exemplary damages on the basis of Category 1.[339] But it is also clear that the absence of aggravating features is a relevant circumstance to be taken into account by a court or jury when exercising its discretion whether to award (and if so, how much)[340] exemplary damages.[341] That the defendant acted on the basis of an honest but mistaken belief, or in good faith, may therefore lead a court or jury to refuse to make an exemplary award altogether.[342] This factor is perhaps reflected also in the view that merely

---

[335] [1993] Q.B. 507, 527B-D, 528E-F, 531D-E.

[336] *Ibid.*, 527B.

[337] See para. 3.101 below.

[338] See, e.g. *Ewing* v. *Vasquez*, 7 May 1985 (Unreported, C.A.) (tenant being difficult to live with); *Holden* v. *Chief Constable of Lancashire* [1987] 1 Q.B. 380, 388D-E (plaintiff acting suspiciously, leading to wrongful arrest).

[339] *Holden* v. *Chief Constable of Lancashire* [1987] 1 Q.B. 380, 388A-D, 388H. See para. 3.38 above.

[340] See para. 3.101 below.

[341] *Holden* v. *Chief Constable of Lancashire* [1987] 1 Q.B. 380, 388D-E.

[342] E.g. *Simper* v. *Metropolitan Police Commissioner* [1982] C.L.Y. 3124; *Kay* v. *James*, 21 April 1989 (Unreported, C.A.). Cf. *Uren* v. *John Fairfax & Sons Pty. Ltd.* (1966) 117 C.L.R. 118, 135, 159. In Northern Ireland, the absence of aggravating features seems almost to entail the refusal of an exemplary award: see *Kelly* v. *Faulkner* [1973] N.I. 31; *Davey* v. *Chief Constable of the R.U.C.* [1988] N.I. 139.

negligent conduct does not establish the state of mind required to sustain an exemplary award.[343]

(2) Assessment

3.86   The assessment of exemplary damages has been a major source of criticism.[344] It is said that these awards are indeterminate and unpredictable,[345] virtually uncontrollable[346] and that they reach levels which are excessive.[347] Indeterminacy is a consequence partly of the fact that the award of an exemplary sum still remains in many instances within the control of a jury, and partly of the inherent subjectivity of the factors which are relevant to assessment. By virtue of section 69(1) of the Supreme Court Act 1981, there is a presumption in favour of jury trial where the claim is one for libel, slander, malicious prosecution and false imprisonment. These are some of the principal torts which give rise to exemplary damages. Moreover, whilst trial by jury is normally inappropriate for a personal injury action, the presence of a claim for exemplary damages is a circumstance which may lead the court to exercise its discretion[348] in favour of one.[349] Actions for battery within Lord Devlin's first category may therefore also be determined by a jury. This has made it difficult to achieve consistency between awards - a difficulty which has been exacerbated by an inability to provide the jury with adequate guidance[350] and by the high barrier which until recently had

---

[343] E.g. *A.B.* v. *South West Water Services Ltd.* [1992] 4 All E.R. 574, 584g-585b (*per* Wright J.); *Barbara* v. *Home Office* (1984) 134 N.L.J. 888. See para. 3.38 above.

[344] See paras. 1.6 above, and Part V below.

[345] E.g. *Broome* v. *Cassell* [1972] A.C. 1027, 1087D (*per* Lord Reid); P.H. Birks, *Civil Wrongs: A New World* (Butterworth Lectures 1990-1), pp. 79-82.

[346] E.g. *Broome* v. *Cassell* [1972] A.C. 1027, 1087E-F, 1090G-1091A (*per* Lord Reid); *Coyne* v. *Citizen Finance Ltd.* (1991) 172 C.L.R. 211, 215-216. But see para. 3.103 below.

[347] This criticism is usually made in the context of defamation cases: see para. 5.12 above. Here also, unfavourable comparisons are sometimes drawn with the levels of awards in personal injury cases: *McCarey* v. *Associated Newspapers Ltd. (No. 2)* [1965] 2 Q.B. 87, 109C-D, G-110B; *Broome* v. *Cassell* [1972] 1027, 1130H; *Rantzen* v. *Mirror Group Newspapers* (1993) 143 N.L.J. 507, 508. But see *Sutcliffe* v. *Pressdram Ltd.* [1991] 1 Q.B. 153, 175D-176D, 186A-C.

[348] Under s. 69(3) of the Supreme Court Act 1981.

[349] *H.* v. *Ministry of Defence* [1991] Q.B. 103, 112E-F.

[350] Previous awards could not be regarded as establishing a norm to which reference might be made in other cases.

to be surmounted before an appellate court could interfere with a jury award.[351] Section 8 of the Courts and Legal Services Act 1990, which empowers the Court of Appeal to substitute its own award for that made by the jury where the damages are excessive, may now change this state of affairs since it will allow the Court to give more guidance as to levels of awards and is likely to generate a body of awards to which reference can be made in subsequent cases.[352]

3.87   However, it is not merely the fact that exemplary awards are often made by juries which creates the danger of indeterminacy. There is evidence that judges, too, have difficulty in assessing these awards.[353] Where the assessment of damages is tied, not to a loss[354] which can be objectively measured, but to subjective factors (such as the gravity of the defendant's conduct) the process is inevitably to some extent a discretionary one. It is more difficult to develop criteria of comparability. It is often stated in the most general terms that exemplary damages are measured by what the defendant ought to pay.[355] In theory, principles of assessment should be generated by the purpose(s) for which an award is made. Since the purpose of an exemplary award is to punish, deter or condemn the defendant's conduct this suggests that damages should be measured either by the gravity of the defendant's conduct, by whatever sum is sufficient to deter it, or by a sum which represents an appropriate symbolic indemnification. These considerations are, of course, extremely difficult to value.[356]

---

[351] Courts were reluctant to intervene, only doing so where the award was one which no reasonable jury could have made: see *Sutcliffe* v. *Pressdram Ltd.* [1991] 1 Q.B. 153, 176D-177A, 187H. Moreover, the court could only substitute its own award where the parties were in agreement.

[352] See para. 3.103 below.

[353] For instance, in the context of an award of aggravated damages (which raises similar problems), the Court of Appeal in *Godwin* v. *Uzoigwe*, [1992] T.L.R. 300, expressed some concern at the way in which the trial judge had arrived at a sum of £25,000: at 14C and 18B of the transcript. But, in substituting a sum of £20,000, the Court of Appeal explained only that this was a more appropriate figure; and cf. *Broome* v. *Cassell* [1972] A.C. 1027, 1097D-E, 1135C.

[354] Or a gain: see Part VII below.

[355] *Phillips* v. *South Western Railway Co.* (1879) 4 Q.B.D. 406, 409; *Broome* v. *Cassell* [1972] A.C. 1027, 1077F, 1086B, 1089B-C, 1126D.

[356] See para. 6.24 above.

3.88   Despite these difficulties, certain principles relevant to the assessment of exemplary awards have been developed by the courts and we examine these below.[357]

(a) The relevance of a compensatory award

3.89   In *Rookes* v. *Barnard* Lord Devlin said that when assessing damages in a case in which exemplary damages are appropriate, the jury should be directed that:

> ...if, but only if, the sum which they have in mind to award as compensation (which may, of course, be a sum aggravated by the way in which the defendant has behaved to the plaintiff) is inadequate to punish him for his outrageous conduct, to mark their disapproval of such conduct and to deter him from repeating it, then it can award some larger sum.[358]

3.90   The importance of this principle of assessment was emphasised by the House of Lords in *Broome* v. *Cassell*.[359] Its essence is that, because an award of compensatory (particularly if it includes aggravated) damages may also serve the purposes of punishment or deterrence, the jury or court should therefore be wary of the risk of double counting. Compensatory and exemplary sums should not be determined separately and then added together.[360] Instead, it is only if what the defendant deserves to pay as punishment exceeds what the plaintiff deserves to receive as compensation that the plaintiff can also be awarded the amount in excess.[361] We understand that counsel sometimes request itemisation of awards, to guide

---

[357] We consider at paras. 6.28ff. below whether there are ways in which the process of assessing exemplary damages can be made more acceptable.

[358] [1964] A.C. 1129, 1228.

[359] [1972] A.C. 1027, 1060A-B, D, 1082H, 1104E, 1116C, 1121G-1122A, 1126C-D. Indeed Viscount Dilhorne, Lord Wilberforce and Lord Diplock (dissenting) thought that the trial judge's direction was inadequate in this respect and that the defendant's appeal should therefore be allowed.

[360] *Ibid.*, 1060C-D, 1062B, 1082B, 1089D-F, 1116G-H, 1126D.

[361] *Ibid.*, 1126D.

the Court of Appeal.[362] However, it may be that insufficient attention is paid to the principle of not adding the separate sums together and that double counting can in fact occur.[363]

(b) No separate award

3.91   Rather than make separate awards of compensatory and exemplary damages the jury or court should award a single sum.[364] This principle is a product of, and goes hand in hand with, the one just discussed. If separate awards are made, the danger is that the sums will simply be added to each other, bringing about precisely the result which the 'if, but only if' direction is designed to avoid. Unfortunately, Lord Devlin's categorisation in *Rookes* v. *Barnard*[365] almost compels this separation[366] and in practice courts and juries now tend to itemize their awards.[367]

(c) Moderation

3.92   Exemplary awards are governed by a principle of moderation.[368] In jury cases the judge should direct the jury as to the danger of its making an excessive award. This principle seems to derive from the feeling that exemplary damages are an exceptional form of civil law punishment which is not subject to the normal safeguards afforded by the criminal process.

---

[362] Although Lord Devlin in *Rookes* v. *Barnard* [1964] A.C. 1129, 1228, indicated that split awards should really only be made in cases where it is difficult for a judge to say whether or not the claim for exemplary damages should be left to the jury.

[363] A jury must be directed in accordance with Lord Devlin's formula if the award is not to be set aside for misdirection. However, the complexity of the direction may mean that *in practice* juries tend to double count, and the levels of damages awarded in defamation cases may be some indication of this.

[364] *Rookes* v. *Barnard* [1964] A.C. 1129, 1228; *Broome* v. *Cassell* [1972] A.C. 1027, 1072C-H, 1082D, 1094H, 1099B, 1116C-1118F, 1126G-H; *A-G* v. *Reynolds* [1980] A.C. 637, 662G-663A (P.C.).

[365] [1964] A.C. 1129.

[366] Cf. *Broome* v. *Cassell* [1972] A.C. 1027, 1100D, 1118D-F.

[367] This seems to be the case at least if one considers awards of damages against the police or at county court level in respect of wrongful eviction, which are frequently split into general, aggravated and exemplary damages. Such itemisation is not *necessarily* evidence of double counting, but according to the House of Lords in *Broome* v. *Cassell* [1972] A.C. 1027, 1072D-H, 1094H, 1116C, it does increase the risk of double counting.

[368] This was Lord Devlin's second consideration: *Rookes* v. *Barnard* [1964] A.C. 1129, 1227-1228.

(d) Wealth of the defendant

3.93   When calculating the appropriate exemplary sum, the court or jury should take into account the means of the defendant.[369] Although there is obvious justice in determining a financial penalty according to the individual's capacity to pay, the courts have provided no guidance as to how evidence of the defendant's means is to be given to the jury.[370]

3.94   There are obvious practical difficulties in determining the precise wealth of the defendant for the purposes of calculating an exemplary award.[371] If the courts were to enter into detailed consideration of this matter a practice might develop of plaintiffs seeking discovery of the defendant's financial affairs whenever an allegation of conduct justifying an award of exemplary damages was made. This might be thought to allow unwarranted intrusions into a defendant's private affairs which would be likely to place the defendant under strong pressure to settle the claim. The expense involved in giving such discovery might be substantial and the process might be particularly difficult to apply to corporate defendants.

3.95   The Ontario Law Reform Commission reported that "[i]n Canadian practice, it appears that wealth is assessed without detailed evidence" and that "[c]ounsel who responded to our inquiries indicated that, in their opinion, judges control investigation into the defendant's wealth carefully, both on discovery and at trial."[372] The Commission accepted that this approach was appropriate on the grounds that any attempt to achieve greater precision in

---

[369] This was Lord Devlin's third consideration: *Rookes* v. *Barnard* [1964] A.C. 1129, 1228. See also, *Benson* v. *Frederick* (1766) 3 Burr. 1845, 97 E.R. 1130; *Manson* v. *Associated Newspapers Ltd.* [1965] 1 W.L.R. 1038, 1045H-1046A.

[370] In the United States, some states place no restrictions on the discovery or proof of wealth evidence, others grant the trial court discretion to adopt appropriate procedures to limit undue harm to a defendant's interest in maintaining privacy of financial affairs (Ohio Code Ann. S. 2307.80(B)(6) (1987). Some states require the plaintiff to make a preliminary showing of evidence that would support such a claim (Iowa Code Ann. S. 668A.1.3 (1986)), while others permit or require the bifurca.

[371] Report on Exemplary Damages (1991), Ontario Law Reform Commission, pp. 50-52; L. Schleuter & K.R. Redden, *Punitive Damages* (1990), vol. 1, p. 203. Cf. also the problems which have surfaced with the introduction of unit fines in criminal cases by the Criminal Justice Act 1991, and which have led the Home Secretary to announce the Government's intention to introduce amending legislation replacing the "rigid and mechanistic" national unit fine system with a discretionary power to raise or lower fines in line with a defendant's income: *The Times*, 11 June 1993; *The Guardian*, 11 June 1993.

[372] Report on Exemplary Damages (1991), p. 51.

assessing punishment according to the defendant's means would inevitably lead to intractable difficulties.

3.96   There seems to be no evidence of this issue having caused any difficulties in English practice to date.[373]   However, it undoubtedly has the potential to do so and it might be thought sensible to introduce express provision to regulate it as part of any reform of the subject.

(e) Joint liability

3.97   In the case of joint defendants the principle of proportionality in punishment[374] means that any exemplary award which is made should be a sum suitable to be inflicted on the defendant who bears the least responsibility for the tort.[375] If this were not the case the plaintiff might be able to collect an inappropriate level of exemplary damages from that person by reason of the principle of joint and several liability.

3.98   Where an award of exemplary damages within Lord Devlin's second category can be regarded as being restitutionary in nature, the principle that the award should be suitable punishment for the defendant who bears the least responsibility can have the strange result of leaving benefits in the hands of the defendant who is most responsible. In practice, the principle places a great premium on the ability of the plaintiff's solicitors to identify the best defendant against which to bring proceedings.

(f) Multiple plaintiffs

3.99   If two or more plaintiffs successfully seek exemplary damages in joint proceedings against a single defendant the correct procedure is for the jury to determine a single sum of exemplary

---

[373] However, in *Singh* v. *London Underground*, *The Independent*, 25 April 1990, the defendant successfully argued that the investigation of its financial structure required by a claim for exemplary damages was a factor which pointed towards trial by jury being unmanageable.

[374] Which demands that the measure of punishment inflicted upon the defendant should bear some relationship to the gravity of her or his conduct.

[375] *Broome* v. *Cassell* [1972] A.C. 1027, 1063D-1064A, 1090E, 1096F-G, 1105D-G, 1118G-1119A, 1122B.

damages which is appropriate punishment for the defendant's conduct.[376] When this sum has been assessed it should be divided equally amongst the successful plaintiffs rather than being multiplied by their number. Whereas a number of victims may serve to multiply the losses which merit a compensatory award, the exemplary award should be appropriate to the defendant's conduct. The fact that the conduct affects more than one person may justify an increase in the punishment inflicted, but the application of a simple mathematical formula would be almost certain to result in over-punishment.

3.100 A likely consequence of this rule in group litigation situations is that plaintiffs who do not participate in the first case to be resolved may find that their entitlement to participate in any award of exemplary damages has been lost.

(g) The plaintiff's conduct and mitigation

3.101 It has been held that a judge is entitled to direct the jury that they are empowered to take the conduct of the plaintiff into account when deciding what sum to award as exemplary damages[377] and it is arguable that the provisions of the Law Reform (Contributory Negligence) Act 1945 apply to such cases. Provocative conduct which results in a wrongful arrest may therefore reduce an award of exemplary damages which is made against the police. This result might be thought to be slightly surprising in view of the requirement that the defendant's conduct be oppressive, arbitrary or unconstitutional before an award of exemplary damages will be available.

3.102 The absence of aggravating features is a factor which is relevant to the amount of an exemplary award,[378] as well as to the question whether such an award should be made at

---

[376] *Riches* v. *News Group Newspapers Ltd.* [1986] Q.B. 256. After *A.B.* v. *South West Water Services Ltd.* [1993] Q.B. 507, the size of the class of plaintiffs is now a reason to refuse an exemplary award altogether. See para. 3.83 above. In *Riches* the plaintiffs were an identified, fairly small class and all of them were before the court.

[377] *Bishop* v. *Metropolitan Police Commissioner*, *The Times*, 5 December 1989. Cf. *McMillan* v. *Singh* (1984) 17 H.L.R. 120, 124, in which the Court of Appeal rejected a judge's holding that exemplary damages could not be awarded in a wrongful eviction case to a plaintiff who had been in arrears of rent at the time of the eviction. Sir John Arnold said that, "it is no defence in a common law claim that you have failed in the transaction, or any associated transaction, to behave with that propriety which enables you to be a successful plaintiff in equity".

[378] *Holden* v. *Chief Constable of Lancashire* [1987] 1 Q.B. 380, 388D-E.

all.[379] A wrong committed in good faith or under an honest mistake may therefore justify a low award, rather than a high one.[380] This factor seems to be relevant to Category 1 awards only, since those made on the basis of Category 2 require that the defendant have acted in the knowledge that, or reckless as to whether, what she or he was doing was wrong.[381]

(h) Guidance of the jury

3.103   Until recently the jury could be given little guidance as to how to reach an appropriate exemplary sum.[382] For instance, no reference could be made to previous awards. However, recent caselaw indicates that the position has changed, although the cases have not concerned exemplary awards. In *Sutcliffe* v. *Pressdram*,[383] the Court of Appeal recognised the need for improved guidance, indicating that in future juries should be made aware of the financial implications of the awards they make in terms which would assist them to understand the real value of large sums. This approach has now been followed in a number of cases involving compensatory sums.[384] More recently, the Court of Appeal has held that section 8 of the Courts and Legal Services Act 1990 empowers it to interfere more readily with jury awards.[385] It also suggested that awards made under this section would in time provide a

---

[379]   See para. 3.85 above.

[380]   E.g. *Eliot* v. *Allen* (1845) 1 C.B. 18, 135 E.R. 441.

[381]   See para. 3.45 above.

[382]   The principles so far discussed in relation to assessment act as constraints on the sum which can be awarded, rather than positively indicating how it should be arrived at.

[383]   [1991] 1 Q.B. 153. This was a case in which the plaintiff sought aggravated, but not exemplary, damages for libel.

[384]   E.g. *Gorman* v. *Mudd*, 15 October 1992 (Unreported, C.A.); *Lewis* v. *Chief Constable of Greater Manchester*, *The Independent*, 23 October 1991 (see transcript); *Rantzen* v. *Mirror Group Newspapers*, (1993) 143 N.L.J. 507.

[385]   *Rantzen* v. *Mirror Group Newspapers*, (1993) 143 N.L.J. 507. The plaintiff, a television presenter and founder of the Childline Charity for sexually abused children, was awarded £250,000 damages for libel by a jury in respect of articles published by the defendants which suggested she had protected and covered up for an alleged paedophile teaching at a private school. Exercising its powers under s. 8 of the Courts and Legal Services Act 1990 and O. 59, r. 11(4), the Court of Appeal intervened and substituted a sum of £110,000. R.S.C., O. 59 r. 11(4), may allow the power to be exercised not only in defamation cases but in any case where juries sit, such as malicious prosecution or false imprisonment. However, because the great majority of civil cases heard with a jury involve libel or slander, it is to be expected that the *Rantzen* approach will have the greatest effect in these cases. See further para. 6.33 below.

corpus to which reference could be made in later cases, thereby establishing some standards as to what were 'proper' awards. In the context of compensatory awards, it was said that juries should not only be invited to consider the purchasing power of any award they made, but should also be asked to ensure that it was proportionate to the damage which the plaintiff had suffered. It should be possible to give similar guidance in the case of exemplary awards.[386]

(3) Miscellaneous rules governing an exemplary award

(a) Vicarious liability

3.104 A public official, such as a police officer, who engages in misconduct is unlikely to bear personal responsibility for any damages awarded because of the doctrine of *respondeat superior*, which, in effect, makes the cost of the award a charge on public funds.[387] On ordinary principles of vicarious liability, an employer is liable for those torts which are committed by employees in the course of their employment.[388] An unlawful act is within the scope of employment even if it is unauthorised, provided that it can be regarded as a mode, albeit an improper one, of carrying out acts which are authorised.[389] Therefore, employers of public officials will often be vicariously liable for torts giving rise to exemplary damages within Lord Devlin's common law categories, and indeed it has been the practice in cases of police misconduct, for instance, for the relevant police authority to pay the damages, including exemplary damages, awarded in respect of that misconduct.

---

[386] Two proposed procedures announced by the Lord Chancellor in December 1992 will further limit the role of the jury in relation to defamation. An 'offer of amends' will allow defendants to curtail proceedings by making an offer recognising that the plaintiff has been defamed and indicating a willingness to pay damages assessed by a judge. A new summary procedure will enable the plaintiff to claim damages up to a fixed ceiling. See *Hansard* (H.L.), 16 December 1992, vol. 541, W.A. 35.

[387] See paras. 3.39-3.43 above.

[388] *Clerk & Lindsell on Torts* (16th ed., 1989), para. 3-16. By virtue of s. 2(1)(a) of the Crown Proceedings Act 1947, the Crown is vicariously liable for the torts of its servants, such as prison officers, as if it were a private person of full age and capacity. By virtue of s. 48(1) of the Police Act 1964, the Chief Constable of a particular police force (or, in London, the Metropolitan Police Commissioner) is vicariously liable "in respect of torts committed by constables under his direction and control in the performance or purported performance of their functions in like manner as a master is liable in respect of torts committed by his servants in the course of their employment".

[389] *Salmond & Heuston on the Law of Torts* (20th ed., 1992), p. 457.

3.105 However, in *Makanjuola* v. *Metropolitan Police Commissioner*,[390] Henry J. held that the plaintiff, who had submitted to a sexual assault by a police officer under a threat by him that he would otherwise make a report which would lead to her deportation, could not hold the Metropolitan Police Commissioner vicariously liable for the policeman's tort since it was clearly a course of conduct of his own and could not be regarded as an improper mode of doing something he was authorised to do. The policeman himself, however, was personally liable in damages, including exemplary damages within Category 1.

3.106 It is unclear what effect the decisions in *Weldon* v. *Home Office*[391] and *Racz* v. *Home Office*[392] will have on the vicarious liability of employers in respect of torts giving rise to exemplary damages, particularly those within Lord Devlin's first category. Relying on dicta of Lord Bridge in *Weldon* v. *Home Office*,[393] the Court of Appeal in *Racz* v. *Home Office*[394] held that the Home Office could not be vicariously liable for the tort of misfeasance in a public office since it involved conduct which was known to be unauthorised or which was actuated by malice, that is by personal spite or a desire to injure for improper reasons. This is exactly the sort of conduct which will typically sustain an award of exemplary damages on the basis of Category 1.

3.107 In other words, the kinds of wrong which are most likely to give rise to exemplary damages are wrongs for which employers are least likely to be vicariously responsible. Unless *Racz* v. *Home Office* can be restrictively interpreted as applying only in respect of the tort of misfeasance in a public office or to torts committed by prison officers, it seems that vicarious liability is now less likely to attach to awards of exemplary damages in respect of wrongs within Category 1. We consider to what extent vicarious liability should exist for awards of exemplary damages at paragraphs 6.42 - 6.44 below.

---

[390] *The Times*, 8 August 1989.

[391] [1992] 1 A.C. 58.

[392] [1992] T.L.R. 624.

[393] [1992] 1 A.C. 58, 164D-F.

[394] [1992] T.L.R. 624.

(b) Survival of cause of action

3.108   As a result of section 1(2)(a) of the Law Reform (Miscellaneous Provisions) Act 1934 no claim for exemplary damages survives for the benefit of the estate of a deceased person.[395] Strong arguments can be levelled against this rule; wrongdoers can, and should, be punished irrespective of whether their victims are alive; a wrongdoer should not escape punishment as a result of a fortuity, and any deterrent effect which may be derived from such an award will be furthered by its survival. On the other hand, if the purpose of such awards is to serve retributive ends or to assuage injured feelings[396] the death of the victim goes most of the way towards removing the purpose of making an award.

3.109   At present an award of exemplary damages can be claimed from the estate of a deceased person.[397] This may also be thought to create problems in so far as punishment is being levied on the innocent heirs of the wrongdoer and no retributive or deterrent effect is any longer available against the wrongdoer. There are, on the other hand, some arguments for maintaining this position. As the value of the estate would have been reduced had the award been made during the wrongdoer's lifetime it is difficult to accept that the estate is being punished, it is simply being deprived of a fortuitous benefit which might otherwise result from the death. Where the rationale of making an award of exemplary damages is the recovery of profits made as a result of the tort, the award should survive against the estate which would otherwise be unjustly enriched by the tort in exactly the same way as the tortfeasor was.

3.110   None of these issues applies to defamation. This is the effect of subsection 1(1) of the 1934 Act under which such a cause of action does not survive against or for the benefit of the estate of a deceased person. The Lord Chancellor's Department consulted on these issues in

---

[395] But see para. 3.19 above.

[396] Note that the bereavement award available under the Fatal Accidents Act 1976 does not survive for the benefit of an estate: Law Reform (Miscellaneous Provisions) Act, s. 1A.

[397] *McGregor on Damages*, (15th ed., 1988), para 717.

1990,[398] but in 1991 announced that, as a result of the wide variety of responses made to the consultation paper, it had concluded not to recommend any change in the law.[399]

(c) Standard of proof

3.111 The standard of proof which is applicable to cases in which exemplary damages are claimed is the balance of probabilities test, as for all civil actions.[400] However, it is arguable that this standard is too low, rendering exemplary damages too readily available. One argument is that if criminal law penalties are only imposed in respect of conduct which is proved beyond reasonable doubt, civil law punishment should be subject to the same condition. English law may have already gone some way down this road. In *Halford* v. *Brookes*[401] it was held that a person should not be determined to be a murderer in civil proceedings unless the criminal law standard of proof had been satisfied. Although the extent to which this rule might apply to tort claims brought in relation to conduct which could amount to other criminal offences is unclear, we think that *Halford* is an exceptional case. It may simply be an extension of the rule in *Hornal* v. *Neuberger Products Ltd.* [402] whereby a jury should be directed even in civil cases that the more serious the allegation, the higher the degree of probability required to prove it.

3.112 Some American states have adopted a compromise position to the effect that the case for exemplary damages should be proved by "clear and convincing evidence",[403] the test applying to the question of the exceptional conduct involved. However, this might create

---

[398] Defamation: Death of a Party to Defamation Proceedings.

[399] The Supreme Court Procedure Committee's Report on Practice and Procedure in Defamation (1991) also concluded that no change in the existing rules was called for: Part VI, pp. 51ff..

[400] But there are some dicta to the contrary. See, for instance, *Mafo* v. *Adams* [1970] 1 Q.B. 548, 556E-F; *Riches* v. *News Group Newspapers Ltd.* [1986] 1 Q.B. 256, 274F, 278F-G, 285A.

[401] [1992] 1 P.I.Q.R. 175.

[402] [1957] 1 Q.B. 247.

[403] Alas. Stat. §09.17.020 (1987); Fla. Stat. Ann. §768.73 (1986); Ind. Code Ann. §34-4-34-2 (1986); Mont. Code Ann. §27-1-221 (1987); Ohio Rev. Code Ann. §2307.80 (1988), (in relation to product liability cases); S.C. Code Ann. §1-33-135 (1988); Ore. Rev. Stat. §41.315 (1987); Ky. Rev. Stat. Ann. §411.184 (1988). Other states have enacted similar provisions in relation to proof of particular issues.

unnecessary complexity, particularly for a jury, if the compensatory and punitive elements of an award of damages were to be subject to different standards of proof.

PART IV

AGGRAVATED AND EXEMPLARY DAMAGES - OVERSEAS LAW

AUSTRALIA

4.1   The theoretical distinction between aggravated and exemplary damages as laid down by Lord Devlin in *Rookes* v. *Barnard*[1] was accepted by the High Court of Australia in *Uren* v. *John Fairfax &nd Sons Pty. Ltd.*.[2] Windeyer J. stated that aggravated damages:

> ...are given to compensate the plaintiff when the harm done to him by a wrongful act was aggravated by the manner in which the act was done: exemplary damages, on the other hand, are intended to punish the defendant, and presumably to serve one or more of the objects of punishment - moral retribution or deterrence.[3]

The judge saw it as logical to regard the state of the defendant's mind as relevant to punishment, but not to the measure of the plaintiff's compensatory damages.[4] Malice is therefore neither necessary nor sufficient, and aggravated damages could in theory be awarded for negligence. However, this is seen as unlikely to happen.[5]

4.2   In New South Wales, section 46 of the Defamation Act 1974 abolished exemplary damages for defamation. It has been observed that since 1974, aggravated damages awards have been liberally awarded by juries, perhaps reflecting a desire to accommodate the punitive element not now available.[6]

---

1   [1964] A.C. 1129 (H.L.).

2   (1966) 117 C.L.R. 118, affirmed by the Privy Council [1969] 1 A.C. 590.

3   *Uren* v. *John Fairfax & Sons Pty. Ltd.* (1966) 117 C.L.R. 118, 149.

4   *Ibid.*, pp. 151-2.

5   See H. Luntz, *Assessment of Damages for Personal Injury and Death* (3rd ed., 1990) para. [1.7.11], n. 20, where the typical causes of action supporting a claim of aggravated damages are noted as trespass to the person and defamation.

6   See J.G. Fleming, *The Law of Torts* (8th ed., 1992), p. 596, n. 643; Discussion Paper on Reform of Defamation Law (1990), the Attorneys General of New South Wales, Queensland and Victoria, p. 29, para. 8.4; *Carson* v. *John Fairfax & Son Ltd.* [1993] 67 A.L.J.R. 634, 670,(*per* McHugh J., H.Ct).

4.3　In *Uren* v. *John Fairfax & Sons Pty. Ltd.*[7] the High Court of Australia refused to adopt the limits placed upon exemplary damages by *Rookes* v. *Barnard* and affirmed that an exemplary award would be appropriate in any case of wanton conduct showing a "contumelious disregard of the rights of the plaintiff."[8]　More recent Australian authority has developed further in directions which would not be permissible in England.　In *Lamb* v. *Cotogno*[9] the High Court of Australia seems to have recognised the possibility of such an award in a case of non-malicious, recklessly committed trespass to the person by a private individual.　The case involved a driver who drove in such a way as to dislodge and injure the plaintiff who was clinging to the car.　In *Coloca* v. *B.P. Australia Ltd.*[10] the Supreme Court of Victoria was prepared to extend the authority of *Lamb* to permit an award of exemplary damages to be made in cases in which allegations were made that employers had negligently exposed employees to dangerous substances in the course of their work.　The judge regarded it as illogical to make the availability of an award of exemplary damages depend on whether the claim was pleaded in trespass or in negligence.

CANADA

4.4　In Canada, too, the distinction between aggravated and exemplary damages as expressed by the House of Lords, has been accepted.[11]　However, in its 1991 Report on Exemplary Damages, the Ontario Law Reform Commission noted that to trigger an award of aggravated damages, Lord Devlin would require proof of the same type of conduct on the part of the defendant as would trigger an award of exemplary damages in Canada - exceptional conduct, such as malevolence, spite or outrageous conduct.[12] The Commission also saw the category of aggravated damages as containing ambiguous and incompatible social goals - compensation, and punishment and deterrence - such as to make the distinction referred to above

---

[7]　(1966) 117 C.L.R. 118.

[8]　The Privy Council approved that approach specifically in relation to libel, [1969] 1 A.C. 590, at 644.

[9]　(1987) 164 C.L.R. 1.

[10]　[1992] Austr. Tort Reports 61, 81-153, 164 (*per* O'Bryan J.).

[11]　*Vorvis* v. *Insurance Corporation of British Columbia* (1989) 58 D.L.R.(4th) 193.

[12]　Report on Exemplary Damages (1991), Ontario Law Reform Commission, p. 28.

problematic.[13] The Commission concluded that the existence of such features created confusion. It recommended that the question of injury to pride and dignity should be approached from a purely compensatory perspective, so that the court should be empowered to award compensatory damages for injuries to pride and dignity as part of the ordinary global award of damages for non-pecuniary loss. Such damages were to be awarded without the need to prove exceptional, malevolent, spiteful or outrageous conduct. It recommended that aggravated damages should be abolished. It was not felt that these recommendations would open a new category of compensatory award, because such payments were already given in some cases, or as part of an award of damages for pain and suffering. The Commission saw the real effect of their proposals as bringing coherence to the law, by rendering less central the question of exceptional conduct for matters of compensation, and removing the question of compensation from the notion of exemplary damages.[14]

4.5   The Commission concluded that it would be premature to make specific recommendations for reform of the law of aggravated and exemplary damages in relation to breach of contract, at least until the debate in Canada about the nature of contractual obligations is resolved.[15]

4.6   In *Vorvis* v. *Insurance Corporation of British Columbia*[16] the Supreme Court of Canada chose not to adopt the *Rookes* v. *Barnard* approach to exemplary damages. Nevertheless awards of exemplary damages were to be confined in Canadian law to cases of extreme conduct which was deserving of condemnation and punishment. Such conduct would have to be shown to be harsh, vindictive, reprehensible or exhibit a malicious motive. Canadian law would not appear to place any absolute bar on the recovery of exemplary damages in cases of breach of contract[17] or of personal injuries based on negligence[18] so long as the general conditions governing the availability of such awards are satisfied. The Ontario Law Reform

---

13   *Ibid.*, p. 29.

14   *Ibid.*, p.30.

15   *Ibid.*, p.101.

16   (1989) 58 D.L.R. (4th) 193.

17   *Ibid.*.

18   *Robitaille* v. *Vancouver Hockey Club Ltd.* (1981) 124 D.L.R. (3d) 228, (Brit. Col. C.A.): a case in which the defendant's conduct was castigated as highhanded, arrogant and displaying a reckless disregard for the rights of the plaintiff.

Commission recommended that exemplary damages[19] be retained and awarded only where the defendant has advertently committed a wrongful act deserving of punishment, and where the defendant's conduct was exceptional.[20]

IRELAND

4.7   Irish law also recognises the concept of aggravated damages as a category of compensatory damages, awarded as a response to particularly offensive conduct by the defendant. In theory, they are distinct from exemplary damages, but in practice, the distinction is far from clear.[21] In *Kennedy* v. *Ireland*,[22] a 'phone-tapping' case, Hamilton P. referred to Lord Devlin's speech in *Rookes* v. *Barnard* and said that he considered that the plaintiffs were entitled to "substantial damages" and that, in the circumstances of the case, it was irrelevant whether they should be described as aggravated or exemplary. It is difficult to see how *Rookes* could be authority for such a proposition.

4.8   The Irish Law Reform Commission has recently attempted to clarify the situation in relation to defamation by recommending an express statutory provision setting out the conditions under which exemplary damages should be awarded.[23] This may more clearly delineate the difference between aggravated and exemplary damages.

---

[19]   The Commission recommended that exemplary damages in Ontario should be referred to as "punitive damages". It did so in order to emphasise the punitive rationale, which the Commission regarded as including important symbolic considerations: Report on Exemplary Damages (1991), pp. 38 and 103.

[20]   *Ibid.*, pp. 38 and 103.

[21]   See B.M.E. McMahon & W. Binchy, *Irish Law of Torts* (2nd ed.,1990), pp. 771 - 778.

[22]   [1988] I.L.R.M. 472, (H. Ct).

[23]   *"(1)   The defendant intended to publish matter to a person other than the plaintiff, knowing that such matter would be understood to refer to the plaintiff and that it would tend to injure the plaintiff's reputation and with knowledge, or a reckless disregard, of its falsity; and*

(2)   The conduct of the defendant has been high handed, insolent or vindictive or has exhibited a disregard for the plaintiff's rights so gross as clearly to warrant punishment over and above that which has been inflicted upon him by an award of compensatory damages. "

See Report on the Civil Law of Defamation, (December 1991), Irish Law Reform Commission, p.68.

4.9   Irish law seems to be in the process of rejecting the rigidity of *Rookes* in relation to exemplary damages. In *Conway* v. *Irish National Teachers' Organisation*[24] the Irish Supreme Court recognised an additional category of case which might justify an award of exemplary damages: where the intended consequences of the defendant's act is the direct deprivation of a constitutional right of the plaintiff.[25] The Irish Law Reform Commission recommendation referred to above - that exemplary damages be retained in cases of intentional defamation in which the conduct of the defendant can be shown to be "highhanded, insolent or vindictive or has exhibited a gross disregard of the plaintiff's rights"[26] - is clearly a far wider and more principled approach than that adopted in *Rookes*.

NEW ZEALAND

4.10   In *Taylor* v. *Beere*,[27] a defamation case, Somers J. referred to Lord Hailsham L.C.'s speech in *Broome* v. *Cassell*[28] to confine exemplary damages to their proper place in relation to aggravated damages:

> It is clear that aggravated damages are given to compensate the plaintiff when the injury or harm done to him by the wrongful act of the defendant is aggravated by the manner in which he did the act. They may include sums for 'loss of reputation, for injured feelings, for outraged morality, and to enable a plaintiff to protect himself against future calumny or outrage of a similar kind' and ' indignation...at the injury inflicted on the plaintiff is a perfectly legitimate motive in making a generous rather than a more moderate award to provide an adequate solatium'....[29]

In this approach, exemplary damages were seen not as an expression of vindictiveness, but as a punishment and a deterrent, to show that tortious conduct does not pay. The distinction was held to form part of the law of New Zealand. Exemplary damages were to be awarded if and

---

24   [1991] I.L.R.M. 497.

25   See also para. 4.22 below.

26   Report on the Civil Law of Defamation (December 1991), Irish Law Reform Commission, p.68.

27   [1982] 1 N.Z.L.R. 81, (C.A.).

28   [1972] A.C. 1027, 1073, and 1077.

29   *Taylor* v. *Beere* [1982] 1 N.Z.L.R. 81, 95.

only if the sum of compensatory and aggravated compensatory damages was not of itself sufficient to inflict a proper punishment on the defendant.

4.11   Contemporaneously, the New Zealand Court of Appeal had to decide whether the Accident Compensation Act 1972, the legislation which established a comprehensive no-fault compensation scheme for personal injury, barred an award of exemplary damages where, as a result of the conduct complained of, the plaintiff may have suffered personal injury.[30] The Court took a policy-based approach, and decided to mould the law of damages to meet social needs. Recognising that the Act had taken over the field of compensation for personal injury, it held that actions for purely punitive purposes would be allowed, and also that since compensatory damages (aggravated or otherwise) could no longer be awarded, exemplary damages would have to take over part of the latter's former role. In other words, since benefits under the Act were in no sense punitive, exemplary damages would have to do not only the work assigned to them by *Broome* v. *Cassell* but also some of the work previously done by the other heads of damages.[31] Therefore, it appears that in New Zealand the legislative regime has caused the distinction between exemplary and aggravated damages to be blurred in relation to personal injury, with exemplary damages actually taking over the role of aggravated damages to some degree. With the recent passing of legislation changing the boundaries of cover of the New Zealand scheme,[32] it appears there may now be more opportunities for plaintiffs to sue in tort outside the act, on the grounds that the injury is either not covered, or that the statutory compensation is inadequate.[33] The effect this will have on aggravated and exemplary damages is unclear.

4.12   In *Donselaar* v. *Donselaar*[34] the Court of Appeal recognised that the assessment of exemplary damages in cases of personal injury would not be easy, since the substratum of compensatory damages had disappeared and with it all practical possibility of taking account of their award in estimating whether and to what extent there should be any addition by way

---

[30]   *Donselaar* v. *Donselaar* [1982] 1 N.Z.L.R. 97.

[31]   *Ibid.*, 107, lines 3-13 (*per* Cooke J.).

[32]   Accident Rehabilitation and Compensation Insurance Act 1992 (N.Z).

[33]   See D.M. Carden, "Accident Compensation and lump sums", [1992] N.Z.L.J. 404.

[34]   [1982] 1 N.Z.L.R. 97.

of exemplary damages.[35] But the new approach was embraced as being necessary. The question whether pure negligence should attract exemplary or aggravated damages did not appear to arise. In *Taylor* v. *Beere*[36] the New Zealand Court of Appeal adopted *Uren* in preference to *Rookes* in a libel action. The Defamation Act 1992, which replaced the Defamation Act 1954, became law on 1 February 1993. Under section 28, punitive damages may only be awarded in defamation actions where a defendant has acted in flagrant disregard of the rights of the plaintiff.

SCOTLAND

4.13 Exemplary damages do not exist in Scottish law. The leading case on this point is *Black* v. *North British Railway Co.*, where Lord President Dunedin refused to award exemplary damages against a railway company because he found:

> ... [n]o authority for any distinction between damages and 'exemplary damages' in the law of Scotland. The very heading under which it is treated in our older books 'Reparation' excludes the idea.[37]

4.14 However, aggravated damages, in the English sense, do exist. In all cases damages are aggravated by the greater gravity of the loss suffered. As we have seen above, cases of this sort may verge upon the punitive in function. Further, in cases of deliberate wrongs damages in Scotland may sometimes be aggravated by the outrageous nature of the conduct complained of.[38] In defamation cases, the conduct of counsel is not accepted as an aggravation unless that conduct has been on the express instructions, or with the privity, of counsel's client.[39]

---

[35] *Ibid.*, 116, lines 40-50 (*per* Somers J.).

[36] [1982] 1 N.Z.L.R. 81.

[37] 1908 S.C. 444, 453.

[38] *Black* v. *North British Railway Co,*, 1908 S.C. 444; D.M. Walker, *The Law of Delict in Scotland* (2nd ed., 1981), p. 461.

[39] See Lord Kilbrandon in *Broome* v. *Cassell* [1972] A.C. 1027, 1133H-1134A.

THE UNITED STATES OF AMERICA

4.15 Because there is clear separation of exemplary[40] and compensatory damages in awards in the United States, there is no category of aggravated damages.[41] Prosser notes that 'aggravated negligence' (covering wilful, wanton and reckless behaviour), can justify exemplary awards,[42] and a number of recent state tort reform statutes permit exemplary awards or increases in exemplary awards where the defendant has acted in a wilful and wanton manner thus further aggravating the damages, knowing that such action would produce such aggravation, or in ways similarly described.[43]

4.16 The American approach to awards of exemplary damages has diverged markedly from the English. Such damages have been awarded frequently in American states on the basis of deliberate tortious conduct[44] or wanton or bad faith breaches of contract. Some states, such as California, Nevada, Montana, Oklahoma, North Dakota, and South Dakota, whose legal systems are codified to a large extent, have express legislative provisions authorizing exemplary damages generally in cases involving aggravated misconduct[45] and there is a large amount of legislation, both state and federal, allowing for such awards to be made in specific circumstances.[46] Such awards have been favoured as a means of enhancing compliance with the law and of giving the successful plaintiff a mechanism which allows the recovery of the costs which would not otherwise be recouped under American procedure. The availability of exemplary awards in product liability cases was well publicised by the jury award of $125

---

[40] In the United States exemplary damages are more commonly referred to as 'punitive damages'.

[41] H. Stoll, "Consequences of Liability: Remedies", Int. Enc. Comp. L. XI/2 Torts (1986), ch. 8, s.109. Cf. C.T. McCormick, *The Law of Damages* (1935), p. 278. Stoll also notes that New Hampshire and Michigan view exemplary damages as an additional compensation for wounded feelings and dignity - i.e. as an award similar to aggravated damages in English law.

[42] William L. Prosser, *Handbook of the Law of Torts*,(4th ed., 1971), 184.

[43] See for example, collected in 2 CCH Products Liability Reporter, (1991), 90,000 et seq, the extracts from products liability statutes from Colorado (Sec. 13-21-102), Georgia (Sec. 51-12-5.1 - 'aggravating circumstances'), and Ohio (Sec. 2315.21 - 'aggravated or egregious fraud').

[44] See American Law Institute, *Restatement of the Law, Second - Torts 2d.* s.908.

[45] See, e.g., Cal. Civ. Code § 3294 (West 1970).

[46] See para 6.14 and Appendix.

million[47] in *Grimshaw* v. *Ford Motor Co.*[48] on the basis of the defendant company's decision to site the fuel tank in its Pinto model in a position which increased the risks to occupants but saved the company money.

4.17 The availability of awards of exemplary damages to juries in America has been regularly cited as one of the reasons for the explosion of litigation commonly identified as the "torts crisis". In fact, research has shown[49] that awards of exemplary damages are nothing like as common or as large in America as the critics of the tort system have claimed, although they have increased in number against corporate defendants. Nonetheless, many states have introduced measures designed to curb excessive awards of exemplary damages. Favoured responses have included increasing the standard of proof; placing caps on the compensation which may be awarded; directing part of the compensation to state funds; banning such awards in certain categories of claim; and granting 'sovereign immunity' against the making of such awards to state governmental bodies. We refer to the American law in more detail at paragraph 6.14 and in the Appendix[50] below when we discuss options for reform.

OTHER APPROACHES

4.18 We noted above that where the harm to personality interests is non-pecuniary (and hence where the loss is incommensurable and difficult to prove), the ideas of compensation, satisfaction and punishment tend to coincide.[51] We now look briefly at French law, where intangible losses are covered by a wide compensatory principle; and German law, which explicitly recognises the concept of satisfaction.

---

[47] Subsequently reduced by the judge to $3.5 million.

[48] (1981) 174 Cal. Rptr. 348.

[49] Collated for the Law Commission by its Consultant, Professor David Owen.

[50] At pp. 179-180 below.

[51] At para. 2.17.

(1) Civil law systems

(a) French law

4.19   Whilst French law does not admit an award of exemplary damages in law,[52] Article 1382 of the French Civil Code articulates a general principle of liability to compensate for 'damage' caused by fault. No distinction is made between physical and pecuniary loss on the one hand (dommage matériel); and non-pecuniary or intangible loss on the other (dommage moral). It is clearly established that dommages moraux may be recovered on the basis of Article 1382,[53] even where these are the only losses suffered.[54] French law thus permits the wide recoverability of intangible losses.[55] Further, the incommensurability and subjectivity of the losses concerned have led French courts to shift from the gravity of the plaintiff's injury to the gravity of the defendant's fault when the assessment comes to be made,[56] although damages are a matter of fact, not law. Some French jurists have rationalised the award of dommages moraux by reference to the punitive principle.[57]

---

[52]   But it has been said that examples of substantial awards in some defamation cases suggest that exemplary damages are awarded in fact: A. Tunc, Introduction, Int. Enc. Comp. L. XI/1 Torts (1986), ch. 1, s.158 and n. 512.   Any decision which in terms justifies the sum of damages awarded by reference to the gravity of the defendant's fault will, however, be quashed by the Court of Cassation.

[53]   See G. Ripert, *La Règle morale dans les obligations civiles* (1949), para. 181; B. Starck, *Droit Civil - Obligations* (1972), para. 115. See M.G. Bridge, "Contractual Damages for Intangible Loss: A Comparative Analysis", (1984) 62 Can. B.R. 323, 332.

[54]   B. Starck, *Droit Civil - Obligations* (1972).

[55]   We observed at para. 2.26 above, that it is possible to see part of the role of the punitive principle in English law in the past as the redress of non-pecuniary harm.

[56]   M.G. Bridge, "Contractual Damages for Intangible Loss: A Comparative Analysis", (1984) 62 Can.B.R. 323,334, and 336, n.49, citing Chalon-sur-Saône, 6 avril 1929, D.H. 1929.359.

[57]   E.g. R. Savatier, *Théorie des obligations* (3rd ed., 1974); G. Ripert et J. Boulanger, *Traité de droit civil (d'après le traité de Planiol)*, vol. II, Obligations (1957), para. 998; G. Ripert, *La Règle morale dans les obligations civiles* (1949), paras. 184-85. See also G. Viney, *Traité de droit civil, les obligations, la responsabilité: conditions* (1982), para. 270.

104

(b) German law

4.20   Exemplary damages are unknown to German law.[58] Nor is there a general delictual principle covering all intentional and negligent harm, as there is in the case of Article 1382 of the French Civil Code. Instead, the German Civil Code[59] refers to specific interests which are protected and to the circumstances in which pecuniary and non-pecuniary harm may be recovered. Although the BGB makes no mention of any interest in the inviolability of the personality, Articles 1 and 2 of the Basic Law[60] recognise a "general right of personality"[61] and this has enabled the German courts to develop a damages remedy in respect of its violation.[62] But German courts have long recognised that the assessment of intangible loss must take into account the defendant's fault, together with other circumstances, such as the means of the parties.[63] Such losses are recoverable only where both the injury to the plaintiff *and* the conduct of the defendant are grave.[64] Furthermore, the Bundesgerichtshof[65] in 1955 justified the award of damages in respect of intangible losses by reference to the principle of satisfaction, and denied only their "direct punitive character".[66] German courts therefore emphasise that damages for non-pecuniary loss must take into account principles of both

---

[58]   B.S. Markesinis, *The German Law of Torts: A Comparative Introduction* (2nd ed., 1990), p. 682.

[59]   The BGB (*Bürgerliches Gesetzbuch*).

[60]   I.e. the German Constitution.

[61]   *Schacht* case (1954) 13 B.G.H.Z. 334.

[62]   *Herrenreiter* case (1958) 26 B.G.H.Z. 349. Incidentally, this has eclipsed civil actions for defamation which are now almost totally unknown in Germany, plaintiffs instead invoking the *Persönlichkeitsrecht*: P.R. Handford, "Moral Damage in Germany", (1978) 27 I.C.L.Q. 849, 865.

[63]   H. Stoll, "Penal Purposes in the Law of Tort", (1970) 18 Am. J. Comp. L. 3, 4.

[64]   P.R. Handford, "Moral Damage in Germany", (1978) 27 I.C.L.Q. 849, 870; B.S. Markesinis, *The German Law of Torts: A Comparative Introduction* (2nd ed., 1990), p. 688.

[65]   The German Supreme Court.

[66]   (1955) 18 B.G.H.Z. 149, 151, 155. In the *Ginseng* case (1961) 35 B.G.H.Z. 363, the Bundesgerichtshof, when recognising the importance of the idea of satisfaction where basic personality rights have been violated, stressed the fact that the defendant's motive had been profit and that this could only be deterred by burdening it with the risk of substantial damages. This seems to be the same idea as that contained in Lord Devlin's second category: see paras. 3.44ff. above.

compensation and satisfaction.[67] It has been said that the Anglo-American cases on exemplary damages would appear to reach comparable results.[68]

(2) Countries with a written Constitution - The United States of America, Canada and Ireland

4.21 We noted above that in the English legal system, which lacks a written Constitution or a Bill of Rights, exemplary damages have played an important role in the protection of civil liberties,[69] and that these damages have been invoked most frequently in relation to torts actionable *per se*.[70] In countries which have a written Constitution, provision is usually made permitting the judiciary to award remedies (including damages) in respect of the violation of constitutionally guaranteed rights and freedoms, or the judiciary have themselves implied such a power from the Constitution.[71]

4.22 It has been held in the United States,[72] Canada,[73] and Ireland[74] that exemplary awards may be made where these constitutional rights have been infringed.[75] Furthermore, there is

---

67 See B.S. Markesinis, *The German Law of Torts: A Comparative Introduction* (2nd ed., 1990), ch. 4, s.3, pp. 669ff..

68 H. Stoll, "Penal Purposes in the Law of Tort", (1970) 18 Am. J. Comp. L. 3, 20.

69 At paras. 2.28 and 3.41.

70 At paras. 2.24-2.25.

71 E.g. in the U.S., s.1983 of the Civil Rights Act 1871 (remedies against state officials) and the decision of the Supreme Court in *Bivens* v. *Six Unknown Named Agents of the Federal Bureau of Narcotics*, (1971) 403 U.S. 388, implying a remedy in damages against federal officials from the Constitution; in Canada: s. 24(1) of the Canadian Charter of Rights and Freedoms (Part 1 of the Constitution Act 1982); in Ireland, the decision in *Meskell* v. *C.I.E.* [1973] I.R. 121, to the effect that breach of a constitutional right guaranteed by the Irish Constitution entitles a person suffering damage thereby to seek redress against the person(s) who infringed the right.

72 *Smith* v. *Wade* (1983) 103 S.Ct 1625.

73 *Lord* v. *Allison* (1986) 3 B.C.L.R. (2d) 300 (S.C.); *Crossman* v. *R.* (1984) 12 C.C.C. (3d) 547 (F.C.T.D.); *Freeman* v. *West Vancouver*, 9 January 1991 (Unreported, B.C.S.C.); *R.* v. *F.* 22 January 1991 (Nfld. S.C.); and *Rollinson* v. *Canada*, 17 January 1991 (Unreported, F.C.T.D.); cited in G. Otis, "Constitutional Liability for the Infringement of Rights *Per se*: A Misguided Theory", [1992] U.B.C. Law Rev. 21.

74 *Garvey* v. *Ireland* [1981] I.L.R.M. 266 (*per* McWilliam J.).

75 But note that the plaintiff must have suffered some actionable loss, i.e. the exemplary award remains parasitic and not independent.

a broad consensus among academics in Canada at least,[76] that the violation of constitutional rights should entitle the victim to a substantial and not merely nominal award of damages, irrespective of whether actual injury has been caused.[77] The arguments used to support this view are similar to those employed in the justification of exemplary damages,[78] namely that a nominal or compensatory award is ineffective to deter constitutional infringements and to vindicate the right concerned;[79] that a substantial award reflects the intrinsic value of rights and marks the value of the interest infringed;[80] and that the availability of substantial awards provides an incentive to plaintiffs to enforce constitutional rights through litigation.[81] However, the U.S. courts have rejected the possibility of substantial awards of damages for the infringement of constitutional rights *per se*,[82] and in Canada also the weight of authority is against such awards.[83] This seems understandable when one considers that exemplary awards may be regarded as already fulfilling part of the function which these claims would serve in the case of particularly egregious violations.[84] The effect of recognising such awards would therefore be significant only in the case of those breaches not giving rise to exemplary awards, for example, negligent or good faith breaches or those where the plaintiff cannot establish (and the court will not presume) some compensable loss.

---

[76] The same view has been expressed in Ireland by T.A.M. Cooney and T. Kerr, "Constitutional Aspects of Irish Tort Law", (1981) 3 D.U.L.J. (N.S.) 1.

[77] I.e. that there should be an award of substantial damages in respect of the infringement of constitutional rights *per se*. See M.L. Pilkington, "Damages as a Remedy for Infringement of the Canadian Charter of Rights and Freedoms", (1984) 62 Can. B.R. 517, 535-542, 570-571; M.L. Pilkington, "Monetary Redress for Charter Infringement" in R.J. Sharpe (ed.), *Charter Litigation* (1987), 307.

[78] See Part V.

[79] See the authorities cited at n. 77 above.

[80] I.e. fulfils a symbolic purpose. E.g. M.L. Pilkington, "Damages as a Remedy for Infringement of the Canadian Charter of Rights and Freedoms", (1984) 62 Can. B.R. 517, 535-542, 570-571; T.A.M. Cooney & T. Kerr, "Constitutional Aspects of Irish Tort Law", (1981) 3 D.U.L.J. (N.S.) 1, 10, 15-16.

[81] E.g. M.L. Pilkington, "Damages as a Remedy for Infringement of the Canadian Charter of Rights and Freedoms", (1984) 62 Can. B.R. 517, 570-571; M.L. Pilkington, "Monetary Redress for Charter Infringement", in R.J. Sharpe (ed.), *Charter Litigation* (1987), 307, 315.

[82] *Carey* v. *Piphus* (1978) 435 U.S. 247, as regards s.1983 of the Civil Rights Act 1871; it is probable that this applies also in the context of *Bivens*-type actions.

[83] G. Otis, "Constitutional Liability for the Infringement of Rights *Per Se*: A Misguided Theory", [1992] U.B.C.Law Rev. 21, 23. But there is some authority in favour of them: see Otis, 24.

[84] See nn. 72-74 above.

PART V

ARE EXEMPLARY DAMAGES EVER JUSTIFIED - ARGUMENTS FOR AND AGAINST

5.1   The remedial armoury of the English law of obligations at present includes both aggravated and exemplary damages. But the availability of exemplary damages in particular has in recent years been called into question.[1] Both the controversy which surrounds them and the complexity of this area of the law make aggravated and exemplary damages a proper subject for reform. Moreover, it is our belief that the limits placed upon the scope of the punitive principle by *Rookes* v. *Barnard*[2] and *A.B.* v. *South West Water Services Ltd.*[3] have produced a body of law which is unprincipled and which precludes any further meaningful development at common law. It is a state of affairs which "... cries aloud ... for Parliamentary intervention."[4]

5.2   Given the weight of opposition to awards of exemplary damages, the first and principal question which arises for consideration is whether these awards are ever justified. In this part we consider the arguments for and against such damages and ask whether the objections to them are powerful enough to warrant their abolition, or whether instead they can be justified as a legitimate legal remedial technique. The answer to this question will govern the choice between the various options which we put to consultees in Part VI: maintaining the status quo, total or partial abolition, or rationalisation. Because some of the objections to exemplary damages are pragmatic, rather than principled, or are concerned only with their assessment,[5] in Part VI we also consider whether there are reforms which might be made to certain ancillary and subsidiary rules which would render exemplary awards more acceptable. Finally, as their history shows,[6] aggravated and exemplary damages are interlinked and any proposals for reform will necessarily reflect this. Those made in relation to exemplary damages will be contingent also upon those made in relation to aggravated damages and vice versa.

---

[1]   See n. 13, para. 1.5 above.

[2]   [1964] A.C. 1129.

[3]   [1993] Q.B. 507.

[4]   *Riches* v. *News Group Newspapers Ltd.* [1986] 1 Q.B. 256, 269C.

[5]   Rather than their availability.

[6]   See paras. 1.12 - 1.13, 2.2 - 2.3 and 3.2, above.

5.3   We set out below some of the objections commonly made to the availability of exemplary damages in civil actions,[7] and then consider the alternative bases upon which such awards might be justified.

ARGUMENTS AGAINST EXEMPLARY DAMAGES

(1) The aim of the law of civil wrongs is solely to provide compensation for loss: exclusivity of the compensatory principle

5.4   There is an *a priori* objection to awards of exemplary damages which is based upon an assumption about the function of remedies for breach of obligations, namely that they exist solely in order to compensate for loss suffered.[8] It is said that the compensatory principle enjoys (or ought to enjoy) a position of exclusivity in relation to civil actions for damages and that the pursuit of other aims, including retribution, deterrence, condemnation and even the removal of gains made by the defendant, is not a legitimate function of the law of civil wrongs. Hence, exemplary damages, which incorporate non-compensatory aims, are exceptional and anomalous.

(2) Punishment is not a legitimate function of the law of civil wrongs and should take place only within the context of the criminal law

5.5   This objection to exemplary damages is a variant of the first, but argues more specifically that, whilst it may be legitimate for the law of civil wrongs to pursue aims other than compensation, punishment[9] is certainly not one of them.[10] The assumption is that punishment should take place only within the criminal law. By having as their object punishment, deterrence or condemnation of the defendant's conduct, exemplary damages thus confuse the civil and

---

7   See the authorities and works cited at paras. 1.5, n.13 and 2.7, n.27.

8   See paras. 1.2-1.3 above.

9   Here meaning retribution, deterrence, condemnation.

10 This would accept, for instance, the possibility of restitutionary damages (on which see Part VII), whilst denying the possibility of an exemplary award.

criminal functions of the law. It is this argument which is invoked most often by those who oppose exemplary awards.[11]

5.6   Secondly, and as a corollary of this, it is argued that punishment ought not to be administered without the evidential and procedural safeguards developed for the protection of offenders by the criminal law.[12] An award of exemplary damages in a civil action deprives the defendant of these protections, and hence it is objected that:

> There is no definition of the offence except that the conduct punished must be oppressive, high-handed, malicious, wanton or its like - terms far too vague to be admitted to any criminal code worthy of the name. There is no limit to the punishment except that it must not be unreasonable. The punishment is not inflicted by a judge who has experience and at least tries not to be influenced by emotion: it is inflicted by a jury without experience of law or punishment and often swayed by considerations which every judge would put out of his mind.... It is no excuse to say that we need not waste sympathy on people who behave outrageously. Are we wasting sympathy on vicious criminals when we insist on proper legal safeguards for them?[13]

5.7   A further objection where there is a maximum financial penalty under the criminal law is that an award of exemplary damages which exceeds it can be seen as undermining Parliament's intentions in so limiting the penalty. These objections might be overcome by the adoption of different evidential and procedural rules and standards for the compensatory and exemplary elements of a civil action. But the difficulty and complexity involved in thereby

---

[11]   It led Lord Devlin in *Rookes* v. *Barnard* [1964] A.C. 1129, 1221 to limit the availability of exemplary awards (although see n. 33, para. 5.13, below); was the reason for Lord Reid's vigorous opposition to exemplary awards in *Broome* v. *Cassell* [1972] A.C. 1027, 1086C-1087G; and was recently reiterated by Sir Thomas Bingham M.R. in *A.B.* v. *South West Water Services Ltd.* [1993] Q.B. 507, 528F-529D.

[12]   E.g. *Broome* v. *Cassell* [1972] A.C. 1027, 1100B-C (*per* Lord Morris), 1123C-D, 1127H-1128C (*per* Lord Diplock), and 1135E-F (*per* Lord Kilbrandon); L.J. Anderson, "An Exemplary Case for Reform", 11 C.J.Q. 233, 249-252.

[13]   *Broome* v. *Cassell* [1972] A.C. 1027, 1087C-F. Other unfavourable comparisons usually made with criminal punishment are the right to silence, the presumption of innocence, the higher standard of proof and the wider availability of legal aid in criminal prosecutions.

accommodating punishment within the civil process outweighs any benefits obtained,[14] and suggests that it ought not to take place at all.

(3) Now that non-pecuniary harm is more freely compensable exemplary damages are no longer necessary

5.8   We noted above that it is possible to regard part of the role of the punitive principle in the past as the redress of certain forms of non-pecuniary harm at a time when such harm was not recognised as a compensable loss,[15] and that the context in which exemplary awards operate continues to be much the same despite the extraction in *Rookes* v. *Barnard* of the compensatory element[16] to previously undifferentiated awards of increased damages.[17] Now that non-pecuniary harm, and in particular certain intangible losses, are more readily recognised as constituting legal 'damage' and hence as compensable,[18] it may therefore be argued that exemplary awards are no longer as necessary as they once were, if indeed at all.

(4) Windfall

5.9   Awards of exemplary damages are also commonly criticised on the basis that they provide the plaintiff with an undeserved windfall.[19] This argument is in part a rephrasing of the contention that the purpose of an award of damages in tort is exclusively compensatory; the plaintiff's receipt of exemplary damages is seen as an unjustified windfall because the

---

[14]   For instance, as regards standard of proof, the higher criminal standard (proof beyond reasonable doubt) would then be applied in relation only to the conduct upon which the claim for exemplary damages is based; whilst the lower civil standard (proof on a balance of probabilities) would continue to apply to the prior question of liability for the wrong itself. This is likely to confuse and incidentally serves to separate and differentiate further the exemplary part of an award.

[15]   See para. 2.26, above.

[16]   I.e. aggravated damages.

[17]   See para. 2.27 and n. 62, para. 3.11, above.

[18]   And this is especially true over the range of wrongs in respect of which exemplary awards have traditionally been made: for example, injury to feelings, mental suffering etc. are recognised heads of compensable loss in the torts of defamation, false imprisonment, and malicious prosecution.

[19]   E.g. *Broome* v. *Cassell* [1972] A.C. 1027, 1086B-C (*per* Lord Reid), 1126D (*per* Lord Diplock); *A.B.* v. *South West Water Services Ltd.* [1993] Q.B. 507, 527E-F, 529A.

plaintiff's only valid interest is in obtaining compensation for losses suffered.[20] It is also a reflection of discomfort with the fact that the plaintiff thereby profits from the wrong done to her or him, being placed in a better position than she or he was before the wrong.

(5) Uncertainty and indeterminacy

5.10   The problems of uncertainty created by awards of exemplary damages arise in a number of different forms. The central assertion is that the difficulties inherent in the present law on exemplary damages, particularly in the application of the overriding principles[21] combined with fact that the assessment of such damages is often in the hands of a jury,[22] make it exceptionally difficult to predict the outcome of such cases. The result can be that major impediments are created to the negotiated settlement of claims of this kind. A plaintiff may be able to obtain a significant tactical advantage in negotiations by seeking exemplary damages.[23] From a different perspective the law gives juries charged with the task of assessing such damages little useful guidance on the level of awards which should be made and this opens the way to allegations that juries may be influenced by inappropriate considerations when fixing their awards.[24] The contrast with the criminal law process which places matters like these in the hands of judges and creates maximum penalties for many offences is seen as very marked. These considerations are put forward as justifying the charge that, particularly in relation to defamation claims, plaintiffs are encouraged to bring unmeritorious claims or to persist in refusing to settle meritorious claims at a realistic figure. It is suggested that this unpredictability in the level of awards of exemplary damages may also mean that an excessive deterrent effect prejudices defendants unfairly, since they are unable to calculate accurately their potential exposure.

---

[20]   See e.g. *McGregor on Damages* (15th ed., 1988), para.406; *Winfield & Jolowicz on Tort* (13th ed., 1989), p. 604. However, some commentators (e.g. L.J. Anderson, "An Exemplary Case for Reform", (1992) 11 C.J.Q. 233, 235) have suggested that the windfall might be justified as a way of counteracting any shortfall which might occur in the capacity of a compensatory award to meet the full losses caused by the tort. See para. 5.19 below.

[21]   See paras. 3.79-3.85 above.

[22]   See paras. 1.6 and 3.86-3.87 above.

[23]   Cf. *Gray* v. *Commissioner of Police*, 30 June 1992 (Unreported, C.A.), where the trial judge remarked disapprovingly that the plaintiff's claim for exemplary damages had perhaps been made only in order to improve his chances of trial by jury.

[24]   See paras. 3.86 and 3.103, above.

5.11 A separate argument is that the risk of having to defend claims and to pay exemplary damages creates considerable uncertainty for business planning and that this uncertainty may produce an excessive deterrent effect which would be likely to disadvantage the national economy; manufacturers may be discouraged from putting useful and innovative products onto the market because of fear of the potential liability. This argument should be capable of being answered, to an extent, by ensuring that only those enterprises whose conduct amounts to a flagrant breach of consumer rights run the risk of having to pay exemplary damages. There can be little argument for such firms not being placed at a competitive disadvantage by the prospect of awards of damages.

(6) Levels of award

5.12 A practical criticism which arises out of indeterminacy in the assessment of exemplary awards is that these damages have reached levels which are excessive.[25] Reference is made to defamation cases, where damages can reach sensational sums;[26] and comparisons are then sometimes made with levels of awards in personal injury actions.[27] This is said to offend the need for a rational relationship between the scale of values applied in the two classes of case.[28] It is objected that:

> ... an evanescent sense of grievance at the defendant's conduct is often grossly over-valued in comparison with a lifelong deprivation due to physical injuries caused by negligence.[29]

---

[25] Cf. Report on Exemplary Damages (1991), Ontario Law Reform Commission, pp. 1 and 21.

[26] See the examples cited at n. 259, para. 3.59 above.

[27] See cases cited at n. 20, para. 1.6 above.

[28] *McCarey* v. *Associated Newspapers Ltd. (No. 2)* [1965] 2 Q.B. 86, 109C-110B (*per* Diplock L.J.); *Coyne* v. *Citizen Finance Ltd.* (1991) 172 C.L.R. 211, 221 (H. Ct of Australia).

[29] *Broome* v. *Cassell* [1972] A.C. 1027, 1130H (*per* Lord Diplock).

(1) Punishment, deterrence and the marking out of conduct for disapproval are legitimate functions of the law of civil wrongs

5.13   At the root of the arguments in favour of exemplary awards is the primary claim that, whilst it may be true that the aim of a civil award of damages is and ought in general to be compensation, the pursuit of retributory, deterrent and condemnatory aims is in certain instances and under certain conditions a legitimate function of the law of civil wrongs.[30] This is certainly true as a matter of historical observation and in any event:

> ... particularly over the range of torts for which punitive damages may be given (trespass to person or property, false imprisonment and defamation being the commonest) there is much to be said before one can safely assert that the true or basic principle of the law of damages in tort is compensation, or, if it is, what the compensation is for (if one says that a plaintiff is given compensation *because* he has been injured, one is really denying the word its true meaning) or, if there is compensation, whether there is not in all cases, or at least in some, of which defamation may be an example, also a delictual element which contemplates some penalty for the defendant. It cannot lightly be taken for granted, even as a matter of theory, that the purpose of the law of tort is compensation, still less that it ought to be, an issue of large social import, or that there is something inappropriate or illogical or anomalous (a question-begging word) in including a punitive element in civil damages, or, conversely, that the criminal law, rather than the civil law, is in these cases the better instrument for conveying social disapproval, or for redressing a wrong to the social fabric, or that damages in any case can be broken down into the two separate elements. As a matter of practice English law has not committed itself to any of these theories: it may have been wiser than it knew.[31]

Moreover, even the most vigorous opponents of exemplary awards recognise that compensatory damages may themselves include an element of punishment, deterrence or

---

[30]   Report on Exemplary Damages (1991), Ontario Law Reform Commission, p. 17; *Uren* v. *John Fairfax & Sons Pty. Ltd.* (1966) 117 C.L.R. 118, 137, 149-150.

[31]   *Broome* v. *Cassell* [1972] A.C. 1027, 1114B-D (*per* Lord Wilberforce).

condemnation.[32] It is argued that these are (in certain circumstances) legitimate objects also where the compensatory sum awarded is inadequate to achieve them alone.[33]

(2) Better protection of rights

5.14 The possibility of a substantial (exemplary) award of damages alerts plaintiffs to a method for the effective private enforcement of important rights;[34] particularly in the case of rights the infringement of which may not give rise to a (compensable) loss, for example torts actionable *per se*. Furthermore, plaintiffs invest considerable time, energy and resources in litigating matters which would otherwise be left uncompensated, even if their claim succeeds. If the plaintiff must prove advertent wrongdoing in order to sustain an exemplary award, the burden on potential claimants is such that the risk of speculative claims is greatly diminished.[35]

(3) Where criminal, regulatory and administrative sanctions are inadequate

5.15 It is being argued increasingly that the inefficacy of criminal, regulatory and administrative enforcement mechanisms justifies the use of exemplary awards in civil actions.[36] In addition,

---

[32] E.g. *Rookes* v. *Barnard* [1964] A.C. 1129, 1228 (*per* Lord Devlin); *Broome* v. *Cassell* [1972] A.C. 1027, 1089D-F (*per* Lord Reid), and 1121H-1122A (*per* Lord Diplock).

[33] Note that even Lord Devlin, who regarded exemplary damages as anomalous, nevertheless favoured their retention not merely on the ground that precedent prevented the House of Lords from removing them from the law completely, but also on the ground that they could in certain circumstances "serve a useful purpose in vindicating the strength of the law": *Rookes* v. *Barnard* [1964] A.C. 1129, 1223, 1226. Cf. *Uren* v. *John Fairfax & Sons Pty Ltd.* (1966) 117 C.L.R. 118, 137.

[34] Report on Exemplary Damages (1991), Ontario Law Reform Commission, pp. 17-18, 56; Review of Restrictive Trade Practices Policy: A Consultative Document (1988), Cmnd. 331, paras. 7.8 - 7.10; Opening Markets: New Policy on Restrictive Trade Practices (1989), Cmnd. 727, paras. 5.16 - 5.18 (but see Annex B, Response 8). Cf. the similar arguments employed by advocates of substantial awards for the infringement *per se* of constitutional rights in Canada: M.L. Pilkington, "Damages as a Remedy for Infringement of the Canadian Charter of Rights and Freedoms", (1984) 62 Can. B.R. 517, 570-571; M.L. Pilkington, "Monetary Redress for Charter Infringement" in R.J. Sharpe (ed.), *Charter Litigation* (1987), 307, 315.

[35] G. Otis, "Constitutional Liability for the Infringement of Rights *Per Se*: A Misguided Theory", [1992] U.B.C. Law Rev. 21, 37.

[36] See, e.g. H.H. Judge Fricker, "Harassment as a tort", (1992) 142 N.L.J. 247 (proposal for the enactment of a new tort of harassment, with exemplary damages available); D. Pannick, "News from the Gutter", *The Times*, 7 February 1992 (proposal for a new right to privacy, with exemplary damages available where there has been flagrant abuse); APIL Preliminary Submission to the Law Commission. Cf. Infringement of Privacy (July 1993), Consultation Paper, Lord Chancellor's Department & the Scottish Office, para. 6.12 (proposal for a new tort of privacy, but exemplary damages not to be

it is considered that the individually enforceable and less condemnatory techniques of the civil law may be preferable in certain circumstances.

5.16   First, some forms of conduct which might be thought to merit punishment do not fall within the controls of the criminal law, or, although technically within the criminal law, may often fail to be prosecuted or to produce what society would regard as an adequate level of punishment. Those who have championed the bringing of civil proceedings against the police have argued that it is rare for the police to initiate prosecutions against their colleagues and that the Police Complaints system is ineffective in comparison to civil proceedings.[37] Civil proceedings are favoured on the basis that they allow an independent assessment and public commentary on the conduct at issue. It is clear from the press coverage that substantial use is being made of proceedings of this nature and it seems likely that the main purpose underlying the bringing of such actions is the vindication of rights and the punishment of those who have abused their position as opposed to the obtaining of compensation. Similarly, it is said to be the case that the police and local authorities are reluctant to prosecute landlords for offences under the Protection from Eviction Act 1977.[38] It may not be wholly unconnected with this that exemplary awards seem to be favoured in wrongful eviction cases based on trespass, particularly in circumstances in which the landlord has flouted warnings concerning the tenant's right not to be evicted without a court order.[39] Finally, cases such as the well publicised *Halford* v. *Brookes*[40] have suggested that a role may exist for the civil law as a fall-back mechanism for use by private individuals to challenge a decision of the police not to initiate criminal proceedings against a private individual.

5.17   It is also commonly argued that the fines imposed by the criminal law for breach of health and safety regulations are inadequate, particularly when death or serious injury has resulted from

---

available for breach).

[37]   R. Clayton & H. Tomlinson, *Civil Actions against the Police* (2nd ed., 1992), pp. 11 ff..

[38]   M. Partington & J. Hill, *Housing Law: Cases, Materials and Commentary* (1991), pp. 265-6.

[39]   Recent examples are *McCaffrey* v. *Ekango* [March 1992] Legal Action 15 and *Ramdath* v. *Daley* [1993] 20 E.G. 123.

[40]   [1992] 1 P.I.Q.R. 175 (the civil proceedings for murder). Other civil cases have been reported concerning allegations of rape and sexual abuse.

the breach.[41]   Again this has produced arguments in favour of using exemplary awards of civil damages as a superior enforcement technique to criminal law prosecutions.

5.18   Finally, it should not be forgotten that some forms of conduct which are reprehensible fall outside the scope of the criminal law: ordinary defamation is an example of this.[42]   Other forms of conduct which are tortious and reprehensible may, if compensation is the measure of damage, only be sanctioned by nominal damages.   In such cases the sanction imposed by normal principles of calculation may be thought to be an inadequate deterrent to such behaviour.

(4) Where compensation is inadequate, or artificial or where it does not effectively remedy the infringement of certain important interests

5.19   In the case of certain forms of wrongdoing a compensatory model of redress may be inadequate to ensure compliance with the law. In other cases a compensatory remedy may be somewhat artificial in that it is difficult to identify or describe the 'loss' involved (and hence also to measure its extent), although it is clear that an interest or right has been infringed. To insist that only identifiable and quantifiable losses can give rise to an award of damages would be to risk removing these interests from the protection of the law.[43]   It may also be argued that the serious violation of certain important and valued interests demands more vigorous, enhanced protection than can be provided by a purely compensatory principle.

---

[41]   E.g. D. Bergman, "Accounting for workplace deaths", [June 1991] Legal Action 7; M. Whitfield, "Cost pressures keep safety on the sidelines", *The Independent*, 9 December 1992.

[42]   Ss. 4 and 5 of the Libel Act 1843 prescribe a common law and a statutory offence of criminal libel. To warrant prosecution, the libel must be sufficiently serious to require the intervention of the Crown in the public interest (*Gleaves* v. *Deakin* [1980] A.C. 477). Leave of a High Court Judge in chambers is required for prosecution for a libel in a newspaper (s. 8 Law of Libel Amendment Act 1888). The sections are rarely invoked - see *Winfield & Jolowicz on Tort* (13th ed., 1989), 605.

[43]   At present they are also protected by aggravated awards and because in certain torts loss is presumed but does not have to be proved.

(a) Vindicating the strength of the law

5.20   Where the defendant deliberately flouts the law, damages in excess of the plaintiff's loss are permissible, since otherwise the law could be broken with impunity.[44] Exemplary damages can therefore serve the valuable social purpose of vindicating the strength of the law. This argument in their favour is particularly relevant with regard to those powerful defendants who are in a special position to interfere with the plaintiff, and who are both able and prepared to disregard the financial consequences of being required to compensate her or him for any loss suffered.

(b) The protection of interests and the vindication of rights

5.21   Certain wrongs or forms of wrongdoing, particularly those involving the serious violation of personality interests,[45] present special difficulties for a compensatory model of redress and may be more effectively remedied by a punitive model.

5.22   First, the serious interference with interests of personality typically gives rise to certain intangible 'harm', such as outrage, humiliation, degradation, insult and so on.[46] The incommensurability and subjectivity of these 'harms' makes them difficult to assess.[47] A purely compensatory model, which looks only to the extent of the loss suffered, faces problems when the assessment comes to be made and a punitive model, which uses other factors (such as the defendant's conduct) as a guide may therefore be more appropriate in these cases.

---

[44]   *Rookes* v. *Barnard* [1964] A.C. 1129, 1226, 1227; *Broome* v. *Cassell* [1972] A.C. 1027, 1077B, 1130D, 1134B-E. The classic example is the Rachman-type landlord who flouts the law and disregards the plaintiff's rights even in the face of police warnings and court injunctions, and where the plaintiff's loss in purely economic and material terms may be very small.

[45]   Such as false imprisonment, malicious prosecution, defamation, nuisance or trespass to land through harassment, trespass to the person by unlawful search. Cf. the recent case of *Baylis* v. *Home Office* [February 1993] Legal Action 16.

[46]   See paras. 2.9 and 2.26 above.

[47]   See paras. 2.11-2.16 above.

5.23   Second, in the case of some wrongs or some forms of wrongdoing, typically those concerning person or personality,[48] it may be difficult and indeed artificial to attempt to identify and describe the 'loss' involved. For instance, plaintiffs suffering unlawful discrimination may find it difficult to point to any particular 'detriment' ordinarily regarded as a proper subject of compensation. Thus, in the case of wrongs which involve serious attacks on person or personality the focus on loss may be somewhat misplaced. It deflects attention from the substance of the plaintiff's complaint, namely the defendant's *treatment* of the plaintiff. This argument is particularly powerful in relation to the actions of government officials exercising extraordinary powers to interfere with the plaintiff's person without her or his consent.[49] Exemplary damages may therefore be justified as an important means of vindicating rights, including civil liberties: they can reflect the fact of infringement, rather than the precise (material) effects upon the plaintiff.

5.24   Similar problems arise in connection with the infringement of property rights where, for instance, the defendant has unlawfully used but not damaged the plaintiff's property. Here, too, it may be difficult to identify the 'loss' involved and the law instead turns from a compensatory to a restitutionary principle.[50]

5.25   Third, it is argued that certain wrongs, because of the nature of the interests involved, require energetic measures of redress and that exemplary damages can provide this enhanced protection.[51] The existence of torts actionable *per se* illustrates how some wrongs incorporate values important enough to deserve protection even without proof of loss. Similar values may be infringed by wrongs not directly concerned with them because of the way in which the wrong was committed. In the case of serious attacks on values which it considers important, the law ought to be especially concerned to prevent and deter such infringement. But a pure compensatory principle may be inadequate to achieve this object, especially if intangible 'harms' (such as injury to feelings), when considered separately from the nature of the conduct causing them or the interest violated, tend to be viewed quite plausibly as a lesser form of

---

[48]   E.g. false imprisonment, malicious prosecution, assault and battery, nuisance and trespass to land involving harassment, discrimination and defamation. See paras. 2.20-2.28 above.

[49]   E.g. the police, prison officers, army officers and, in certain circumstances, medical officers.

[50]   See Part VII below.

[51]   Cf. P. Ollier & J. Le Gall, Various Damages, Int. Enc. Comp. L. XI/2 Torts (1986), ch.10, s.70 and s.105.

injury than serious personal injury caused by negligence.[52] A simple comparison of the *injury* involved produces small compensatory sums for intangible harms and leaves them inadequately protected. Exemplary damages are therefore justified in order to prevent and deter more effectively the serious infringement of important values.

(c) Symbolising the importance of legally protected interests

5.26   Money awards for wrongs are inevitably seen as an indication of the value attached to the interest infringed. Further, some interests are and ought to be valued over and above the concern to avoid loss caused through their infringement - they ought not to be infringed at all. Here, the emphasis should be not merely on the precise effects of the wrong upon the plaintiff, but also upon the fact of infringement. A compensatory model may fail to convey this in that it individualises the wrong and suggests that the law is primarily concerned with an interest in not being harmed, rather than that the infringement of certain values is objectionable in itself. Exemplary damages are justified as a means of conveying this message - they are a legitimate technique for symbolising the importance of legally protected interests, by marking out the defendant's conduct or treatment of the plaintiff for disapproval.[53]

(d) Restraining abuses of power

5.27   We have mentioned that exemplary damages can protect interests and vindicate rights and that this is particularly important and effective in relation to the actions of government officials exercising extraordinary powers to interfere with the plaintiff's person without consent.[54] Exemplary damages thus subject relationships of power to a valuable scrutiny and operate as a restraint of abuses of power by those with a peculiar capacity to interfere with person and personality. Where persons in a position of authority engage in arbitrary or oppressive

---

[52]   Cf. the views of Lord Diplock in *McCarey* v. *Associated Newspapers Ltd. (No. 2)* [1965] 2 Q.B. 86, 108E, 109C-G; and in *Broome* v. *Cassell* [1972] A.C. 1027, 1130H.

[53]   Although a declaration of rights or an award of nominal damages can also act as a symbolic vindication of rights these may often now appear to be more of an insult than a vindication: cf. *Kehoe* v. *New York Tribune Inc.* (1930) 241 N.Y.S. 676 (A.D. 1st Dept.). Cf. also the role of nominal damages in the past as a means of resolving disputes concerning property rights, where the plaintiff was often interested only in avoiding the appearance of having tacitly abandoned or renounced her or his right: H. Stoll, Consequences of Liability: Remedies, Int. Enc. Comp. L. XI/2 Torts (1986), ch.8, s.84.

[54]   See para. 5.23 above.

behaviour, there is a need for such objective scrutiny. However, the punitive principle at present restrains abuses of power in a haphazard manner, operating where government officials are involved for example, but not where store detectives and security guards are involved.

PROVISIONAL CONCLUSIONS

5.28 The range of views on the question of the availability of exemplary damages is at heart a product of radically different perceptions of the role of the law of civil wrongs, in particular tort law, and of its relationship to criminal proceedings. The opposing views are best summarised in the speeches of Lord Reid[55] and Lord Wilberforce[56] in *Broome* v. *Cassell*.[57] In essence the debate is whether the purpose of tort is exclusively to provide compensation, that is true monetary replacement for losses incurred, or whether deterrent, restitutionary and punitive functions have a role to play.[58] It will almost certainly be impossible to achieve a consensus on the acceptability of exemplary damages in the absence of agreement as to which of these perceptions is correct.

5.29 There can be little doubt that the majority of English commentators on this debate writing since *Rookes* v. *Barnard* have supported the views of Lord Devlin[59] and Lord Reid.[60] However, a significant number of difficulties are created by this approach and it has been

---

[55] Who was of the view that punishment (retribution, deterrence, condemnation) is not a legitimate function of the law of tort and should take place only within the criminal law. He therefore favoured their abolition, although he believed it was for Parliament, not the judiciary, to achieve this: *Broome* v. *Cassell* [1972] A.C. 1027, 1086B-1087G.

[56] Who was not prepared to adopt the *a priori* assumption made by Lord Reid and perceived a wider role for civil proceedings: *ibid.*, 1114A-E. He accepted (at 1114F) that the opponents of exemplary awards "have, marginally, the best of it in logic", but was impressed by the vitality of the principle not only in England, but in Australia, Canada and New Zealand, as well as the United States.

[57] [1972] A.C. 1027.

[58] See paras. 5.4, 5.5-5.7 and 5.13, above. The question is also whether tort law should be viewed as being concerned with the reparation of harm or with, in addition, the protection of interests from invasion.

[59] But see n. 32, para. 5.13, above.

[60] E.g. The Report of the Committee on Defamation (1975), Cmnd. 5909, paras. 351-360; The Supreme Court Procedure Committee's Report on Practice and Procedure in Defamation (1991), section IV; and A. Ogus, *The Law of Damages* (1973),p p. 32-4.

rejected in other common law jurisdictions.[61] Moreover, we believe it would be unwise to restrict the remedial scope of the law of civil wrongs by reference to an *a priori* assumption as to its natural limits.[62] To assert that the role of the law of civil wrongs is only to provide compensation, or less restrictively that it does not at least include punitive aims, is to assume what is at issue and fails to address the question of policy involved. We therefore believe that it is now appropriate to reconsider whether the opposition to exemplary awards is justified and we invite the views of consultees on this important question.

5.30   At the most general level it can be argued that the approach of Lord Devlin and Lord Reid is based on an oversimplification which tends to equate the law of tort in general and its functions with that part of the law of tort which devotes its attention to the protection of accident victims. The perception that the law of tort is concerned primarily with compensation has gathered force during the course of the last century, with the growth of personal injury actions and the development of the tort of negligence (where the compensatory principle clearly prevails);[63] the transfer from the jury to the judiciary of the power to award and assess damages in the majority of civil actions;[64] and the increasing recognition of non-pecuniary harm as a *compensable* loss. But whilst personal injury litigation has indeed been primarily concerned with compensation, exemplary damages have long been a feature of other areas of tort, in particular defamation and species of trespass which exist to protect rights as much as financial and bodily interests. These suggest that tort law has historically been concerned with the protection of interests as well as with reparation for harm.

---

[61] See paras. 4.1-4.6, and 4.10-4.12, above.

[62] Cf. P.B.H. Birks, *Civil Wrongs: A New World* (Butterworth Lectures 1990-1), p. 79; and Report on Exemplary Damages (1991), Ontario Law Reform Commission, pp. 39-40.

[63] E.g. *Hicks* v. *Chief Constable of South Yorkshire* [1992] 2 All E.R. 65, 68b; *Kralj* v. *McGrath* [1986] 1 All E.R. 54, 61F-G. This phenomenon has helped to create the impression that tort law is primarily concerned with compensating carelessly inflicted losses. The concentration of modern tort courses on negligence may also serve to marginalise non-compensatory and specific forms of relief.

[64] See paras. 1.6 and 3.86, above. Because judges are required to articulate their decisions they may find compelling the view that the assessment of damages should be placed on a more 'rational' or more exact basis. This hope may be misplaced in the context of non-pecuniary, particularly intangible, harm. Cf. *Godwin* v. *Uzoigwe*,[1992] T.L.R. 300, where the C.A. confessed that they had some difficulty in ascertaining how the trial judge had reached the sum of £25,000 awarded; and then proceeded to substitute a smaller sum of £20,000, reached by reasoning only that "this is a serious case which calls for a substantial award" (see pp. 15C, 18C of the transcript).

5.31   It can also be contended that much of the writing[65] on the subject of damages has distorted the true picture by identifying compensation as the aim of damages in tort and by marginalising as anomalies those areas of the subject which do not conform to this picture: a more accurate picture would accept that a variety of purposes are served by the different measures of damages recognised as appropriate for the different kinds of tort. Recent writing[66] has challenged the validity of the exclusion of remedies of account from the ambit of the subject of damages and has shown that restitutionary, as opposed to compensatory, aims lie behind significant areas of what is traditionally classified as compensatory forms of damages.[67] As a matter of empirical observation at least therefore, the claim that the law of civil wrongs is concerned only with compensation for losses is simply false.[68]

5.32   Moreover, the perceived overlap and conflict with the criminal law[69] can be regarded as misplaced. The view that a tort action in which exemplary damages are awarded constitutes a substitute crime seems plausible enough when one considers the aims of retribution, deterrence and condemnation in isolation. Considered in this way, exemplary damages may appear to duplicate and simulate the criminal law. But this ignores the way in which they operate and the reasons why they are invoked. The potential consequences of a criminal prosecution and conviction are vastly different from those of a civil action in which exemplary damages are available. A criminal prosecution entails, in many instances, a threat of imprisonment and, whilst the symbolic aspect of exemplary damages is important, it cannot be said to involve the serious stigma to which a criminal prosecution gives rise. Nor can it be said that the material implications of a criminal conviction, such as its effect on employment prospects, have an equivalent in the award of exemplary damages. Further, a civil action

---

[65]   See, e.g. *McGregor on Damages* (15th ed., 1988), para. 9; A. Ogus, *The Law of Damages* (1973), p.17; *Winfield & Jolowicz on Tort* (13th ed., 1989), p. 600.

[66]   P.B.H. Birks, *Civil Wrongs: A New World* (Butterworth Lectures 1990-1); A.S. Burrows, *Remedies for Torts and Breach of Contract* (1987).

[67]   See Part VII below and *Strand Electric Engineering Co. Ltd.* v. *Brisford Entertainments Ltd.* [1952] 2 Q.B. 246 (para. 7.10) and *BBMB Finance (Hong Kong) Ltd.* v. *Eda Holdings Ltd.* [1990] 1 W.L.R. 409.

[68]   But it does not, of course, follow from this that exemplary damages *ought* to be available. The positive justification for exemplary awards is considered below.

[69]   See paras. 5.5-5.7 above.

recognises the status of the plaintiff as an aggrieved individual,[70] a factor which may be of particular importance in the case of wrongs committed by state officials;[71] and the fact that the law gives individuals access to mechanisms whereby they can enforce their own rights by litigation may be thought to be a fundamental feature of a free society. Once one accepts that an award of exemplary damages does not transform the civil wrong into a common law crime or characterise the defendant as a criminal any more than the fact that compensation orders can be made in criminal proceedings transforms the crime into a civil wrong,[72] the objection that it deprives the defendant of the protections afforded by the criminal law simply falls away.[73] The pursuit of punitive aims has an entirely different meaning in civil proceedings.[74] This becomes clear if exemplary damages are justified by reference to the role which they can play in the redress of interests recognised as deserving of protection by the law, but which may not be adequately protected by a pure compensatory principle.[75]

5.33   For these reasons, although we recognise the argument that the inadequacy of criminal, regulatory and administrative enforcement mechanisms justifies the use of exemplary damages in civil actions as an alternative means of more effectively deterring and condemning criminal behaviour,[76] we would not wish to place reliance upon it. If the penalty exacted by the criminal law is thought to be an inadequate response to particular conduct it is arguable that the attention of law reformers should be directed to improving the criminal law and that individuals should not be free to sidestep it by use of civil proceedings.[77]

---

[70]   But this can be criticised as condoning an intensely personalised form of retribution. See L.J. Anderson, "An Exemplary Case for Reform", 11 C.J.Q. 233, 250.

[71]   Since the state controls a criminal prosecution.

[72]   See the Powers of Criminal Courts Act 1973, ss. 35, 37, 38. In *R. v. Chappell* (1984) 6 Cr. App. R.(S.) 214 it was held that non-actionable loss may be the subject of a compensation order.

[73]   Similarly, if the desirability of protections is based upon the implications of a criminal prosecution and conviction, rather than upon the fact of punishment *per se*.

[74]   Cf. Lord Hailsham's deprecation of the use of the word 'fine' to denote an award of exemplary damages because "[d]amages remain a civil, not a criminal, remedy": *Broome* v. *Cassell* [1972] A.C. 1027, 1082B-C.

[75]   This focuses on the deterrent and symbolic, rather than any retributory, aspect of an exemplary award.

[76]   See paras. 5.15-5.18 above.

[77]   But even if reliance is placed upon the argument that exemplary damages are justified where the criminal, regulatory and administrative law is inadequate, it still does not follow that the tort is thereby converted into a common law crime. It simply illustrates the resourcefulness of the law in ensuring

5.34   The remaining argument against the availability of exemplary awards is that which says they are no longer necessary because non-pecuniary - in particular, intangible - 'harm' is now more readily recognised as a *compensable* loss.[78] We are not attracted by this argument. Instead, we are at present, subject to the views of consultees, persuaded by the arguments set out at paragraphs 5.19 - 5.26 above, that a pure compensatory principle may in certain circumstances be inadequate or artificial and that exemplary damages are an important and valuable means of protecting interests which would not otherwise be effectively redressed by compensation or which demand enhanced protection. Consequently, we are at present inclined to accept the claim that deterrence and condemnation *are* legitimate functions of the law of civil wrongs, as a means of achieving these aims.[79] We thus believe that exemplary damages can be justified in certain circumstances and provisionally favour their being available.

5.35   Because the criticism that exemplary damages represent an undeserved windfall is based on the premise that a plaintiff in a civil action is entitled to expect only compensation for losses suffered,[80] it also loses some of its force if it is accepted that other purposes can justify an award of damages.[81] The recognition of these other purposes does not, however, entirely explain why the sum awarded to achieve them should be paid over to the plaintiff, rather than to some other body. We find the argument that the possibility of an exemplary award alerts plaintiffs to a method for the effective private enforcement of important rights appealing.[82] But we also consider, at paragraph 6.38 below, possible reforms in relation to this issue should consultees disagree. Nevertheless, even if it is thought that an award of exemplary damages ought to be paid to a body other than the plaintiff, we do not believe that this in itself affects the basic question of whether exemplary damages ought in principle to be available. If it is

---

compliance with its own precepts.

[78]   See para. 5.8 above.

[79]   See para. 5.13 above. But we would not wish to emphasise a retributory function. This does not, however, mean that retributory principles have no role whatsoever to play - they may generate principles of assessment for controlling the levels of exemplary awards. See para. 6.24 above.

[80]   See para. 5.9 above.

[81]   In truth many of the arguments which criticise the 'windfall' which may result from awards of exemplary damages are actually concerned with the uncertainty as to the sum of damages which is likely to be awarded and the prospect of an unduly excessive sum being awarded in defamation proceedings. See paras. 5.36-5.37 below.

[82]   See para. 5.14 above.

accepted that non-compensatory purposes can justify an award of damages, we believe that there are a number of possible ways of proceeding. The options upon which we seek the views of consultees are considered in Part VI below.

5.36 We do not believe that the objections to exemplary awards based on uncertainty of assessment and excessive levels invalidate our provisional conclusion. Uncertainty in assessment is capable of being surmounted by clarifying the principles upon which the assessment of exemplary damages is to be made. Modification of ancillary rules is also a possibility which should be considered - options are improved guidance for juries, a reallocation of tasks from jury to judge, or the adoption of fixed awards or statutory limits. We consider these, and other reforms, below.[83] Uncertainty can perhaps also be reduced somewhat by means of greater appellate control over exemplary awards. This is already likely after the introduction of section 8 of the Courts and Legal Services Act 1990, which allows the Court of Appeal to substitute its own award in jury cases without the agreement of the parties, where it considers the award to be excessive.[84] The recent decision in *Rantzen* v. *Mirror Group Newspapers*[85] suggests that the power contained in section 8 will be used to exercise greater control over exemplary awards in the future.

5.37 The power contained in section 8 and the emerging caselaw under it may also mean that excessive levels of exemplary damages will no longer be relied upon as an objection to this form of award. In any event, we consider it to be unfair. Defamation cases have on occasion produced sensational sums,[86] but there is little evidence that the level of damages being awarded in areas of tort other than defamation is generally regarded as a problem. Outside defamation the highest awards of exemplary damages have occurred in cases of police misconduct.[87] Awards of exemplary damages in the discrimination sphere were until very

---

83 At paras. 6.24-6.35.

84 See para. 6.30 below.

85 (1993) 143 N.L.J. 507.

86 See para. 3.59, n. 259 above. But even as regards defamation the criticism has been said to be unfounded: *Broome* v. *Cassell* [1971] 2 Q.B. 354, 388G-389B (C.A.).

87 A short search of cases recorded on LEXIS revealed three case between 1982 and 1991 which resulted in awards of between £20,000 and £25,000 being made against the police, but several others in the range of £1,000 to £2,000. An equivalent search for wrongful eviction cases revealed no exemplary award of more than £3,000 and several as low as £250 (many of these would have been tried by judge alone, subject to the old county court limits).

recently controlled by the fact that there was a statutory maximum placed on the overall award which may be made by an Industrial Tribunal in such proceedings.[88] The aggregate amount of compensatory, aggravated and exemplary damages could not exceed £10,000 in such cases.[89] Research conducted into awards of this kind made between 1988 and 1990 revealed only four cases out of 249 in which exemplary damages were awarded.[90] Three of these awards were for £2,000 and one for £1,000.[91]

5.38   In conclusion, we do not accept the *a priori* argument that the purpose of the law of civil wrongs is exclusively to provide compensation and find the argument that 'punishment' ought to take place within the criminal law or only in conjunction with the protections afforded by the criminal law unconvincing. We further believe, subject to the views of consultees, that the pragmatic objections to the assessment of exemplary awards are in the process of or are capable of being surmounted. It is our provisional view that the argument that exemplary damages have a useful role to play is persuasive, but in Part VI we present the full range of options (including the abolition of exemplary awards) for consultees' consideration.

---

[88] Sex Discrimination Act 1975 ss. 65(1)(b), (2) and 66(4); Race Relations Act 1976 ss. 56(1)(b), (2) and 57(4).

[89] Employment Protection (Consolidation) Act 1978, s. 75; and the Unfair Dismissal (Increase of Compensation Limit) Order 1991, S.I. 1991, No. 466. The Unfair Dismissal (Increase of Compensation Limit) Order 1993, S.I. 1993, No. 1348, with effect from 1 June 1993, raised this limit to £11,000.

[90] Many of the 249 cases would have fallen outside of Lord Devlin's categories.

[91] (Jan/Feb 1992) 41 Equal Opportunities Review 30. The E.C.J. has now held in *Marshall* v. *Southampton & S.W. Hampshire A.H.A.*, 2 August 1993, that the statutory ceiling upon *compensation* for victims of discrimination is unlawful in the case of public sector employees. County court limits which confined aggravated and exemplary awards in housing cases have also been removed recently (see para. 3.46 above). It might be argued that the removal of these limits creates a new danger that excessive awards of aggravated and, in the housing cases, exemplary damages, will be made in the future. But the police cases do not seem to have produced excessive awards. In Canada, research conducted on behalf of the Ontario Law Reform Commission led it to conclude that anecdotal claims about high levels of exemplary awards could not be substantiated and that, on the contrary, awards of exemplary damages were made in only relatively modest amounts: Report on Exemplary Damages (1991), ch. 4.

PART VI

AGGRAVATED AND EXEMPLARY DAMAGES - OPTIONS FOR REFORM AND CONSULTATION ISSUES

6.1 The level of legal protection extended to interests of personality[1] and the form which it takes is a matter of policy for each legal system. We have seen how these interests are protected to a greater or lesser extent in other jurisdictions.[2] In English law aggravated damages by definition protect these interests and exemplary damages have in practice done so in those cases falling within Lord Devlin's categories. Violation of personality rights and the intangible losses to which they typically give rise are thus at present remedied in some cases by non-compensatory money awards, which on the one hand introduce restrictions upon the recoverability of intangible losses but on the other offer enhanced protection to them. In other cases they are remedied within a compensatory framework, for instance where mental distress is recognised as a permissible head of compensable loss. We have also seen that the violation of property and certain other rights is protected by monetary awards without proof that loss has been suffered.[3] Although, as we have said in Part V, the issues of the reform of aggravated damages and exemplary damages are interlinked, they are not identical and we consider them separately in this part of the paper. However, as will become clear, proposals for the reform of exemplary damages will be contingent upon those made in relation to aggravated damages, and vice versa.

EXEMPLARY DAMAGES

6.2 In considering reform of the English law of exemplary damages there are three areas of discussion. First, is the status quo satisfactory, or should such damages be totally or partially abolished, or be placed on a more rational basis? Secondly, can improvements to be made to the assessment of such awards? Thirdly, we consider and seek consultees' views on a number of more minor technical reforms which might serve to improve the law.

---

[1] See paras. 2.11-2.28 above.

[2] See Part IV above.

[3] Such rights and interests are also protected by restitutionary awards; see Part VII below.

(1) The availability of exemplary damages

6.3   We shall consider four options: maintaining the status quo, abolishing exemplary damages (either totally or partially), and putting such damages on a principled basis. This last option, which is the one we provisionally favour subject to the views of consultees, would expand the availability of exemplary damages in English law.

(a) Maintain the status quo

6.4   It might be thought that, in spite of the anomalies present in the existing English law, no change is called for. English law might be thought to have developed a narrow set of circumstances in which exemplary damages may be awarded which seems to work adequately and to allow for the possibility of useful development. Any reform would raise the possibility of considerable disputes as to the correct solution and might well introduce new and more difficult anomalies and impede future developments.

6.5   It is difficult to maintain this position on any basis of principle. Those who believe that the role of the law of tort is exclusively to compensate victims for their losses would take the view that the present law permits an anomaly to survive simply because Lord Devlin was not prepared to reject long-established authority. On the other hand, those who believe that tort law has purposes other than compensation will almost certainly regard Lord Devlin's three categories, the rules regarding the qualifying torts and the overriding principles as drawing the boundaries of the operation of exemplary damages too narrowly and in an unprincipled way. The recent introduction, in *A.B.* v. *South West Water Services Ltd.*,[4] of the requirement that exemplary damages may only be awarded in respect of a cause of action for which such an award had been made prior to *Rookes* v. *Barnard* contributes to the perception of the law as unprincipled. This requirement limits such awards to torts where an award happened actually to have been made in a reported case before *Rookes* v. *Barnard*, and means that such awards will no longer be possible for common law wrongs identified since 1964, as arguably in the case of economic duress.[5] As *Rookes* v. *Barnard* shows, intimidation is part of an evolving area of unlawful interference with business and as such cannot be accommodated satisfactorily

---

4   [1993] Q.B. 507, on which see paras. 3.35 and 3.55ff. above.

5   *Universe Tankships* v. *I.T.W.F.* [1983] 1 A.C. 366.

within a defined list of torts. Furthermore, in the absence of express authorisation[6] such awards will also no longer be possible for post 1964 statutory wrongs, such as those in the anti-discrimination legislation.

(b) Total abolition

6.6   Such an approach would coincide with the views of Lord Reid and many commentators.[7] Had the House of Lords in *Rookes* v. *Barnard* and, in particular, Lord Devlin not felt constrained by the weight of authority to the contrary, exemplary awards would no longer be a feature of English law. The adoption of this approach is dependent on acceptance of the arguments discussed in paragraphs 5.4 - 5.12 above. First, the aim of the civil law of wrongs is solely to provide compensation for loss, and punishment is not a legitimate function of this area of the law and should take place only within the context of the criminal law. Exemplary awards are punitive and accordingly confuse the functions of the civil and criminal law. Secondly, exemplary awards provide the plaintiff with an undeserved windfall. Thirdly, now that non-pecuniary harm, and in particular that resulting from violation of rights of personality,[8] is more readily recognised as a 'loss' which can be made the subject of compensatory damages, exemplary damages are no longer necessary.[9] Fourthly, exemplary damages are unacceptably uncertain. Levels of award are unpredictable and difficult to assess. Those who accept these arguments see such damages as an unacceptable anomaly which serves no useful purpose.

(c) Partial abolition

6.7   A less radical version of the previous suggestion might result in the removal of exemplary damages from particular areas of tort. Practice in United States jurisdictions has produced a variety of express statutory bans on awards of exemplary damages in particular circumstances,

---

6   As for example in the Copyright, Designs and Patents Act 1988, discussed at para. 3.54 above.

7   See e.g. *McGregor on Damages*, (15th ed., 1988), para. 406. The Faulks Committee on the Law of Defamation proposed the abolition of exemplary damages in defamation actions: Report of the Committee on Defamation (1975), Cmnd. 5909, para. 360.

8   I.e. injury to reputation, deprivation of liberty, and injury to feelings. See paras. 2.9-2.10 and 2.26-2.27 above.

9   If this were to be accepted we would favour retention of aggravated damages. See para. 6.48 below.

which we summarise in the Appendix.[10] This would leave the law free to develop into new areas in a principled way, but would remove exemplary damages from any areas in which they can be shown to have caused unacceptable difficulties. It might be argued that the obvious candidate for such treatment is defamation, in which aggravated compensatory damages may reach very high levels. It can be said that reputation *per se* (that is, when not combined with deprivation of liberty, for example, as in false imprisonment) should no longer enjoy the level of protection it has previously enjoyed,[11] and the freedom of expression concerns reflected in Article 10 of the European Convention on Human Rights are now surfacing as an opposing principle. We understand that few of the widely publicised defamation cases in recent years have in fact involved exemplary damages. The Faulks Committee on Defamation[12] in its report in 1975 recommended that legislation should abolish awards of exemplary damages in defamation cases[13] and a Working Group of the Supreme Court Procedure Committee reporting in 1991[14] repeated the call for the abolition of exemplary damages in defamation cases. A further situation where a prohibition of exemplary damages might be seen as desirable arises out of the recent proposals to create a new tort of privacy, which do not at present provide for exemplary damages.[15] Against these arguments, it must be noted that in defamation the possibility of large awards may influence the behaviour of the tabloid press; and in the case of both defamation and (if accorded the protection of the civil law) privacy, exemplary awards may protect intangible personality interests more effectively. However, partial abolition along these lines would allow the police misconduct and discrimination cases, in which there is a real risk of serious misconduct giving rise to small or nominal awards, to survive. In fact, the approach set out at (d) below, which we provisionally favour, could also work in tandem with express statutory bans in particular areas. We seek consultees' views on this approach, and on any other areas of tort where an express statutory ban on awards of exemplary damages is seen as desirable.

---

[10] At pp. 179-180 below.

[11] See para. 3.59.

[12] Report of the Committee on Defamation (1975), Cmnd. 5909.

[13] Paras. 351-360. The Committee cited the approach of Lord Reid in *Broome* v. *Cassell* (see para. 5.6 above) with approval and took the view that it was irrational to punish the person who published defamatory matter to make a profit, but not the person who acted out of malice.

[14] Supreme Court Procedure Committee Report on the Practice and Procedure in Defamation (1991).

[15] See Infringement of Privacy (July 1993), Consultation Paper, Lord Chancellor's Department & the Scottish Office, especially para. 6.12.

(d) Putting exemplary damages on a principled basis

6.8   We believe that the arguments[16] in favour of some form of exemplary damages are convincing. In particular we consider that there is intrinsic value in protecting personality rights and in empowering citizens to enforce those rights. It would also appear, in the light of the use which has been made of exemplary damages in recent years, particularly in housing, discrimination and police malpractice cases, that there are practical objections to abolishing them. These considerations have led us provisionally to favour this option. There are, however, several possible ways of proceeding. The precise scope of any reform would depend on the principle upon which exemplary damages are justified. If it is the principle that punishment, deterrence and the marking out of conduct for disapproval are legitimate functions of the law of civil wrongs, a reform permitting such awards for all torts and other civil wrongs committed deliberately, maliciously or possibly recklessly, might be justifiable.[17] If, on the other hand, non-compensatory awards are only justified because there is a need for the law to provide redress in respect of the intangible personality interests and other interests (in particular property rights) it protects, but for which a compensatory model of redress is inadequate or artificial, exemplary damages would only be justified in a narrower range of circumstances. On either view, it will be necessary to decide whether legislation should make provision for such awards according to a generally drawn statutory test, a test which confined the availability to specific wrongs, a detailed legislative scheme, or a combination of these perhaps building on the substance of the existing law and Lord Devlin's categories.

6.9   If new areas of exemplary damages were to be introduced it would be necessary to decide whether legislation to introduce such remedies should also codify the existing law with the intention of removing some of the problems which bedevil the present system. Subject to consultees' views, we provisionally favour this approach.

---

[16]   See paras. 5.13-5.14 and 5.19-5.26 above.

[17]   The Ontario Law Reform Commission linked their recommended "advertent exceptional conduct" criterion of availability for exemplary damages specifically to a retributory (punitive) aim or justification: Report on Exemplary Damages (1991), p. 38.

(i) A generally drawn statutory test

6.10   Legislation might provide that exemplary damages should be generally available, for instance whenever a defendant was shown to have acted maliciously or otherwise outrageously. Additionally it could conceivably be provided that such damages could be awarded where it was proved that a wanton or reckless disregard of safety had occurred. The first formula would open the door to awards against persons other than public servants where profit-making was not the motive, thereby covering any gap left by a possible abolition of aggravated damages.[18] The second might provide an answer to some of the problems which have been raised concerning the inadequacy of criminal prosecutions for serious breach of safety duties.

6.11   A number of models for such a general provision exist. In English law sections 97(2) and 229(3) of the Copyright, Designs and Patents Act 1988[19] entitle the court to make an award of such additional damages as the justice of the case requires in the light of all the circumstances, particularly the flagrancy of the defendant's infringement and any benefit accruing to the defendant from the infringement. The American Law Institute's *Restatement of the Law of Torts, Second* published in 1979 provides:-

§908   "(1) Punitive damages are damages, other than compensatory or nominal damages, awarded against a person to punish him for his outrageous conduct and to deter him and others like him from similar conduct in the future.

(2) Punitive damages may be awarded for conduct that is outrageous, because of the defendant's evil motive or his reckless indifference to the rights of others. In assessing punitive damages, the trier of fact can properly consider the character of the defendant's act, the nature and extent of the harm to the plaintiff that the defendant caused or intended to cause and the wealth of the defendant."

6.12   The advantages of such a general test are as follows. First, it would remove the limitations contained in Lord Devlin's first two categories, which have been criticised on the ground that they generate an illogical distinction between wrongful arrest by a store detective and that by

---

[18]   See paras. 6.48ff. below.

[19]   Para. 3.54 above.

a policeman (Category 1); and between malicious but profit-seeking conduct and purely malicious conduct (Category 2). Secondly, and most importantly, scope would be left for the development of the law on a case-by-case basis. It would liberate the common law from the self-imposed restrictions and complexities produced by *Rookes* v. *Barnard* and the subsequent case law, and leave the courts free to develop this area of the law in a principled way. While such a general provision would expand the availability in principle of exemplary damages, it is arguable that the requirement that the wrong be committed deliberately or with reckless indifference to the rights of the plaintiff, would mean that the question would only arise in a small proportion of tort cases.[20] This broad approach does, however, depend on acceptance of the principle that punishment, deterrence and the marking out of conduct for disapproval are legitimate functions of the law of civil wrongs.

6.13 The disadvantage of this approach is, however, that it might create considerable uncertainty in the law until such time as litigation provided guidance as to its effects. Unless combined with legislative provision on some of the other issues considered at paragraphs 6.28 - 6.35, and 6.36 - 6.47 below, it would also be criticised for all the reasons (the functions of the civil law, unpredictability and lack of safeguards) which have been given by the critics of the existing law for favouring the abolition of exemplary damages. Further, the limitations of Lord Devlin's categories do at present exclude all those deliberate crimes committed by private individuals which are also torts (for example, assault, murder, rape). A general test could catch all these deliberate crimes. Such a test might also be considered less desirable on the ground that it does not focus so obviously[21] upon the personality interests[22] which it is possible to argue are especially deserving of the enhanced protection which exemplary damages

---

20 Thus, Rustad's and Koenig's study of product liability cases in the United States between 1966 and 1991 located 355 punitive damages verdicts out of many thousands of actions: M. Rustad, "Demystifying Punitive Damages in Products Liability Cases: A Survey of a Quarter Century of Trial Verdicts (1991), discussed in Faculty Workshop Typescript, Suffolk University Law School, 14 November 1991, co-author T. Koenig. Other empirical investigators reported similarly small numbers: e.g. Landes & Posner, "New Light on Punitive Damages", [Sept/Oct 1986] Regulation 33, 36 (2%); and the Rand Institute for Civil Justice, M. Peterson, S. Sarma, and M. Shanley, "Punitive Damages: Empirical Findings" R-3311-ICJ (1987) (0.1%) See also U.S. General Accounting Office, "Product Liability: Verdicts and Case Resolution in Five States, (1989), Report to the Chairman, House of Representatives' Sub-Committee on Commerce, Consumer Protection and Competitiveness, Committee on Energy and Commerce.

21 But see Part II and para. 3.6 above.

22 See paras. 2.9-2.10, 2.26-2.27 above.

provide,[23] and may for this reason be too wide. Subject to the views of consultees, we incline to the view that a general test, or at least, a general test alone, would not create sufficient certainty to be a worthwhile reform.

(ii) A detailed legislative scheme

6.14   An alternative approach would be closely to define the circumstances in which an award of exemplary damages might be made and the conditions which should govern its making. In the United States, a variety of statutes, both federal and state, provide expressly for exemplary or multiple damages to be awarded in a wide range of specific situations.[24] We tend to prefer such a detailed scheme, but seek consultees' views both on the general approach and on the more specific questions set out below. We also note that the other possible reforms examined at paragraphs 6.28 - 6.47 below are relevant to the proposal we now outline. On this approach it is first necessary to identify those areas of law in relation to which awards of exemplary damages should, but are not, available. Secondly, the principle upon which such awards should be based would have to be determined.

6.15   There are a number of situations in which wrongful conduct does not at present give rise to an exemplary award but in which it arguably should. The first is wrongful arrests, assaults and other arbitrary or oppressive behaviour by persons in a position of authority but who are not government officials, such as store detectives, security guards, and possibly the employees of public utilities.[25] The second is flagrant misconduct, including breach of anti-discrimination

---

23   See para. 5.25 above.

24   See, e.g. Clayton Act § 4, 15 U.S.C. § 15 (treble damages); Fair Credit Reporting Act, 15 U.S.C. § 1681(n) (punitive damages); Omnibus Crime Control and Safe Streets Act of 1968, 18 U.S.C. § 2520(c)(wiretapping - punitive damages); Cal. Civ. Code § 3340 (West 1970)(wrongful injuries to animals - punitive damages); Iowa Code Ann. § 639.14 (1950)(malicious attachment - punitive damages); Iowa Code Ann. § 709.14 (1950) (conversion of logs or lumber - double damages); Mass. Gen. Laws Ann. ch 231, § 93 (1959)(libel and slander - punitive damages); S.C. Code Ann. § 66071.13 (Supp. 1974)(unfair or deceptive trade practices - treble damages); Tex. Rev. Civ. Stat. art. 8306, § 5 (1967)(wrongful death of workman - punitive damages); Utah Code Ann. § 76-6-412 (Supp. 1973)(receiving certain stolen property - treble damages); Va. Code Ann. § 8-650 (1950)(knowingly making unauthorized use of another's picture - punitive damages). In addition to these express statutory provisions, the courts have implied punitive damages into a number of federal statutes. See, e.g. Federal Civil Rights Act of 1871, 42 U.S.C. § 1983 (deprivations of civil rights under colour of state law); Jones Act, 46 U.S.C. § 688 (wrongful death in admiralty). The constitution of at least one state expressly provides for punitive damages in certain cases. Tex. Const., art. 16 § 36 (punitive damages for wrongful death resulting from wilful act or omission or gross negligence).

25   Since these often have statutory rights of entry to premises.

legislation by persons other than government officials, and fraud. A third, but more problematic, group of cases consists of deliberate unsafe product design and breaches of health and safety legislation resulting in personal injuries, and 'cynical' breaches of contract. We invite views as to which of these types of conduct should be covered by any proposed legislative formula. Negligence and breach of contract, which raise particular problems, are considered below.[26]

6.16   Turning to the principle upon which exemplary damages should be based, one possible approach reflecting the first category of excluded cases referred to above would centre on the relationship of power which exists when personality rights are deliberately infringed, as well as on the malicious or otherwise outrageous behaviour of the defendant. Thus, it might be provided that exemplary damages shall be available in any civil action where it is proved that (a) the parties were in a relationship of inequality at the time of the wrong, and (b) there has been conscious and deliberate wrongdoing by the defendant which shows a contumelious disregard for the plaintiff's rights.

6.17   Concerns about the uncertainty of the broad concept could be addressed by providing that a relationship of inequality is presumptively established where certain specified relationships exist. These could include some or all of the following: landlord and tenant, government or public official (including the police) and citizen, employer and employee,[27] persons exercising statutory power and the object of that power, newspaper or magazine and a citizen who is the subject of material published by the newspaper or magazine. In other cases, for instance in the case of store detectives and security guards, it would be for the person seeking an exemplary award to show that the relationship qualified. Where the plaintiff belongs to a statutorily protected class, as in the case of the victim of unlawful discrimination or of wrongful harassment or eviction by a landlord, this is unlikely to be a difficult hurdle to surmount, although it would be possible for such persons to be included in the presumptively unequal category. Such a test would require refinement and may (see paragraphs 6.28 - 6.47 below) require supplementation, but it would clearly identify the symbolic and practical functions of exemplary damages which we support. We seek consultees' views on this proposal and on which relationships should be presumed to fall within it.

---

[26]   See paras. 6.20 and 6.21 below.

[27]   Consideration would have to be given as to how to treat *potential* employees, who are also protected by the anti-discrimination legislation.

6.18   In order to ensure that the intangible interests now protected by aggravated damages are covered, it could also be provided that rights of personality[28] are capable of giving rise to exemplary damages. This could be done by a list of the torts we have identified in earlier parts of this paper[29] as important in protecting such rights: defamation, false imprisonment, trespass to the person, malicious prosecution, intimidation, discrimination and assault and battery, as well as any other torts for which exemplary damages are to be available.[30] The common feature would be that the tort, or the way in which it is committed, constitutes a personal wrong.[31] We do not at present consider that a closed list would be entirely satisfactory because that would, in effect, replicate the cause of action test in *A.B.* v. *South West Water Services Ltd..* The position of harassment which may be emerging as a tort[32] but has not clearly done so yet[33] illustrates the problem. However, we have no doubt that a list produced after consideration of the full range of possible candidates and embodied in a modern statutory provision, or examples of *types* of torts, would be more acceptable than one which is simply the product of the accidents of litigation and the state of the authorities in 1964 when *Rookes* v. *Barnard* was decided. We invite consultees to comment.

6.19   The above approach does not, moreover, necessarily include interference with property rights which are at present actionable *per se*. It would be possible either to include interference with such rights and possibly with other specified analogous rights, for instance confidentiality, or to leave the protection of such rights and interests to the restitutionary awards considered in Part VII. Furthermore, although it is arguable that deliberate breaches of health and safety legislation would be included on the ground that the plaintiff would be likely to be a member of a statutorily protected class, it is less clear whether deliberate unsafe product design would be included. If, therefore, it is decided to cover such cases, it may be that specific reference to the disregard of plaintiffs' safety would be required. We seek consultees' views on these

---

28   I.e. injury to reputation, deprivation of liberty, and injury to feelings. See paras. 2.9-2.10 and 2.26-2.27 above.

29   See paras. 2.25-2.28 above.

30   The proposed new tort of privacy would also appear to qualify in principle. See Infringement of Privacy (July 1993), Lord Chancellor's Department & the Scottish Office.

31   See paras. 3.57-3.62 above.

32   *Thomas* v. *N.U.M.* [1986] Ch. 20 ; *Khorasandjian* v. *Bush* [1993] 3 W.L.R. 476.

33   *Patel* v. *Patel* [1988] 2 F.L.R. 179; *News Group Newspapers Ltd.* v. *SOGAT* [1986] I.R.L.R. 227.

matters. One obvious question is whether conduct constituting the tort of negligence should be capable of giving rise to an exemplary award and we consider this below.

(iii) Negligence

6.20   Whichever option is chosen, we raise for consideration whether behaviour which is merely negligent or which constitutes the tort of negligence should be included. We have noted the arguments in favour of inclusion at paragraphs 3.69 - 3.72 above. We have not formed a provisional view on this issue, but we consider that reference to 'reckless disregard' or 'reckless indifference' in relation to plaintiffs' rights would catch conduct which was more than careless but less than deliberate or exceptional. If exemplary damages were to become available in mass disaster cases, we think there is a strong case for requiring that some percentage of the damages awarded as a consequence be paid into a central fund for the victims of mass disasters generally.[34] We seek consultees' views on these aspects.

(iv) Breach of contract

6.21   We have seen that exemplary damages have never been available for breach of contract and that there are several arguments for maintaining this position.[35] First, contract typically protects commercial and pecuniary interests rather than interests of personality. Often intangible personality losses would, in any event, not be regarded as in the contemplation of the parties. Secondly, many breaches of contract are made for commercial reasons and it is difficult to draw the line between 'innocent' breach for which there would be only compensation and 'deliberate' or 'cynical' breach in respect of which there would also be the possibility of an exemplary award.[36] The possibility of exemplary awards could also lead to greater uncertainty in the assessment of damages in commercial and consumer disputes. The making of a profit in excess of that which the plaintiff might have made had the contract been

---

[34]   See para. 6.38 below.

[35]   See para. 3.76 above, and, on aggravated damages, see paras. 3.15-3.16 above.

[36]   See also paras. 7.16 and 7.17 below and *Surrey C.C.* v. *Bredero Homes Ltd., The Times* 16 April 1993 (Transcript pp. 13-15 and 22, *per* Dillon and Steyn LJJ.).

performed may, moreover, require skill and initiative which economic theory[37] or policy suggests should not be taken from the defendant save in exceptional cases. Not all contracts are specifically enforceable and, in the case of those which are not, it is arguable that the parties should have the option of breaking the contract and of paying damages in lieu if they are able to find a more remunerative use for the subject matter of their promise. Where the contract is specifically enforceable or made between fiduciaries, as we shall see, restitutionary damages, which may deter the breach of contract, may be awarded. Finally, in cases where a contract is intended to prevent distress, give peace of mind or provide enjoyment, or where the plaintiff's distress is directly caused by physical loss arising from the breach of contract, damages are recoverable. To that extent contract has the means of protecting personality interests. Subject to the views of consultees, our provisional view is that these considerations mean that there should be no reform of the present law in relation to breach of contract.

(v) Group Actions

6.22   If exemplary awards were to be available in cases involving a class of plaintiffs, as in the mass disaster cases, it would be necessary to develop mechanisms for determining whether, and how, any exemplary award is to be shared among the victims, and whether an award made to one plaintiff should go to reduce an equivalent award sought in later proceedings. We seek consultees' views on these additional questions.

(vi) Name

6.23   Finally, we raise for consideration the question whether the expanded form of exemplary damages should be renamed, to shift the focus from punitive aspects to reflect the multi-faceted function disclosed in our examination of the present law. One possible label is 'extra damages'. However, the implication that such damages will always be in addition to compensatory damages may be unfortunate since there are cases where only an intangible interest in personality is affected or where a property interest actionable *per se* is infringed without causing loss. We seek consultees' views on this suggestion, and other possible labels.

---

[37]   R. Posner, *Economic Analysis of Law*, (3rd ed., 1986), 107; R.L. Birmingham, "Breach of Contract, Damage Measures and Economic Efficiency" (1970) 24 Rutgers L.Rev. 273. Cf. P. Birks, "Restitutionary damages for breach of contract: *Snepp* and the fusion of law and equity", [1987] L.M.C.L.Q. 421, 440-42; D. Friedmann, "The Efficient Breach Fallacy", (1989) 18 J.L.S. 1.

(2) The assessment of exemplary damages

(a) Principles of assessment

6.24 We noted in paragraph 3.87 above that the identification of the purposes for which an exemplary award is made should in theory generate principles which guide assessment. Since the approach we favour does not interpret the main or justifiable purpose of an exemplary award as being to punish, this does suggests that damages should not be measured solely by the gravity of the defendant's conduct. If exemplary damages are primarily justified in cases involving the deliberate infringement of personality rights which the law ought to protect, a hybrid principle of measurement of damages is indicated. This would be made up of elements going to deterrence and to a symbolic indemnification. We seek consultees' views on such a principle, noting, however, that difficulties in setting values on such elements render it of limited practical use.

6.25 In addition, the following principles relating to the assessment of exemplary damages arise for consideration:[38]

(i) The relevance of a compensatory award

6.26 In *Rookes* v. *Barnard*, Lord Devlin said that the sum awarded to a plaintiff as compensation might itself be adequate to punish, deter or mark disapproval of the defendant's conduct.[39] Exemplary awards should therefore take into account the punitive effect of the compensatory award, and in this way the amount of compensation awarded to a plaintiff is relevant to the assessment of any exemplary sum. In *Broome* v. *Cassell*, Lord Hailsham considered this principle to be a vital one, which would retain its value even if Lord Devlin's categories were to be wholly rejected.[40] However, the Ontario Law Reform Commission noted that the punitive effect of a compensatory award would be ineffective where the award was paid by an insurer, and consequently recommended that exemplary damages should be assessed without

---

[38] The issues raised in paras. 6.45 and 6.46-6.47 below are also relevant to assessment.

[39] [1964] A.C. 1129, 1228. See paras. 3.89-3.90 above.

[40] [1972] A.C. 1027, 1060A-D.

regard to the sum awarded to the plaintiff as compensation.[41] We seek the views of consultees on the relevance of the compensatory award.

(ii) Moderation

6.27 We also invite consultees to consider whether the assessment of exemplary damages should continue to be guided by a principle of moderation.[42] This might be justified on the practical ground that the assessment of exemplary damages is inevitably a discretionary process, and that without such a principle there would otherwise be little control upon levels of awards.

(b) Can the mechanics of assessment of exemplary damages be improved?

6.28 One, if not the major, problem raised by the existing law of exemplary damages is that such awards are unpredictable. There are several possible ways of reducing this problem if some form of exemplary damages is to remain available.

(i) Judge and jury

6.29 In general both criminal law penalties, such as fines, and the damages awarded in civil cases are calculated by judges. However, it is commonly the case that awards of exemplary damages made in respect of defamation, false imprisonment and malicious prosecution will be calculated by a jury because the right to jury trial has been retained in relation to these torts.[43] The existence of jury trial in such cases exacerbates the difficulties caused by exemplary damages. It may mean that juries have to be directed in relation to difficult principles of the law of damages; that juries are given the discretion to choose to award damages on what is or appears to be a punitive basis without being subject to any real control or having any experience as to the appropriate level of award to make; and that, because the jury will give no reasons for its award, it will be difficult for an appeal court to reject its decision.

---

[41] Report on Exemplary Damages (1991), p. 54. The Commission pointed out that the fact that the defendant was insured would have an impact upon the defendant's wealth, a factor which *was* relevant to assessment.

[42] See para. 3.92 above.

[43] See paras. 1.6, 3.86 and 3.103.

6.30   An additional difficulty which used to exist concerning the role of judge and jury was that if
        the Court of Appeal was of the view that the jury's award was either excessive or inadequate
        it could only substitute its own view of what would be an appropriate award if all the parties
        to the appeal agreed. In the absence of such agreement the court could only direct that the
        case should be retried before a different jury. However, provision has now been made by
        section 8 of the Courts & Legal Services Act 1990 for rules to be made for the Court of
        Appeal to have power to substitute "such sum as appears to the court to be proper" for the
        jury's award.[44] It should be noted that, whilst the new provision does not extend the
        grounds on which the Court of Appeal is entitled to interfere with the jury's award, it has
        created a new climate.   Thus, in *Rantzen* v. *Mirror Group Newspapers*[45] an award of
        £250,000 was reduced to £110,000. The Court of Appeal said that where freedom of
        expression is at stake, even at common law, the influence of the European Convention of
        Human Rights required the courts to subject large awards of damages to a more searching
        scrutiny than had been customary in the past. An almost limitless discretion in the jury failed
        to provide a satisfactory measurement for deciding whether restriction on freedom of
        expression was justified under the Convention. The Court also said that reference could be
        made at trials to awards made by the Court of Appeal in the exercise of its powers under
        section 8.

6.31   The task of assessing exemplary damages might be allocated to the judge rather than the jury,
        with the expectation that judges might award more moderate sums and that in time judicial
        knowledge of the awards which are being made would lead to a generally understood level of
        acceptable figures. Given the intangibles involved in the assessment of an appropriate award
        of damages for torts such as defamation it might, however, be over optimistic to assume that
        transferring responsibility for the calculation of such awards from jury to judge would lead in
        the short term to a uniform level of moderate awards. The best that can be hoped for is
        probably, in the words of the Irish Law Reform Commission,[46] that "the problem has to be
        approached on the assumption, which appears reasonable to us, that judges by their training
        and experience are in a better position to arrive at a sum which bears an appropriate
        proportion to the seriousness of the libel or slander."

---

[44]   See R.S.C., O. 59 r. 11(4).

[45]   (1993) 143 N.L.J. 507.

[46]   Report on the Civil Law of Defamation (December 1991), para. 10.3.

6.32   The recommendation made by the Faulks Committee in 1975 might be adopted. The Committee recommended that the jury's role in defamation cases should be confined to determining whether the final award should be contemptuous, nominal, moderate or substantial, with the actual figure being chosen by the judge.[47] The difficulty with such a recommendation lies in the vagueness of the terms used. The Irish Law Reform Commission, having provisionally favoured a more limited version of the Faulks Committee's proposals,[48] was convinced, as a result of comments received during consultation, that this would create more difficulties than it would solve. The Commission was particularly impressed by the argument that the distinction between the categories would be difficult to draw and to maintain, especially in the course of defamation proceedings, and was concerned that the distinction might lead to appeals being made on both the categorisation and the ultimate assessment of the damages. The Commission ultimately chose to recommend that the power to assess damages should be transferred to the judge, subject only to the proviso that the jury should have power to determine that only nominal damages should be awarded.[49]

6.33   The matter was considered by the Ontario Law Reform Commission in its report on Exemplary Damages. It recommended that there be no reallocation of tasks[50] because (a) there was no indication that arbitrary or excessive jury awards had been made in Ontario, (b) it would be inconsistent to remove the power from the jury to assess exemplary damages as it assessed compensatory damages, and (c) leaving assessment to the jury provided a community standard of the appropriate measure of such damages. The Commission went on to note that the power of assessment did not have to be unlimited, recommending that the judge could give guidance on quantum, that counsel could make submissions to the judge or jury on quantum, and that appellate courts should have power to substitute their own awards when setting aside an exemplary award. Subject to the views of consultees, we provisionally conclude that there should be no reallocation of tasks. However, we also seek consultees' views on any limitations which might be imposed on juries exercising their powers, noting that

---

47   Report of the Committee on Defamation (1975), Cmnd. 5909. para. 513.

48   The Irish version suggested that the role of the jury should be confined to stating whether the damages awarded should be nominal, compensatory or punitive: Irish Law Commission Consultation Paper on the Civil Law of Defamation (March 1991)..

49   *Ibid.*, paras. 10.4 and 10.6.

50   Report on Exemplary Damages (1991), Ontario Law Reform Commission, pp. 49-50.

appellate court powers of substitution already exist.[51] *Rantzen* v. *Mirror Group Newspapers* indicates that at appellate level there is now a judicial willingness to use available powers to control levels of damages appropriately in defamation cases.[52]

(ii) Fixed awards

6.34   It has been suggested from time to time that excessive damages could be addressed by the introduction of fixed awards,[53] for example by a cap on damages or the use of a formula to establish amounts. We think that any introduction of fixed awards of exemplary damages, in order to avoid the possibility of excessive damages, would be likely to encounter difficulties. It could well lead to some wrongdoers undertaking a cost benefit analysis with the intention of allowing for the risk of having to pay exemplary damages as the price of their conduct, and the deterrent and punitive purposes underlying the award of exemplary damages might thus be lost.[54] Victims of such conduct might feel that the law had placed a price on their right not to have a tort committed against them. In addition, it is likely that any limit would be arbitrary, in that it would deprive the court of the flexibility inherent in the present system. This flexibility currently allows the court to tailor the punishment to the circumstances of the wrongdoer and the wrong, and to take into account recent changes in the value of money. There is also a separate difficulty, revealed by the debate on penalties for breach of industrial safety legislation, of fixed penalties being regarded as an inadequate response to the particular conduct in issue (although this is not seen as a reason for not limiting criminal law penalties).

6.35   Some American states have capped awards of exemplary damages according to a formula.[55] For example, the limits of an exemplary award may be set at the higher of a fixed sum or two or three times the compensatory award. This would seem likely to create difficulties. An

---

[51]   See para. 3.103 above.

[52]   See para 6.29 above.

[53]   L.J. Anderson, "An Exemplary Case for Reform", (1992) 11 C.J.Q. 233, 257.

[54]   *Broome* v. *Cassell* [1971] 2 Q.B. 354, 389C-D (C.A.). This difficulty could be overcome if restitution of profits was allowed in addition to any exemplary award which was made.

[55]   Ala. Code §6-11-21 (1987); Tex. (Trial, Judgment and Appeal) Code Ann. §41.007; Col. Rev. Stat. §13-21-102 (1987); Va. Code Ann. §8.01-38.1 (1988); Ga. Code Ann. §51-12-5.1 (1987); Fla. Stat. Ann. §768.73; Okla. Stat. Ann. tit. 23, §9 (1987); Kan. Stat. Ann. §60.3701 (1988); Ohio Rev. Code Ann. §2307.80 (1988).

exemplary award calculated on such a basis in a case of defamation for which aggravated compensatory damages are to be awarded would be capable of producing an excessive figure, (although this would not, of course, arise if aggravated damages were abolished altogether). The choice of the appropriate fixed sum would be likely to be controversial, but without this element being included in the formula exemplary awards might cease to be available in cases in which a small compensatory award or a nominal one would be made.

(3) Other possible reforms

(a) Survival

6.36   We have previously outlined how, as a result of section 1(2)(a) of the Law Reform (Miscellaneous Provisions) Act 1934, no claim for exemplary damages survives for the benefit of the estate of a deceased person, and the strong arguments levelled against this rule.[56] Further, at present an award of exemplary damages can be claimed from the estate of a deceased person.[57] It needs to be considered whether the current rules governing the survival of actions featuring exemplary damages strike the correct balance in terms of the deterrent, punitive and restitutionary aims underlying such awards. A better balance might be achieved by repealing the exceptional rules which currently apply and permitting the standard rules concerning the survival of causes of action to operate. We seek consultees' views on such an option.

(b) Standard of proof

6.37   We have outlined the arguments for altering the standard of proof in cases with a punitive element.[58] It needs to be considered whether the proposals for a move to make the conduct upon which the claim for exemplary damages is based subject to the criminal standard of proof (proof beyond reasonable doubt), or a compromise standard part way between criminal and civil, such as 'clear and convincing evidence', are justified and realistic, and in what context; or whether the existing position requiring proof on balance of probabilities, with flexibility

---

[56]   See paras. 3.108-3.110 above.

[57]   Para. 3.109 above.

[58]   See paras. 3.111 and 5.6 above.

allowing for a higher standard where necessary,[59] requires no change. We seek comment on these aspects.

(c) Remove the windfall to the plaintiff

6.38   If exemplary damages are to be retained in some form, consideration needs to be given to whether some, or all, of the award should be diverted from the successful plaintiff to other purposes. Several American states have enacted legislation under which a part of any exemplary damages awarded is payable to the state or to another public fund.[60] We have previously noted suggestions as to how exemplary damages arising from group actions could be distributed.[61] A variation could be the establishment of a central fund into which a percentage of exemplary damages arising from mass disaster cases would be paid and then distributed. We provisionally favour that option if exemplary damages are to become available in mass disaster cases, because not all the plaintiffs may be before the court, and we do not think that fact should be a positive reason for denying the award. One important question which then arises is how such a fund would be administered and by whom. We seek consultees' views on these proposals.

(d) Insurance

6.39   If awards of exemplary damages are intended to influence an individual's conduct directly it is arguable that insurance should not be available for such awards. It might be argued that the result of permitting insurance against exemplary damages is both illogical and unfair in so far as the effect of the award is shifted to innocent third parties, other insured, who did not participate in the misconduct. It is deemed to be against public policy for an individual to insure against the risk of being held liable in criminal proceedings. However, it is apparently the case that newspapers can obtain insurance against the possibility of their having to pay exemplary damages and that insurance cover in respect of such damages may be available in

---

[59]   See *Hornal* v. *Neuberger Products Ltd.* [1957] 1 Q.B. 247.

[60]   Iowa Code Ann. §668A.1 (1987); Fla. Stat. Ann. §768.73 (1986); Mo. Ann. Stat. §537.675 (1987); Colo. Rev. Stat. §13-21-102 (1987); Ill. Ann. Stat. Ch 110, ¶2-604.1 (1987); Ga. Code Ann. §51-12-5.1 (1987); Ore. Rev. Stat. §18.540 (1988).

[61]   See paragraphs 3.70-3.71 (personal injury cases) and 6.22 above.

other areas. Other jurisdictions which grant wider recognition to exemplary damages have allowed insurance to cover product liability and road accident claims.[62]

6.40   It therefore needs to be considered whether it is acceptable for the punitive effect of exemplary damages to be shifted by insurance from the shoulders of the person who bears primary responsibility for the conduct. Central to this issue is the question whether the deterrent effect of the damages is greatest if the penalty is imposed on the individual responsible for the conduct or is shifted to others, such as the employer or insurance company, who may be better placed to influence future conduct. The Association of Personal Injury Lawyers in its preliminary submission to the Commission adopted the view that an award of exemplary damages should ultimately be paid by the tortfeasor rather than the insurer, but that the plaintiff's interest in the money should be protected by a provision which entitled the damages to be collected from the insurer, with the insurer having a right of recoupment against the insured.

6.41   Research conducted for the Commission suggests that some insurers in the United States, who formerly insured against such losses under the general liability provisions of insurance contracts, have tried to avoid the risk by excluding responsibility for such losses. The cases in the United States are almost evenly split on the issue of whether to prohibit insurance against such damages, on grounds of public policy, with a significant body of cases favouring the outlawing of insurance contracts for personal exemplary damages liability.[63] However, even states which generally prohibit insurance contracts against exemplary damages liability ordinarily permit such contracts in cases of true vicarious liability.[64] Statutes in at least two states provide that insurance contracts are not to be construed as covering exemplary damages (as in policy clauses, for example, that provide insurance for 'all sums which the Insured shall

---

[62]   In *Lamb* v. *Cotogno* (1987) 164 C.L.R. 1 the High Court of Australia upheld an award of exemplary damages against a motorist whose compulsory third party insurance policy was available to meet any such award.

[63]   Recent cases include *Home Ins. Co.* v. *American Home Products. Corpn.* (1990,2nd Cir.), 902 F.2d 1111; *U.S. Fire Ins. Co.* v. *Goodyear Tire & Rubber. Co.* (1990. 8th Cir.), 920 F.2d 487. *Contra*: *Whalen* v. *On-Deck Inc.*,(1986) 514 A. 2d 1072.

[64]   See, e.g. *Oliver* v. *Producers Gas Co.* 798 P.2d 1090. On insurance generally, see G.M. Giesel, "The Knowledge of Insurers and the Posture of the Parties in the Determination of the Insurability of Punitive Damages",(1991) 39 Kan. L. Rev. 355 ; G.L. Priest, "Insurability and Punitive Damages", (1989) 40 Ala. L. Rev. 1009; E.A. Obler, "Insurance for Punitive Damages: A Reevaluation", (1976) 28 Hastings L.J. 431.

become legally obligated to pay as damages'), unless such contracts expressly so provide.[65] In Texas, exemplary damages coverage is prohibited in professional liability insurance contracts for medical doctors.[66] In Ohio, exemplary damages are prohibited in contracts for uninsured and underinsured motorist insurance.[67] We seek consultees' views on these options.

(e) Vicarious liability

6.42 Similar arguments to those in relation to insurance can be made in relation to vicarious liability. The principal justification which is usually given for the existence of vicarious liability is to ensure that adequate funds are available to pay compensation. As compensation is not the aim of an exemplary award this justification is untenable in this context. It is also difficult to conceive of any reason based on retributive principles for awarding exemplary damages against an innocent employer by means of the mechanism of vicarious liability.

6.43 Any justification for the practice must therefore be based on deterrent, symbolic and restitutionary principles. The central justification in terms of deterrence can only be that the employer is the person best placed to respond to the deterrent effect of awards of exemplary damages in the sense of ensuring that his employees do not commit such conduct in future. The lesson to be derived from a penalty imposed upon an individual may be less widely learned. An award of exemplary damages also serves an important symbolic function in marking out the severity of the disapproval of the conduct. A further justification for allowing vicarious liability to apply to exemplary damages is that plaintiffs may be advantaged because they may not have to identify the particular individual within the employer's workforce whose misconduct forms the basis of the claim; for example, an individual who is the victim of police misconduct will not have to identify the particular officer involved.[68] The deterrent effect of tort may be increased by this consideration since otherwise no exemplary damages would be likely to be awarded.

---

[65] Hawaii Rev. Stat. § 431-458; Montana Code Ann. § 33-15-317.

[66] Tex. Ins. Code art. 5.15-1, § 8.

[67] Ohio Rev. Code Ann. § 3937.18.

[68] The plaintiff in *Racz* v. *Home Office*, [1992] T.L.R. 624, e.g., could not identify the individual prison officers who had assaulted him: p. 3 of the transcript.

6.44   Principles of restitution may also argue in favour of an employer's vicarious responsibility for awards of exemplary damages. To the extent that an employee's misconduct, in pursuit of corporate profit, has violated the rights of others, the profits 'earned' by the activity may be regarded as tainted, and not properly belonging to the enterprise. 'Innocent' shareholders therefore have no fair claim to such 'illicit profits' which may be seen as a form of unjust enrichment not belonging to them at all. Where actual restitutionary relief is unavailable, exemplary damages serve roughly to recoup from the corporation's coffers the unjust rewards of the employee's misdeeds. There are also constitutional reasons for holding that *government* should, as it is now, be vicariously liable for the misconduct of its officials. The Ontario Law Reform Commission adopted the view that the punishment of an innocent defendant violates basic principles of retributive justice and recommended that an employer should only be vicariously liable to pay exemplary damages in respect of an employee's conduct in situations in which the employer has tacitly approved that conduct.[69] We seek consultees' views on these options.

(f) Joint liability - multiple defendants

6.45   In situations of joint liability, particularly in cases of defamation, we think that considerable advantages might be obtained from the introduction of a provision along the lines of subsection 14(4) of the Irish Civil Liability Act 1961.[70] Under such a provision the standard principles of joint and several liability would not operate in relation to awards of exemplary damages. As a result an exemplary award which was appropriate punishment to be inflicted on one defendant (such as the author of defamatory statements) would not be reduced by the fact that others who were jointly liable, such as the printers or publishers, bore a lesser responsibility or did not have the wealth to make an award at a figure appropriate to the author appropriate to them. A publisher who reproduced another person's work in all innocence would be jointly liable for any award of compensatory damages which was made, but not for any exemplary award. A significant advantage gained by such a provision would be the lessening of the unpredictability as to the quantum of any exemplary award in cases featuring joint defendants

---

[69]   Report on Exemplary Damages (1991), pp. 58 and 105.

[70]   "Where the court would be prepared to award punitive damages against one of concurrent tortfeasors, punitive damages shall not be awarded against another of such tortfeasors merely because he is a concurrent tortfeasor, but a judgment for an additional sum by way of punitive damages may be given against the first-mentioned tortfeasor". Canadian law has adopted several, as opposed to joint and several, liability in relation to awards of exemplary damages.

149

and the associated need for plaintiff's advisers to ensure that proceedings are commenced against the appropriate defendants. It would also lead to a clearer separation of compensatory and exemplary awards. We seek consultees' comments on our suggestion.

(g) Evidence of the defendant's wealth

6.46   We discussed this above at paragraphs 3.93 - 3.96. It needs to be considered whether special rules should be devised concerning the availability of evidence as to the defendant's wealth when exemplary damages are sought.

6.47   The options would appear to be to leave the matter to judicial discretion; to allow unrestricted discovery of such material; to allow discovery of such material only when a prima facie case meriting exemplary damages has been made out; or to subject cases in this area to split trials so that the defendant's means could be considered only after the issue of liability had been concluded in the plaintiff's favour. The Ontario Law Reform Commission, having considered this range of possibilities, took the view that it should continue to be the case that no detailed inquiry into the defendant's finances should be undertaken.[71] We provisionally support this latter option, and seek consultees' views on this proposal.

AGGRAVATED DAMAGES

6.48   An issue which we raise for consideration is whether, as the Ontario Law Reform Commission recommended,[72] interests of personality can and should be protected only by a strict compensatory model of redress. We have suggested that the requirement of exceptional conduct necessary to sustain an aggravated award makes it difficult to see these awards as purely compensatory. This requirement could be abandoned and injury to feelings and the like approached from a purely compensatory perspective in which, subject to remoteness, the court would simply ask whether the plaintiff had actually been caused intangible loss by the defendant's wrongful conduct.

---

[71]   Report on Exemplary Damages (1991), pp. 52 and 104.

[72]   *Ibid.*, pp. 27-30, 103.

A Compensatory model

(a) Arguments in favour of abandoning the exceptional conduct requirement in aggravated damages

6.49   In favour of this approach, it might be argued that a true injury to feelings, or to pride and dignity and the like, is worthy of legal protection regardless of whether or not the defendant's wrongful conduct is also exceptional.[73] On this view, the requirement of exceptional conduct represents an unreasonable bar to the recovery of intangible losses and should be removed. Further, if it does introduce a punitive element into aggravated awards and if the objections to the presence of the punitive principle in civil actions are accepted,[74] then this would also suggest its abandonment. In any event, now that injury to feelings, mental distress and the like are recognised as a permissible head of loss in many actions and are also more freely recoverable, the "link to the especially bad conduct of the defendant seems unhelpful and unnecessary."[75] Finally, the removal of the exceptional conduct requirement effectively entails the abolition of aggravated damages, and this might be welcomed on the ground that the distinction between aggravated and exemplary damages has been a source of confusion and complexity in the law.[76]

(b) Arguments against abandoning the exceptional conduct requirement in aggravated damages

6.50   The abandonment of exceptional conduct and the recourse to a purely compensatory model of redress in respect of intangible losses howsoever caused would, however, generate a number of problems. First, if exceptional conduct is conduct from which the law is prepared to infer loss or which gives rise to a presumption of loss,[77] then a strict compensatory model (which is interested more in the *fact* of loss) will effectively increase the plaintiff's burden. Plaintiffs

---

[73]   *Ibid.*, p. 29.

[74]   See paras. 5.4-5.12 above.

[75]   A.S. Burrows, *Remedies for Torts and Breach of Contract* (1987), p.209.

[76]   It has also been argued by Burrows, *ibid.*, that the distinction between 'mental distress damages' and aggravated damages is a source of confusion.

[77]   See para. 3.26 above.

will be put to proof of loss in precisely those cases where loss is most difficult to prove.[78] If the court were to require evidence of loss, rather than to deem it, plaintiffs might be induced to go beyond injury to feelings and seek to establish some physical or psychiatric illness,[79] which would of course in turn increase the importance of medical evidence and also the costs of litigation.[80]

6.51   Second, the problems of subjectivity and proof are acute in relation to intangible losses.[81] The removal of exceptional conduct as a precondition to their recoverability opens the door to trivial and bogus claims and generates further problems regarding the susceptibility or peculiar sensibility of the plaintiff. The need for intangible losses to be subjected to some kind of objective test is made more imperative by the fact that any words or conduct accompanying a wrong could happen to injure the plaintiff's feelings. One method of objectifying the loss is to insist on culpable conduct.

6.52   Third, the gravity of the defendant's conduct acts as a guide to assessment. Neither exact determination of the loss suffered nor precise valuation is possible where the loss is non-pecuniary. It was this which, in Lord Devlin's view, explained the relevance of the defendant's conduct to the assessment of damages 'at large'.[82] If injury to feelings was to be approached from a purely compensatory perspective, this would consequently lead to difficulties of assessment. The process of compensatory assessment purports to be more definite and less discretionary than that for aggravated damages : the court or jury must simply attempt to

---

[78]   See paras. 2.13-2.16 above.

[79]   See, for instance, *Gardiner* v. *Manpower (U.K.) Ltd.* [August 1991] Legal Action 23, a discrimination case where the plaintiff introduced a medical report which described her condition as 'phobic anxiety' requiring therapy. The I.T. held that this severe injury went well beyond the injury to feelings which an ordinary person experiences from an insult or degradation and, distinguishing *Noone* v. *North West Thames R.H.A.* [1988] I.R.L.R. 195, awarded the plaintiff the statutory maximum damages. This may also be a reflection of the low level of awards for injury to feelings in discrimination cases, which encourages plaintiffs to describe their injury as more severe.

[80]   Cf. Report on Exemplary Damages (1991), Ontario Law Reform Commission, p. 29; M.G. Bridge, "Contractual Damages for Intangible Loss: A Comparative Analysis", (1984) 62 Can.B.R. 323, 359.

[81]   See paras. 2.13-2.16, above. These are problems of proof from the perspective of the court and the defendant.

[82]   *Rookes* v. *Barnard* [1964] A.C. 1129, 1221. See paras. 3.2 and 3.21 above.

measure and value the loss. It would be difficult to subject intangible losses to this process, whereas the gravity of the defendant's conduct can be used as a criterion of comparability.[83]

6.53   Fourth, we have seen that the requirement of exceptional conduct excludes aggravated damages from the tort of negligence and negligently committed wrongs.[84] If a purely compensatory model was adopted in the case of intangible loss, the question would arise as to whether damages should be available in respect of all wrongs or only some. If the latter, what form would restrictions take? We would value consultees' views on these questions and on the questions raised above, as to proof and assessment of loss.

6.54   Finally, it may be asked whether a pure compensatory model would adequately protect the interests concerned. Aggravated (and exemplary) damages offer *enhanced* protection for the *serious* violations of personality which occur when the defendant's conduct is exceptional. The Ontario Law Reform Commission's recommendation was made against a background in which exemplary damages are more widely available than they are in English law. In Canada, as we have seen,[85] exemplary damages are available wherever the defendant's conduct is exceptional, and hence the abolition of aggravated damages would still leave the relevant interests protected by exemplary damages. In this country, on the other hand, aggravated damages are wider in this respect than exemplary damages. Their removal could leave a serious gap in terms of the protection of these interests in cases which fall outside Lord Devlin's categories. If it is accepted that compensatory damages cannot adequately protect personality rights, this would suggest that aggravated damages should only be abolished if at the same time the restrictions placed upon exemplary damages by *Rookes* v. *Barnard*[86] and *A.B.* v. *South West Water Services Ltd.*[87] are removed. In view of our provisional conclusion that exemplary damages should be retained and put on a principled basis, we have also formed the provisional view that the exceptional conduct requirement should be abandoned and that aggravated damages should be assimilated within a compensatory framework. We invite

---

[83]   The problem is perhaps that Lord Devlin, or his judgment as it has subsequently been interpreted, elevated the *relevance* of the defendant's culpable conduct to the status of a *requirement*.

[84]   See para. 3.14 above.

[85]   See para. 4.4 - 4.6 above.

[86]   [1964] A.C. 1129.

[87]   [1993] Q.B. 507.

consultees' comments on this approach and on the question whether, if a purely compensatory model is adopted in the case of intangible loss, damages should be available for such losses irrespective of what wrong has caused them. If only some wrongs should give rise to damages awards for such losses, which should these be?

PART VII

RESTITUTIONARY DAMAGES

INTRODUCTION

7.1   There is increasing recognition that the principle of unjust enrichment in English law is the basis of independent restitutionary claims, which deprive the defendant of benefits received at the expense of the plaintiff.[1] There is also increasing awareness that restitutionary claims may overlap with other kinds of claim and that remedies in tort and for breach of contract or an equitable obligation must, in appropriate cases, take account of the restitutionary principle. Restitutionary claims are likely to overlap with tortious claims where the defendant has benefited by the wrongful use of the plaintiff's property. They may also overlap with breach of contract but, although available in certain circumstances, face particular difficulties because of concern that they would reallocate risks and obligations which had been freely agreed.[2] In the earlier sections of this paper we have argued that punitive damages have been used for the infringement of personality interests in part because of the difficulties the compensatory model has in dealing with intangible losses. In this part we shall see that restitutionary remedies have been used for infringements of economic and proprietary interests which pose difficulties for the compensatory model.

7.2   Although it is arguably possible to discern a general principle in the cases requiring a person to make restitution of benefits acquired through a wrongful act,[3] this has not yet been recognised by the courts.[4] In the present state of legal development what we have[5] are discrete categories associated with the doctrine of 'waiver of tort', and restitution of benefits

---

[1]   *Lipkin Gorman* v. *Karpnale Ltd.* [1991] 2 A.C. 548

[2]   R. Goff & G. Jones, *The Law of Restitution* (3rd ed., 1986) p. 468.

[3]   *Ibid.*, p. 606, 613. See also P. Birks, *An Introduction to the Law of Restitution* (1985), ch. X; A.S. Burrows, *Remedies for Torts and Breach of Contract* (1987), ch. 6; A.S. Burrows, *The Law of Restitution* (1993), pp. 393-396, 418-419; *Chitty on Contracts* (26th ed., 1989), para. 2071.

[4]   See e.g. *Stoke-on-Trent City Council* v. *W. & J. Wass Ltd.* [1988] 1 W.L.R. 1406, 1415-1416 (*per* Nourse L.J.); *Surrey C.C.* v. *Brodero Homes Ltd. The Times*, 16 April 1993 (C.A.).

[5]   *A.G.* v. *Guardian Newspapers (No. 2)* [1990] 1 A.C. 109, 286 (*per* Lord Goff).

acquired by criminal acts,[6] breach of fiduciary relationships, breach of confidence and certain breaches of contract. Even in the context of these discrete categories, there is debate as to whether particular remedies, such as the account of profits or equitable compensation,[7] are restitutionary.

7.3   There is also debate as to the juridical basis of such remedies; that is, whether all or some of the benefit based remedies are generated by independent restitutionary claims or whether at bottom the basis of the cause of action is in fact the tort, equitable wrong or breach of contract.[8] It is thus necessary to ask whether the particular tort or other 'wrong' is capable of giving rise to a restitutionary remedy, and, if so, whether it is based on an independent claim or is dependent on the tort or wrong. The relationship of independent restitutionary claims based on the principle of unjust enrichment to the compensatory model differs from that of exemplary damages. In such cases the non-compensatory remedy simply corresponds to its cause of action. If the *aim* of the law is not compensatory but restitutionary, the fact that the remedy is not compensatory might not be thought to require justification in the same way as it does for remedies for torts and breaches of contract. In any event, even if the remedy is restitutionary, in some cases, for instance, where the plaintiff's money or property has come into the hands of the defendant, the view that the compensatory principle occupies a position of paramountcy is not problematic, since the plaintiff has lost the money or the property. In other cases, however, restitutionary remedies may be awarded where there is no 'loss' in this sense. It is in these cases that it is said by some that the cause of action is in fact the tort, the equitable wrong or the breach of contract and not an independent restitutionary cause of action.

7.4   To establish a restitutionary claim, it must be shown that the defendant has benefited (or has been 'enriched') and that the benefit was 'at the expense of' the plaintiff. In this part of the

---

6   R. Goff & G. Jones, *The Law of Restitution* (3rd ed., 1986), ch. 33. The Criminal Justice Act 1988, s. 71 permits courts to make confiscation orders where the defendant in criminal proceedings has benefited by obtaining money or property from an indictable offence or an offence listed in Sched. 4 to the Act. In deciding whether to make such an order the court may take into account the fact that the victim is intending to institute civil proceedings; *ibid.*, s. 72(3).

7   *Nocton* v. *Lord Ashburton* [1914] A.C. 932; *Bartlett* v. *Barclays Bank Trust Co. Ltd.* [1980] Ch. 515; *Parker-Tweedale* v. *Dunbar Bank Plc. (No 1)* [1990] 3 W.L.R. 767, 773-774. See also I.E. Davidson, (1982) 13 Melb. U. L. Rev. 349; P.M. McDermott,"Jurisdiction of the Court of Chancery to award Damages", (1992) 108 L.Q.R. 652; Gummow J. " Unjust Enrichment, Restitution and Proprietory Remedies", in P.D. Finn, *Essays on Restitution* (1990), 47, 62-64.

8   See para. 7.11 below.

paper we consider the present law, the questions of principle which must be addressed in considering reform and the options for reform.

THE PRESENT LAW

7.5   Restitutionary awards have been most commonly made in cases concerning what have been termed the 'proprietary torts':[9] conversion,[10] other wrongful interference or trespass to goods,[11] trespass to land[12] and for the infringement of intellectual property rights.[13] They have also been made in cases concerning fraud or deceit,[14] intimidation,[15] passing off,[16] inducing breach of contract[17] and the equitable wrongs of breach of confidence[18] and breach of fiduciary duty[19] and their appropriateness in nuisance has been recognised.[20]

---

[9]   *Stoke-on-Trent City Council* v. *W. & J. Wass Ltd.* [1988] 1 W.L.R. 1406, 1416 (*per* Nourse L.J.).

[10]   *Lamine* v. *Dorrell* (1705) 2 Ld Raym. 1216, 92 E.R. 303; *Re Simms* [1934] Ch. 1.

[11]   *Oughton* v. *Seppings* (1830) 1 B. & Ad. 241, 109 E.R. 776; *Strand Electric & Engineering Co. Ltd.* v. *Brisford Entertainments Ltd.* [1952] 2 Q.B. 246, 254-255 (*per* Denning L.J.; Somervell and Romer L.JJ. analysed the award as compensatory).

[12]   *Powell* v. *Rees* (1837) 7 Act. & E. 426, 112 E.R. 530. See also *Penarth Dock Engineering Co. Ltd.* v. *Pounds* [1963] 1 Lloyd's Rep. 359; *Bracewell* v. *Appleby* [1975] Ch. 408.

[13]   Account of profits: *Hogg* v. *Kirby* (1803) 8 Ves. J. 215, 223, 32 E.R. 336, 339; *Colburn* v. *Simms* (1843) 2 Ha. 543; 67 E.R. 224; *My Kinda Town Ltd* v. *Soll* [1983] R.P.C. 15; *Potton Ltd.* v. *Yorkclose Ltd.* [1990] F.S.R. 11. Damages and account of profits: Patents Act 1977, ss. 61-62; Copyright, Designs and Patents Act, 1988, ss. 96, 97, 229.

[14]   *Hill* v. *Perrott* (1810) 3 Taunt. 274, 128 E.R. 109; *Billing* v. *Ries* (1841) Car. & M. 26, 174 E.R. 392; *Kettlewell* v. *Refuge Assurance Co.* [1908] 1 K.B. 545; [1909] A.C. 243. See also *Mahesan* v. *Malaysia Government Officers' Co-operative Housing Society Ltd.* [1979] A.C. 374 (remedies arising in respect of a bribe).

[15]   *Astley* v. *Reynolds* (1731) 2 Str. 915, 93 E.R. 939; *Universe Tankships Inc of Monrovia* v. *I.T.W.F.* [1983] 1 A.C. 336.

[16]   *My Kinda Town Ltd* v. *Soll* [1983] R.P.C. 15 (*per* Slade J.).

[17]   *Lightly* v. *Clouston* (1808) 1 Taunt. 112, 127 E.R. 774; *Foster* v. *Stewart* (1814) 3 M. & S. 191, 105 E.R. 582. But see Winfield's criticisms: *The Province of the Law of Tort* (1931), pp. 174-175.

[18]   *Seager* v. *Copydex Ltd. (No. 2)* [1969] 1 W.L.R. 809; *Jeffries* v. *News Group Newspapers Ltd.* 18 July 1990 (*per* Ferris J., Unreported).

[19]   *Phipps* v. *Boardman* [1967] 2 A.C. 46; *English* v. *Dedham Vale Properties Ltd.* [1978] 1 W.L.R. 930 (although better seen as an example of breach of statutory duty); *Guinness Plc.* v. *Saunders* [1990] 2 A.C.663. See also *Surrey C.C.* v. *Bredero Homes Ltd.*, *The Times* 16 April 1993 (*per* Steyn L.J.).

Sections 27 and 28 of the Housing Act 1988 create a tortious remedy of a restitutionary character for "unlawful eviction". The damages awarded under this provision are measured according to the increase in the value of the landlord's property resulting from the eviction.

7.6 It has been held that a restitutionary award cannot be made in respect of infringement of a right to hold a market.[21] Libel has been held not to give rise to a restitutionary award in the United States[22] but may give rise to an award of exemplary damages in England if the defendant commits the tort knowingly or with reckless disregard as to whether his conduct is wrongful for the purpose of obtaining some material advantage.[23] In the case of certain intellectual property rights neither damages nor an account of profits can be awarded for innocent infringement.[24] Although restitutionary notions have undoubtedly influenced the 'deliberate recourse to wrongdoing for profit' category of exemplary damages, as has been seen, exemplary damages are not limited to restitution of profits and other gains received at the expense of the plaintiff. However, it would appear that the effect of the category is that in practice restitutionary awards may be made in respect of gains made by deliberate wrongdoing by the commission of those torts which fall within the *Rookes* v. *Barnard* second category. In principle, therefore, a restitutionary award should be available for battery.[25]

---

20 *Carr-Saunders* v. *Dick McNeill Associates Ltd.* [1986] 1 W.L.R. 922 (although as there was no evidence of profit no award was made). Cf *Stoke-on-Trent City Council* v. *W. & J. Wass Ltd.* [1988] 1 W.L.R. 1406, 1410G.

21 *Stoke-on-Trent City Council* v. *W. & J. Wass Ltd.* [1988] 1 W.L.R. 1406, above.

22 *Hart* v. *Dutton* (1949) 93 N.Y.S. 2d, aff'd (1949) 98 N.Y.S. 2d. 773. R. Goff & G. Jones, *The Law of Restitution* (3rd ed., 1986), p. 613 and A.S. Burrows, *Remedies for Torts and Breach of Contract* (1987), p. 269 consider that no reasons of principle preclude such an award although it appears to be assumed that where there is no deliberate libel the only question is compensation of the plaintiff: *McCarey* v. *Associated Newspapers Ltd. (No. 2)* [1965] 2 Q.B. 86, 101, 104-105, 107; *Broadway Approvals Ltd.* v. *Odhams Press Ltd. (No. 2)* [1965] 1 W.L.R. 805, 818-819, 820, 825.

23 *Broome* v. *Cassell* [1972] A.C. 1027. See paras. 3.44-3.51 above for discussion of this category of exemplary damages.

24 Patents Act 1977, s. 62; *Slazenger & Sons* v. *Spalding & Bros.* [1910] 1 Ch. 257 (trade mark). See also *Spalding & Bros.* v. *A.W. Gamage Ltd.* (1915) 84 L.J. Ch. 449 (passing off) and generally A.S. Burrows, *Remedies for Torts and Breach of Contract* (1987), pp. 264-265. But the position is different for copyright and infringement of design right where an account of profits may be ordered: Copyright, Designs and Patents Act 1988, ss. 97, 229, 233. On innocent trespass and breach of confidence see notes 54 and 60 below.

25 H. Street, *Principles of the Law of Damages* (1962), p. 254 suggests that battery could give rise to quasi-contract (i.e. restitution) where, for instance, a boxer deliberately fouls to obtain the winner's purse or a defendant cuts off a prince's (or a pop star's) hair without permission and sells off the locks for large sums.

7.7   In general the gain to a defendant from a breach of contract is irrelevant to the quantification of damages.[26] However, an innocent party who has rendered part performance before the contract was discharged may claim a restitutionary award as an alternative to the normal compensatory remedies for breach of contract by seeking a *quantum meruit* or, where there has been a total failure of consideration, the recovery of money paid to the defendant. Apart from these cases, the defendant's gain will be relevant in sales of land because the effect of the contract is that the purchaser has an equitable interest in the land and is accordingly entitled to the proceeds of any wrongful sale to a third party.[27] It will also be relevant where there has been a breach of a contractual duty of confidence[28] or where the breach of contract involves the use of or interference with the plaintiff's property.[29] These are all cases of specifically enforceable contracts and it is arguable that the defendant's gains should be relevant in all cases where the contract is, in principle, specifically enforceable.[30]

(1) Nature of the benefit

7.8   It is necessary for the defendant to have received either a definite sum of money, directly from the plaintiff or by the sale or use of the plaintiff's property,[31] or a benefit which can be readily assessed in money,[32] for example where the defendant has made profits or saved

---

26   *The Siboen* [1976] 1 Lloyd's Rep. 293, 337 (profits from alternative charter irrelevant); *Tito* v. *Waddell (No. 2)* [1977] Ch. 106, 332 (the question is not one of making the defendant disgorge what he has saved by committing the wrong); *Surrey C.C.* v. *Bredero Homes Ltd., The Times* 16 April 1993.

27   *Lake* v. *Bayliss* [1974] 1 W.L.R. 1073; *Tito* v. *Waddell (No. 2)* [1977] Ch. 106, 332.

28   *Peter Pan Mfg. Corpn.* v. *Corsets Silhouette Ltd.* [1964] 1 W.L.R. 96.

29   *Penarth Dock Engineering Co. Ltd.* v. *Pounds* [1963] 1 Lloyd's Rep. 359; *Wrotham Park Estate Co. Ltd.* v. *Parkside Homes Ltd.* [1974] 1 W.L.R. 798.

30   S.M. Waddams, *The Law of Damages* (1983) paras. 969-974; S.M. Waddams, "Restitution as Part of Contract Law", in A.S. Burrows ed., *Essays on the Law of Restitution* (1991), 197, 207-213.

31   *Lamine* v. *Dorrell* (1705) 2 Ld Raym. 1216, 92 E.R. 303; *Powell* v. *Rees* (1837) 7 Ad. & E. 426, 112 E.R. 530 (sale of thing taken from land); *Phillips* v. *Homfray* (1871) 6 Ch. App. 770 (profits from coal tortiously taken and sold).

32   Disputes concerning the correct basis for the valuation of a landlord's interest in property have arisen under s. 28 of the Housing Act 1988. See, for example, *Jones* v. *Miah* [1992] E.G.C.S. 51.

expense by using the plaintiff's property,[33] and possibly services to which the plaintiff was entitled,[34] or by the infringement of certain other protected interests.[35] As indicated the courts have not yet recognised a general principle providing for restitution of profits made or expense saved by reason of the infringement of interests protected by tort or contract law.

7.9   The position of 'negative benefits' by the saving of expense is not, however, free from difficulty. First, a majority of the Court of Appeal in *Phillips* v. *Homfray*[36] held that trespass to land could only give rise to an action for money had and received where property or the proceeds of property belonging to the landowner has been appropriated by the defendant. Thus, no such award lay in respect of the mining expenses the defendant saved by his use and occupation of the plaintiff's land. This case has been widely criticised[37] as being unprincipled because "a gain or acquisition to the wrongdoer by the work and labour of another does not necessarily, if it does at all, imply a diminution of the property of such other person".[38] The decision has not been followed in the United States and Canada,[39] has not influenced restitutionary awards arising from breach of contract and may require reconsideration in the light of more modern English decisions concerning the wrongful use of property.

---

[33] *Rumsey* v. *The North East Ry. Co.* (1863) 14 C.B. (N.S.) 641, 143 E.R. 596 (saving of costs of carriage); *Penarth Dock Engineering* v. *Pounds* [1963] 1 Lloyd's Rep. 359; *Bracewell* v. *Appleby* [1975] Ch. 408; *Peter Pan Mfgn. Corp.* v. *Corsets Silhouette Ltd.* [1964] 1 W.L.R. 96 (profits made from manufacturing process using confidential information) - these last two are cases of account of profits and perhaps do not belong.

[34] *Lightly* v. *Clouston* (1808) 1 Taunt. 112, 127 E.R. 774; *Foster* v. *Stewart* (1814) 3 M. & S. 191, 105 E.R. 582.

[35] E.g. confidentiality and fiduciary relationships.

[36] (1883) 24 Ch. D. 439.

[37] R. Goff & G. Jones, *The Law of Restitution* (3rd ed., 1986), pp. 16, 608-610; G.E. Palmer, *The Law of Restitution*, (1978), vol. I, para. 2.5; P.D. Maddaugh & J.D. McCamus, *The Law of Restitution* (1990), pp. 518-521; *Chitty on Contracts* (26th ed., 1989), para. 2073. Cf. P.B.H. Birks, *An Introduction to the Law of Restitution*, (Rev. ed., 1989) pp. 323-325.

[38] (1883) 24 Ch. D. 439, 471-2 (*per* Baggallay L.J., dissenting).

[39] *Edwards* v. *Lee's Administrators* (1936) 96 S.W. 2d 1028 ; *Raven Red Ash Coal Co.* v. *Ball* (1946) 39 S.E. 2d 231; *Daniel* v. *O'Leary* (1976) 14 N.B.R. (2d) 564.

7.10   Secondly, cases of saving expense have been analysed in compensatory terms. For instance, in *Strand Electric & Engineering Co. Ltd.* v. *Brisford Entertainments Ltd.*,[40] where damages were awarded in respect of theatre equipment wrongfully used by the defendant, the assessment was by reference to a reasonable hiring charge for the equipment. Although Denning L.J. said that as this sum was payable even where the owner suffered no loss it was not compensatory but based on the fact that the defendant had the benefit of the use of the equipment and had saved the expense of hiring alternative equipment,[41] Somervell and Romer L.JJ. preferred to base the award on the loss to the owner in not being paid the fee he would have charged for the use of the goods,[42] i.e. they saw it as compensation. There are, however, difficulties with the compensatory analysis. First, it is irrelevant that there was no market for such property so the plaintiff could not have hired it out. It is also irrelevant that the plaintiff would in no circumstances have allowed the defendant to use the property and in such situations it is artificial to treat the hire charge as compensation for the plaintiff's loss.[43] Thirdly, in some cases the determination of the reasonable hire is determined by taking into account the profit made by the defendant from the use of the property, i.e. her or his benefit.[44] Support for the view that such cases are in fact only defensible on the basis of restitutionary principle and that the argument that they can be justified on the basis of a loss of bargaining opportunity is a fiction has recently been provided by Steyn L.J. in *Surrey C.C.* v. *Bredero Homes Ltd.*.[45]

---

[40]   [1952] 2 Q.B. 246.

[41]   [1952] 2 Q.B. 246, 254-255. See also *Penarth Dock Engineering Co. Ltd.* v. *Pounds* [1963] 1 Lloyd's Rep. 359, 361-362; *Bracewell* v. *Appleby* [1975] Ch. 408, 419-420.

[42]   [1952] 2 Q.B. 246, 252, 257. See also *Hillesden Securities Ltd.* v. *Ryjack Ltd.* [1983] 1 W.L.R. 959; *Bracewell* v. *Appleby* [1975] Ch. 408 at 420; R.J. Sharpe & S.M. Waddams, "Damages for lost opportunity to bargain",(1982) 2 O.J.L.S. 290. But see *Surrey C.C.* v. *Bredero Homes Ltd.*, *The Times* 16 April 1993 (*per* Steyn L.J.).

[43]   *Wrotham Park Estate Co. Ltd.* v. *Parkside Homes Ltd.* [1974] 1 W.L.R. 798 (breach of restrictive covenant); *Jefferies* v. *News Group Newspapers Ltd.* 18 July 1990 (Unreported, Ferris J.) (breach of confidence).

[44]   *Bracewell* v. *Appleby* [1975] Ch. 408; *Wrotham Park Estate Co. Ltd.* v. *Parkside Homes Ltd.* [1974] 1 W.L.R. 798.

[45]   *The Times*, 16 April 1993. His Lordship was only considering the *Wrotham Park* case (above) but his reasoning is more generally applicable.

(2) At the expense of the plaintiff

7.11   Where the claim is for the recovery of money or the value of property taken or services rendered, it is often characterised as an independent restitutionary claim.[46] The defendant's benefit is said to be at the expense of the plaintiff in the sense that it has been extracted from the plaintiff. The fact that there has also been a tort or breach of contract is said to be irrelevant to the cause of action. Where the claim is for the profits made or the expense saved by the defendant's use of the plaintiff's property or infringement of the plaintiff's interest, the position is said to differ. Here it is said that there is no 'subtraction' from the plaintiff but the benefit is nevertheless 'at her or his expense' in the sense that it accrues by reason of the wrong, which is accordingly the basis of the cause of action.[47] In these cases it is said that any restitutionary claim is dependent on the tort or other breach of obligation; restitutionary principles are said to be operating at a secondary level. The theoretical issue need not concern us but this view is not universally accepted.[48] It does not accord with the way English law classifies claims in other contexts.[49] It may in any case be of no practical importance if, as appears to be the case, those who would distinguish the two classes of case accept that the policies affecting tort and contract claims are relevant to claims categorised as independent[50] and that common law or statutory bars may apply to claims categorised as dependent.[51] The real issue is the extent of the remedy in any case in which restitution is considered, and it is to this which we now turn.

---

[46]   P. Birks, *An Introduction to the Law of Restitution* (Rev. ed., 1989), pp. 23-4, 39-44, 313-315; A.S Burrows, *The Law of Restitution* (1993), pp. 16-23. See generally R. Goff & G. Jones, *The Law of Restitution* (3rd ed., 1986), pp. 12-26.

[47]   P. Birks, *An Introduction to the Law of Restitution*, (Rev. ed., 1989), pp. 316-326; A.S. Burrows, *The Law of Restitution* (1993), pp. 376 ff.

[48]   See J. Beatson, *The Use and Abuse of Restitution* (1991), pp. 25-28, 208-210, 230-235.

[49]   See *Letang* v. *Cooper* [1965] 1 Q.B. 232, 242. On the contract and tort borderline, see e.g. *Coupland* v. *Arabian Gulf Petroleum Co.* [1983] 1 W.L.R. 1136, 1152-1153; *Midland Bank Trust Co. Ltd.* v. *Hett, Stubbs and Kemp* [1979] Ch. 384.

[50]   P. Birks, *An Introduction to the Law of Restitution* (Rev. ed., 1989), pp. 179-180; *Universe Tankships Inc. of Monrovia* v. *I.T.W.F.* [1983] 1 A.C. 366; *Thavorn* v. *Bank of Credit and Commerce International* [1985] 1 Lloyd's Rep. 259, 264.

[51]   A.S. Burrows, *The Law of Restitution* (1993), pp. 376, 440-448; *Chesworth* v. *Farrar* [1967] 1 Q.B. 407. Cf. P. Birks, *An Introduction to the Law of Restitution* (Rev. ed., 1989), pp. 347-351.

(3) The extent of the remedy

7.12   In the case of torts and equitable wrongs susceptible to a restitutionary award the question is whether the plaintiff will be entitled to the profits earned by the defendant as a result of the wrong or whether she or he will be restricted to the market value of the property (in the case of wrongful sale) or the hire value (in the case of wrongful user). In the case of breach of contract the question may also arise as to the extent of restitutionary relief where the plaintiff has made a bad bargain. Is relief by way of recovery of money or *quantum meruit* limited by reference to the contract price and is other restitutionary relief limited by reference to the damages that would have been awarded for loss of expectation?

7.13   Restitutionary awards only extend to those gains made by the defendant which are attributable to the plaintiff's property or the infringement of an interest recognised as analogous.[52] To the extent that a gain is so attributable it will be regarded as 'at the expense of' the plaintiff.

(a)   In the case of a direct transfer of money from the plaintiff to the defendant or the sale of the plaintiff's property by the defendant the money transferred[53] or the proceeds of sale[54] will normally be attributable to the plaintiff's interest.[55]

---

[52]   E.g. passing off is regarded as an injury to the plaintiff's property in the goodwill of her or his business (*Draper* v. *Trist* [1939] 3 All E.R. 513, 526) and confidential information has been said to be proprietary (see F. Gurry, *Breach of Confidence* (1984), pp. 46-56 but cf. *Attorney-General* v. *Guardian Newspapers Ltd. (No. 2)* [1990] 1 A.C. 109, 281). On the position of bribes, which may appear anomalous, see *Mahesan* v. *Malaysia Government Officers' Co-operative Housing Society Ltd.* [1979] A.C. 374; *Logicrose Ltd.* v. *Southend United F.C. Ltd.* [1988] 1 W.L.R. 1256. See further A.M. Tettenborn, "Bribery, Corruption and Restitution - the Strange Case of Mr Mahesan", (1979) 95 L.Q.R. 68; C.A. Needham, "Recovering the Profits of Bribery",(1979) 95 L.Q.R. 536.

[53]   *Clarke* v. *Shee* (1774) 1 Cowp. 197, 98 E.R. 1041; *Neate* v. *Harding* (1851) 6 Ex. 349, 155 E.R. 577..

[54]   *Lamine* v. *Dorrell* (1701) 2 Ld Raym. 1216, 92 E.R. 303; *Heilbut & Rocca* v. *Nevill* (1870) L.R. 5 C.P. 478 (realisation of converted bill of exchange); *Phillips* v. *Homfray* (1871) 6 Ch. App. 770; [1892] 1 Ch. 465, 474 (coal taken and sold); *Smith Kline & French Laboratories Ltd.* v. *Long* [1989] 1 W.L.R. 1, 9-11 (*per* Slade L.J.). In the case of misappropriation of goods by unauthorised mining the cost of raising the mineral may be deducted (*McGregor on Damages* (15th ed., 1988), para. 1329) and an innocent defendant is entitled to deduct the cost of severing the mineral (*McGregor, op. cit.*, paras. 1323-1329) and, although this is not entirely clear, probably an additional sum by way of profit for the defendant's work: *McGregor, op. cit.*, para. 1330; H. Street, *Principles of the Law of Damages* (1962), 217.

[55]   Cf. P. Birks, *An Introduction to the Law of Restitution* (Rev. ed., 1989), pp. 138, 316, 320.

(b)   Where the defendant uses the plaintiff's property we have seen that a reasonable hiring fee will be recoverable even if the plaintiff would not have hired the property to the defendant and could not have hired it to anybody else.

(c)   Where the defendant has used the plaintiff's property to make profits, there is the question whether all or part of the profits may be recovered. In such cases the question of attribution may be more complex. If the defendant could not have made the profit without using the plaintiff's property, in principle an account of profits (including, in an appropriate case, an unrealised profit[56]) will be available. However, in many cases, including those where the profit is in part attributable to the defendant's property[57] or to the defendant's work and skill, this is a laborious and expensive process.[58] The fact that the defendant could have made the gain without using the plaintiff's property, that the plaintiff's only way of exploiting the property was to hire it out or to sell it, that the defendant could have compelled the plaintiff to grant a licence to use the property and that the defendant's infringement of the plaintiff's right was not deliberate[59] are factors that indicate the inappropriateness of an account of profits as opposed to a remedy based on 'user' or 'saving of expense'.

7.14   In cases of breach of fiduciary duty and breach of confidence the plaintiff's interest has been described as proprietary and similar principles apply.[60]

---

[56]   *Potton Ltd.* v. *Yorkclose Ltd.* [1990] F.S.R. 11.

[57]   *Edwards* v. *Lee's Administrators* (1936) 96 S.W. 2d 1028 (recovery of proportion of profits defendant made from charging for admission to "Great Onyx Cave" under plaintiff's land: the apportionment reflected the fact that part of the cave was under the defendant's land).

[58]   *Price's Patent Candle Co. Ltd.* v. *Bauwen's Patent Candle Co. Ltd.* (1858) 4 K. & J. 727, 730, 70 E.R. 302, 303; *A.G.* v. *Guardian Newspapers Ltd. (No. 2)* [1990] 1 A.C. 109, 292; *My Kinda Town* v. *Soll* [1983] R.P.C. 15, 55, 407, 432. See further A.S. Burrows, *Remedies for Torts and Breach of Contract* (1987), pp. 267-268; *Copinger & Skone James on Copyright* (13th ed., 1991), para. 11-76.

[59]   See n. 25 above.

[60]   Fiduciary duties: *Phipps* v. *Boardman* [1967] 2 A.C. 46, 107, 115. Cf. 127-128; *Reading* v. *Attorney-General* [1951] A.C. 507 (note the allowance for services rendered); *English* v. *Dedham Vale Properties Ltd.* [1978] 1 W.L.R. 93. Confidentiality: *Seager* v. *Copydex Ltd.* [1967] 1 W.L.R. 923; (No. 2) [1969] 1 W.L.R. 809 (innocent breach of confidence; award of information's value as between willing seller and willing buyer); *Peter Pan Mnfg. Corp.* v. *Corsets Silhouette Ltd.* [1964] 1 W.L.R. 96 (account of profits ordered where manufacture would not have been possible without using the confidential information); *A.G.* v. *Guardian Newspapers Ltd. (No. 2)* [1990] 1 A.C. 109, 262, 266,

7.15 In the case of the infringement of non-property interests it may be more artificial to think in terms of a reasonable 'user' fee for say the publication of a libel or a breach of confidence and in some contexts, for instance battery,[61] to negotiate for a fee may be contrary to public policy. But as indicated these objections may not extend to an award based on the saving of expense to the defendant.[62] Where profits are sought the difficulties of attribution may be greater. Thus, on the assumption that restitutionary awards are in principle available in respect of libel, a plaintiff who is libelled by a newspaper or who is incidentally libelled by the defendant may find it very difficult to show that the profits of the newspaper or other defendant are attributable to the libel. There would be similar problems if it were to be recognised that restitutionary claims are in principle available in respect of negligence. It is difficult to regard the expense saved, for instance by not taking appropriate safety precautions in a factory, as attributable to the plaintiff as opposed to the entire class of foreseeable potential plaintiffs.

7.16 In cases in which restitutionary awards are in principle available in respect of a breach of contract similar problems of attribution may arise. Thus, where for example S, who has agreed to sell goods to B, in breach of contract sells the goods to a third party for more than their market price, the normal compensatory measure of damages will be the difference between the contract price and the market price at the date of the breach. It is arguable that any extra profit over and above that which is made by the contract breaker is the result of the defendant's skill and initiative and not 'at the plaintiff's expense', and should not accordingly be taken from the defendant save in exceptional cases, such as where there is a fiduciary duty between the parties or where the contract is specifically enforceable.

7.17 Problems of attribution do not, however, arise where the restitutionary alternative to damages for breach of contract is a claim for the recovery of money paid or a *quantum meruit*. Where the plaintiff seeks the recovery of money or the award of a *quantum meruit* there is no question of the recovery of the defendant's consequential profits. In such cases the issue concerns the relevance of the contract price. It has been held that it is no objection to a claim

---

276, 281.

[61] See para. 7.6 above.

[62] *Jeffries* v. *News Group Newspapers Ltd.* 18 July 1990, (Unreported, *per* Ferris J.).

for the recovery of money that it will rescue the plaintiff from an unprofitable bargain.[63] It has also been held that relief by way of *quantum meruit* is not limited to a proration of the contract price[64] or the contract price itself.[65] Although this has been criticised as inconsistent with the contract and as reallocating contractual risks,[66] proration is difficult in a complex contract and may be unfair because it takes no account of fixed costs which may be incurred at the early stages of a contract or of economies of scale which may have affected the determination of the contract price but be lost on part performance.[67] The case for stating that the contract price should operate as the ceiling for a *quantum meruit* is stronger because it can be said that receipt of the *total* price that would have been paid under the contract fully protects the expectations of the innocent part-performer.

ARGUMENTS FOR AND AGAINST RESTITUTIONARY AWARDS

7.18   The survey of common law developments above shows that it is not the case that the only function of the civil law has been to compensate. Apart from the many examples of restitutionary awards in particular contexts and exemplary damages within the *Rookes* v. *Barnard* categories, the availability of injunctive and specific relief is not entirely explicable in compensatory terms. In the context of restitutionary awards, the question is whether the time is now ripe for the recognition of a general principle requiring a person to make restitution of benefits acquired through a wrongful act and, if so, whether this development should be undertaken by legislation or left to the common law. We shall first list the arguments for and against restitutionary awards and then consider the options for reform and in particular whether this is an area in which statutory intervention is desirable.

---

63   *B.P. Exploration Co. (Libya) Ltd.* v. *Hunt (No. 2)* [1979] 1 W.L.R. 783, 800. See also *D.O. Ferguson & Associates* v. *Sohl, The Times*, 24 December 1992 (C.A.) (payment in excess of value of part work done recovered from contractor even though site owner, using another builder, had the work completed at a cost that was less than the balance of the contract price due). See generally, *Chitty on Contracts*, (26th ed., 1989), para. 2059; G.H. Treitel *The Law of Contract*, (8th ed., 1991), pp. 833, 932-933.

64   *Newton Woodhouse* v. *Trevor Toys Ltd.*, 20 December 1991 (Unreported, C.A.).

65   *Lodder* v. *Slowey* (1900) 20 N.Z.L.R. 321, 358 aff'd. [1904] A.C. 442 (P.C.); *Rover International Ltd.* v. *Cannon Film Sales Ltd.* [1989] 1 W.L.R. 912.

66   R. Goff & G. Jones, *The Law of Restitution* (3rd ed., 1986), pp. 466-8.

67   *Newton Woodhouse* v. *Trevor Toys Ltd.* 20 December 1991, (Unreported, C.A.); *Chitty on Contracts*, (26th ed., 1989), para. 2142.

(1) Arguments for restitutionary awards

1.   If it can be shown that the defendant has gained a benefit and that benefit would not have been gained but for the wrong to the plaintiff, to allow the defendant to retain that benefit (or that part of the benefit which is not reflected by a loss to the plaintiff) is to permit the defendant to profit from the wrong.[68] In *McCarey* v. *Associated Newspapers Ltd. (No. 2)* Diplock L.J. said of the profit making exception to the compensatory principle that: "[T]he law is mocked if it enables a man to make a profit from his own wrong-doing. This is not punishment; it is merely preventing the defendant from obtaining a reward for his wrong-doing. But equally it is not compensation; the plaintiff is the accidental beneficiary of a rule of law based on public policy rather than on the reparation of private wrongs".[69]

2.   Restitution is a method of deterring the deliberate (and possibly the opportunistic) exploitation of wrongdoing while avoiding several of the dangers (in particular indeterminacy) associated with exemplary damages.

3.   In the case of taking or making use of property or a similar interest, whether or not loss has been caused there has been an infringement of the owner's right to exclusive enjoyment of the property or interest. The interests recognised as similar to property interests are ones in which the remedies are available irrespective of whether there is actual damage or an intent to injure, where the courts grant *in specie* protection by injunction and which commonly[70] involve the misappropriation of trade values seen in the market-place as items of wealth. If such interference only leads to compensation and the prevention of future infringement, proprietary and analogous

---

[68] *A.G.* v. *Guardian Newspapers Ltd. (No. 2)* [1990] 1 A.C. 109, 262, 266, 286.

[69] [1965] 2 Q.B. 86, 107. See also *My Kinda Town* v. *Soll* [1983] R.P.C. 15, 55 ("The purpose of awarding an account of profits ... is not to inflict punishment... [i]t is to prevent an unjust enrichment of the defendant..."); *Potton Ltd.* v. *Yorkclose Ltd* [1990] F.S.R. 11, 15.

[70] But not always: see *A.G.* v. *Guardian Newspapers Ltd. (No. 2)* [1990] 1 A.C. 109 (confidential information about the security services); *Jeffries* v. *News Group Newspapers Ltd.* 18 July 1991 (confidences about matrimonial relationship).

rights would arguably be inadequately protected.[71] For instance, there would be no civil remedy for the temporary misappropriation of property or for a breach of confidence which causes no loss, as possibly where the fact that the plaintiff has made a large anonymous donation to charity is revealed.[72]

4.   Often there will be loss of value by reason of the use of property or other interest which it is difficult to identify and prove. This may be the case where the infringement takes the form of competitive activity.[73] Again, paths in popular beauty spots may be damaged by the number of users although it cannot be said that any individual inflicts identifiable loss.

5.   Restitution is a method of protecting interests on which it is difficult to put a compensatory value, for instance reputation and confidentiality.[74] It may be the only way of protecting a contracting party who has expressly or impliedly obtained an undertaking from the party in breach that he would not pursue a particular activity at all or for profit.[75]

6.   Restitution is a method of protecting relationships such as fiduciary relationships in which there is inequality and the potential for abuse.

(2) Arguments against restitutionary awards

1.   Just as exemplary damages are regarded by some as a pure and undeserved windfall to the plaintiff, so too are restitutionary damages. This is particularly the case where the defendant's profits are claimed in circumstances in which the plaintiff could not

---

[71]   In the context of intellectual property, it has been argued that restitution is a positive incentive to creators to produce the ideas or works in question: W.J. Gordon, "Of Harms and Benefits: Torts, Restitution and Intellectual Property", (1992) 21 J.L.S. 449.

[72]   *A.G.* v. *Guardian Newspapers Ltd. (No. 2)* [1990] 1 A.C. 109, 255-256 (*per* Lord Keith).

[73]   See *Stoke-on-Trent City Council* v. *W. & J. Wass Ltd.* [1988] 1 W.L.R. 1406, 1410 (*per* Nourse L.J.), where there was no clear evidence directly linking the plaintiff's market's comparative lack of success to the success of the defendant's market. See also the fourth argument against restitution, below.

[74]   *A.G.* v. *Guardian Newspapers Ltd. (No. 2)* [1990] 1 A.C. 109, 255 (*per* Lord Keith).

[75]   P. Birks, (1993) 109 L.Q.R. (forthcoming).

(or would not) have made those profits but, given the difficulties of attribution discussed above, it is a more general problem. In such cases restitution operates in a quasi-punitive manner and the objections to the use of the civil law as a means of punishment also apply.[76]

2.   In cases of the wrongful use of property and trespass, restitutionary awards are not confined to cases of deliberate wrongdoing and cannot therefore be justified on the basis of deterrence.

3.   The policy considerations which have led to certain rights being treated as analogous to property rights are unclear and do not justify an enhanced remedy as compared with the remedies available for infringement of other rights protected by the civil law.

4.   Restitutionary awards may inhibit enterprise and discourage economic activity[77] since they will retrospectively remove the fruits of an activity from a person who, as in the case of the proprietary torts, may not have known that she or he was infringing the rights of another. Where property is misused this may be justifiable because of the owner's right to exclusive enjoyment but in the case of other interests protected by the law, it does not follow from the fact of protection that the protection should extend beyond compensation and protection from future infringement.[78] The extent of protection depends on the nature of the right.

5.   In the case of breach of contract several arguments have been made against the general availability of restitutionary awards. First, many breaches of contract are made for commercial reasons and it is difficult to draw the line between 'innocent' breach for which there would be only compensation and 'cynical' breach in which there would

---

[76] So do the concerns about multiple plaintiffs; in the case of a defendant's gain which has been made 'at the expense of' several plaintiffs, a restitutionary award would have to attribute the gain between the plaintiffs according to some principle.

[77] *Surrey C.C.* v. *Bredero*, *The Times*, 16 April 1993 (Unreported. Transcript p. 22 *per* Steyn L.J.).

[78] *Stoke-on-Trent City Council* v. *W. & J. Wass Ltd.* [1988] 1 W.L.R. 1406, 1418-1420 (*per* Nicholls L.J.).

also be the option of restitution in the way suggested by some commentators.[79] This would lead to greater uncertainty in the assessment of damages in commercial and consumer disputes. Secondly, in seeking restitution the plaintiff might be evading the requirements of the mitigation rule. Thirdly, a restitutionary award is in reality a monetized form of specific performance but not all contracts are specifically enforceable. Fourthly, there may be difficulties of attribution. The making of a profit in excess of that which the plaintiff might have made had the contract been performed may require skill and initiative which should not be taken from the defendant save in exceptional cases.

PROVISIONAL CONCLUSION

7.19   We do not believe that the only function of the civil law should be to compensate and it is our provisional view that restitutionary awards are *prima facie* justified if certain conditions are satisfied. Although the case in favour of restitutionary awards would be strengthened if exemplary damages were abolished, we do not consider that it depends on such abolition.

7.20   Subject to the views of consultees, our provisional view is that for there to be a restitutionary award the following conditions must be satisfied. First, there must have been either interference with a proprietary right or an analogous right (such as confidentiality and the rights enjoyed by the beneficiary of a fiduciary relationship) or deliberate wrongdoing which could have been restrained by injunction. Secondly, the gains made by the defendant must be attributable to the interest infringed.[80] To this extent the rejection of restitution in respect of the deliberate infringement of the right to hold a market[81] is unfortunate. It may be a reflection of the relative underdevelopment of restitutionary principles rather than of the application of distinct considerations of policy that differentiate this from other rights recognised as justifying restitutionary awards. However, the explanation may also in part be historical since the categories in which restitutionary awards have been made have traditionally been seen as separate. We recognise the difficulties in deciding which interests should be

---

[79]   *Surrey C.C.* v. *Bredero Homes Ltd.*, *The Times*, 16 April 1993 (Unreported. Transcript pp. 13-15 and 22 *per* Dillon and Steyn L.J.J.).

[80]   See para. 7.13(c) above.

[81]   *Stoke-on-Trent City Council* v. *W. & J. Wass Ltd.* [1988] 1 W.L.R. 1406.

treated as analogous to property rights so as to justify restitutionary awards even where the infringement is not deliberate.

7.21   In the case of breach of contract we incline to the view that the distinction that appears to be drawn between specifically enforceable contracts and contracts between fiduciaries where a restitutionary award may be made, and other contracts where the gain to a defendant from breach is irrelevant, reflects an appropriate balance of the respective interests of the parties.

OPTIONS FOR REFORM AND CONSULTATION ISSUES

7.22   We invite the views of consultees on the following questions:

1.   Should it be possible for restitutionary awards to be made in respect of all gains made by reason of a wrong where the test of attribution is satisfied? A general approach of this sort might either include or exclude gains made by reason of breach of contract but, for the reasons above, we provisionally believe that only gains made by reason of contracts that are either in principle specifically enforceable or between parties in a fiduciary relationship should be included.

2.   Should restitutionary awards only be available in respect of the 'proprietary torts' and infringements of interests recognised as analogous to property interests? If this approach were to be adopted and to be implemented by legislation, it would either be necessary to define the 'analogous' interests (which would then constitute a closed list and preclude further judicial development) or to accept a broad statutory approach that would leave discretion in the court. Both alternatives raise the question of the relative advantages of statutory and case by case development considered at 4 below.

3.   Should restitutionary awards be available in respect of gains made by conscious wrongdoing? Again a general approach of this sort might either include or exclude gains made by reason of breach of contract but, for the reasons above, we provisionally believe that gains made by reason of contracts that are either specifically enforceable or between parties in a fiduciary relationship should be included. Although, in one respect this approach would constitute a widening of the existing law, unless combined with 2 above it would exclude restitution of gains made by the innocent infringement of property rights which is now available. The analogy of the statutory provisions concerning infringement of patents, which suggest that neither

171

damages nor an account of profits may be made in the case of innocent infringement, is not entirely apposite because in cases of trespass and wrongful interference with goods compensatory damages are available in respect of an innocent infringement.

4.   Should development be left to the courts which, despite decisions such as *Stoke-on-Trent City Council* v. *W. & J. Wass Ltd.*,[82] are increasingly receptive to restitutionary awards or should it be by legislation? If the latter should it be by a detailed legislative scheme or by a general formula, possibly modelled on the statutory provisions concerning intellectual property rights?

---

[82]   [1988] 1 W.L.R. 1406.

PART VIII

SUMMARY OF CONSULTATION ISSUES AND PROVISIONAL RECOMMENDATIONS

8.1   We have considered:

(i)   the problems of intangible losses, the need to redress interference with interests of personality, and how these aspects have affected the development of punitive damages;

(ii)   the present law relating to aggravated damages and exemplary damages - our survey covering availability and assessment - and the relationship between both, and an in-depth analysis of the leading cases: *Rookes* v. *Barnard*,[1] *Broome* v. *Cassell*[2] and *A.B.* v. *South West Water Services Ltd.*;[3]

(iii)   how overseas jurisdictions deal with aggravated and exemplary damages;

(iv)   the arguments for and against exemplary damages; and

(v)   restitutionary damages, including the state of the present law, and the arguments for and against restitutionary awards.

We shall now set out the issues on which we seek the views of consultees, and our provisional conclusions.

8.2   We have concluded that the purpose of civil law remedies and the law of tort is not exclusively to provide compensation. Our approach to the options for reform is influenced by this (paragraphs 5.38 and 7.19).

8.3   We note that at present the law protects a number of interests in respect of which it is either difficult or impossible to give a monetary equivalent. We raise for consideration whether

---

[1]   [1964] A.C. 1129.

[2]   [1972] A.C. 1027.

[3]   [1993] Q.B. 507.

personality rights and intangible losses and property and analogous rights can and should be protected by only a strict compensatory model of redress (paragraph 2.29).

EXEMPLARY DAMAGES

8.4 We consider the current law and conclude that it is in an unsatisfactory and unprincipled condition, particularly in the light of the adoption of the 'cause of action' test in *A.B.* v. *South West Water Services Ltd.*.[4] We therefore reject the suggestion that the status quo be maintained (paragraph 6.5).

8.5 We present the arguments for and against the total abolition of exemplary damages (paragraphs 5.4 - 5.26 and 6.6).

8.6 We seek consultees' views on partial abolition as an option, noting that such an approach could work in tandem with the approach we provisionally favour, of putting exemplary damages on a principled basis (paragraph 6.7).

8.7 We note our belief that the arguments in favour of the civil law continuing to recognise the punitive principle in some form are convincing, in particular, their value in protecting personality rights. We also note the practical objections to abolishing exemplary damages and provisionally conclude, subject to the views of consultees, that exemplary damages should be retained, but put on a principled basis. We note that the nature of such rationalisation and the extent to which such damages should be available depend on whether the principle seen to justify exemplary damages is that punishment and deterrence are legitimate functions of the law of civil wrongs, or that there is a need to provide redress for breach of intangible personality interests. The legislation making provision for rationalising exemplary damages could contain a general or a specific test (paragraph 6.8).

8.8 We provisionally favour codifying the existing law at the same time as the rationalised remedy is introduced (paragraph 6.9).

8.9 We then consider two models for the rationalisation of exemplary damages. The first is a legislative model providing for the general recognition of such damages, leaving scope for the

---

4 [1993] Q.B. 507.

development of the law by traditional common law methods (paragraphs 6.10 - 6.13). The second is a legislative model closely defining the circumstances in which an award of exemplary damages might be made and the conditions which would govern the process. We provisionally favour this option (paragraph 6.14).

8.10   We seek consultees' views on the relative merits of the two models and on the types of conduct which should be covered by any proposed legislative formula (paragraph 6.15). As regards the principle upon which exemplary damages might be based, we suggest a test which would centre on a relationship of inequality. We also give examples of situations where the relationship might be presumptively established. These include landlord and tenant, government or public official and citizen, employer and employee, persons exercising statutory power and the object of that power, and newspaper or magazine and a citizen who is the subject of material published by the newspaper or magazine. We seek consultees' views on these, and on how rights of personality could be more specifically protected (paragraphs 6.16 - 6.18).

8.11   We ask for consultees' views on whether the suggested approach should cover interference with property rights actionable *per se* and analogous rights, deliberate breaches of health and safety legislation, negligence and breach of contract (paragraphs 6.19 - 6.21). Our provisional view is that there should be no reform of the position in relation to breach of contract (paragraph 6.21).

8.12   We also seek consultees' views on whether and how exemplary awards should be shared amongst a class of victims, and whether exemplary damages paid to one plaintiff should reduce an equivalent award in later proceedings (paragraph 6.22).

8.13   We raise for consideration the possibility of renaming exemplary damages, to shift the focus from retributory aspects (paragraph 6.23).

PARTICULAR ISSUES

8.14   We ask consultees to consider the possible principles which it is thought should govern the assessment of exemplary damages (paragraphs 6.24 to 6.27).

8.15   We consider alternative reforms aimed at reducing perceived existing problems with the law of exemplary damages. The first of these is whether judges should take over the role of juries in assessing the damages. We provisionally reject such an option, subject to the views of consultees (paragraph 6.33).

8.16   We consider that too many difficulties would attach to the option of fixing awards, either by capping, or by the use of a formula (paragraphs 6.34 - 6.35).

8.17   We consider other possible reforms, and seek comments from consultees on the following issues:

(a)   the possibility of repealing the rules which currently apply to survival of actions for exemplary damages (paragraph 6.36);

(b)   a proposal to make exemplary damages subject to a stricter standard of proof than that normally used in civil cases, substituting the criminal standard of proof, or some sort of compromise standard, such as 'clear and convincing evidence' (paragraph 6.37);

(c)   whether part of any exemplary damages award should be made payable to the state or to another public fund (paragraph 6.38);

(d)   whether it is acceptable for the punitive effect of exemplary damages to be shifted by insurance from the shoulders of the person who bears primary responsibility for the conduct. We raise a number of options followed in the United States for consideration (paragraphs 6.39 - 6.41);

(e)   what situations justify an employer being vicariously liable to pay exemplary damages in respect of the conduct of an employee (paragraphs 6.42 - 6.44);

(f)   a legislative proposal governing joint liability to ensure that an exemplary award inflicted on one defendant would not be reduced by the fact that others who were jointly liable bore lesser responsibility or did not have sufficient wealth, which we see as desirable (paragraph 6.45); and

(g)   whether special rules should be devised concerning the availability of evidence as to the defendant's wealth where exemplary damages are sought. Subject to consultees' views, we provisionally support the view that it should continue to be the case that no detailed inquiry into the defendant's finances should be undertaken (paragraph 6.47).

AGGRAVATED DAMAGES

8.18   We raise for consideration whether intangible interests of personality can be protected by a strict compensatory model of redress (paragraph 6.48). We provisionally conclude that aggravated damages should be abolished by means of the removal of an exceptional conduct requirement and a strict compensatory model should apply (paragraph 6.48). We seek consultees' views on this and on the following questions:

(a)   what problems of assessment and proof, if any, might be raised by the abolition of aggravated damages (paragraph 6.50 - 6.52);

(b)   should damages be available in respect of all wrongs or only some (paragraph 6.53); and

(c)   would the proposed abolition of aggravated damages and the adoption of a compensatory model of redress have to be carried out in conjunction with the reform of the law of exemplary damages, to ensure that any gaps are closed (paragraph 6.54).

RESTITUTIONARY DAMAGES

8.19   We consider that restitutionary damages are *prima facie* justified if there has been either interference with a proprietary right or with an analogous right, and the gains made by the defendant are attributable to the interest infringed (paragraph 7.20).

8.20   We seek consultees' views on a general approach whereby restitutionary damages could be made in respect of all gains made by reason of a wrong where the test of attribution is satisfied. This could in principle include gains made by reason of breach of contract, but we provisionally conclude that those contracts should be either specifically enforceable or made between parties in a fiduciary relationship (paragraph 7.21). We consider that the distinction drawn between specifically enforceable contracts and contracts between fiduciaries where a restitutionary award may be made and other contracts where the gain to a defendant from breach is irrelevant reflects an appropriate balance of the respective interests of the parties (paragraph 7.22(1)).

8.21   We ask if restitutionary damages should only be available in respect of the 'proprietary torts' and infringements of interests recognised as analogous to property interests (paragraph 7.22(2)).

8.22   We ask if restitutionary damages should be available for gains made by conscious wrongdoing. We note, as in paragraph 8.20 above, that the distinction drawn between specifically enforceable contracts and contracts between fiduciaries where a restitutionary award may be made and other contracts where the gain to a defendant from breach is irrelevant reflects an appropriate balance of the respective interests of the parties. Therefore, our provisional view is that gains in these circumstances should not include gains made by reason of breach of contract (paragraph 7.22(3)).

8.23   We ask if development of restitutionary damages should be left to the courts or made by statutory provision. If the latter is favoured, we ask whether there should be a detailed legislative scheme or a general formula (paragraph 7.22(4)).

APPENDIX

EXAMPLES OF AMERICAN STATUTORY BANS ON AWARDS OF PUNITIVE DAMAGES

At Federal level:

a. The Federal Tort Claims Act, 28 U.S.C. § 2674, provides in part that the U.S. "shall be liable [for] tort claims, in the same manner and to the same extent as a private individual under like circumstances, but shall not be liable for . . . punitive damages."

b. Foreign states, even though subject to liability for compensatory damages to a limited extent, are expressly protected against liability for punitive damages. 28 U.S.C. § 1606.

c. The securities acts, which allow private civil actions for certain violations, expressly limit relief to actual damages, 15 U.S.C § 77K(e) & (g), § 77e, § 77www(b), § 78bb(a), although a few courts have allowed such damages under accompanying state law claims.

d. Courts have interpreted a small number of other federal statutes as allowing only actual, compensatory damages, thereby precluding punitive damages. 15 U.S.C. § 1709(e) (regulating interstate land sales disclosures); 47 U.S.C. § 206 (regulating radio and telegraph communications); 12 U.S.C. § 1821(e)(3)(A), (B) (regulating financial institution recovery and reform).

At state level:

Such damages are generally prohibited, unless otherwise provided by statute, by the New Hampshire Rev. Stat. Ann. § 507. A handful of miscellaneous statutes authorize such awards in this state.

Statutes banning such awards in relation to limited topics have included: Retracted libels (Georgia Code Ann. § 51-5-11; South Dakota Cod. L. Ann. § 20-11-7); Strict liability for mining accidents (Wisconsin Stat. Ann. § 107.31); Administrators [and executors] of estates. (Wisconsin Stat. Ann. § 895.02 and Mississippi Code Ann. 91-7-235); Personal representatives of descendants (Georgia Code Ann. § 9-2-41); Breach of contract (Georgia Code Ann. § 13-6-10; Kentucky Rev. Stat. Ann. § 411.184(4) and Montana Code Ann. § 27-1-220; (most states have similar common-law prohibition, with several generally recognized exceptions); Breach of promise to marry, alienation of affections, criminal conversation (Illinois Ann. Stat. ch. 40, ¶¶ 1803, 1903, 1953); Medical and legal malpractice (Illinois Ann. Stat. ch. 170, ¶ 2-1115 and Or. Rev. Stat. § 18.550 (health practitioners)); Claims against bond, trust account, or letter of credit (Iowa Code Ann. § 523B.3); Victims of crime (Iowa Code Ann. § 910.1); Electronic surveillance (Louisiana Rev. Stat. Ann. § 15:1312); Libel and slander (Massachusetts Ann. Laws ch. 231, § 93); Drugs and food approved by federal Food and Drug Administration, unless defendant procured approval by fraud (New Jersey Stat. Ann. § 2A:58c-5(c); Ohio Rev. Code Ann. §2307.80(C) (drugs); Oregon Rev. Stat. § 30.927 (drugs) and Utah Code Ann. § 78-18-2 (drugs); Uniform Commercial Code transactions (UCC § 1-106(1)).

Statutory Protection of Governmental Bodies from Punitive Damages

American practice has, in marked contrast to English law, provided significant protection against awards of punitive damages to governmental bodies. The federal government and about one-third of the states have express legislation prohibiting punitive damages against the federal or state government, and, in some state statutes, against political subdivisions or public entities, and, in at least one, against governmental employees. See Alabama Code § 6-11-26 (state, counties, municipalities, and agencies, except certain medical agencies); Alaska Stat. § 09.50.280 (state); California Govt Code Ann. § 818 (public entities); Idaho Code § 6-918 (government entities); Indiana Code Ann. § 34-4-16.5-4 (governmental liability for personal injuries and wrongful death); Iowa Code Ann. § 25A.4 (state); Maryland Tort Claims Act, Md. State Govt Code Ann. § 12-104; Massachusetts Ann. Laws ch. 258, § 2 (public entity - property damage, injury, or death); Minnesota Stat. Ann. § 3.736 (state), § 466.04 (political subdivisions); Montana Code Ann. § 2-9-105 (state and governmental entities); New Hampshire Rev. Stat. Ann. § 507-B:4 (property damage and personal injury claims against government entity); New Jersey Tort Claims Act, N.J. Stat. Ann. § 59:9-2; South Carolina Tort Claims Act, S.C. Code Ann. § 15-78-120; Texas Civ. Prac. & Rem. Code § 101.024 (tort liability of governmental units); Utah Code Ann. § 63-30-22 (governmental entities); Wisconsin Stat. Ann. § 893.80 (claims against governmental bodies or officers, agents, or employers); Puerto Rico Laws Ann. tit. 21, § 3403(L)(municipal corporations). The leading American text on the subject states that "In the absence of a statute on punitive damage liability, or where immunity has been abolished, or is inapplicable on the facts, most courts which have considered the question have refused to make punitive awards for the wrongful acts of agents or employees against public entities for public policy reasons because the cost ultimately falls on the innocent citizen." 1 Schlueter & Redden, *Punitive Damages* (2nd ed.,1989) at 138 (citing, inter alia, *Newport* v. *Fact Concerts, Inc.*, 453 U.S. 247 (1981); *Rohweder* v. *Aberdeen Prod. Credit Ass'n*, 765 F.2d 109 (8th Cir. 1985); *Smith* v. *Northeast Ill. Reg'l Commuter R.R. Corp.*, 569 N.E.2d 41 (1991); *Annotation, Punitive Damages from Municipality*, 19 A.L.R.2d 903 (1951). Note, however, that a small number of cases have found an exception to a governmental entity's general immunity from punitive damages in a limited number of egregious circumstances.

****

Printed in the United Kingdom for HMSO.
Dd.294484, 10/93, C18, 3397/5, 5673, 260507.